# Anarchists in the Academy

# Anarchists in the Academy

Anarchists in the Academy

Dani Spinosa

## Machines and Free Readers in Experimental Poetry

The University of Alberta Press

Published by

The University of Alberta Press
Ring House 2
Edmonton, Alberta, Canada T6G 2E1
www.uap.ualberta.ca



LIBRARY AND ARCHIVES CANADA CATALOGUING IN PUBLICATION

Spinosa, Dani, 1986–, author
Anarchists in the academy : machines and free readers in experimental poetry / Dani Spinosa.

Includes bibliographical references and index.
Issued in print and electronic formats.
ISBN 978-1-77212-376-0 (softcover).—
ISBN 978-1-77212-405-7 (PDF)

1. Experimental poetry—21st century—History and criticism. 2. Anarchism in literature. 3. Semiotics and literature. 4. Poetics. 5. Criticism. I. Title.

PN1059.E94S65 2018 809.1'911
C2018-900806-7

First edition, first printing, 2018.
First printed and bound in Canada by Houghton Boston Printers, Saskatoon, Saskatchewan.
Copyediting by Lesley Peterson.
Proofreading by Kirsten Craven.
Indexing by Siusan Moffat.



The University of Alberta Press is committed to protecting our natural environment. As part of our efforts, this book is printed on Enviro Paper: it contains 100% post-consumer recycled fibres and is acid- and chlorine-free.

The University of Alberta Press gratefully acknowledges the support received for its publishing program from the Government of Canada, the Canada Council for the Arts, and the Government of Alberta through the Alberta Media Fund.

Canada | Canada Council for the Arts | Conseil des Arts du Canada | Alberta Government

*For my mother, who made our house a TAZ,*
*complete with communal garden, basement grocery co-op,*
*renegade theatre company, independent fashion and costume design,*
*a radical sense of wonder, and the knowledge that*
*no matter how different we all became,*
*we could get ice cream together.*

# Contents

# Acknowledgements

THIS BOOK EXISTS because Andy Weaver played "Ursonate" one day in his Introduction to Poetry lecture, and then let me bother him for another decade. Without his guidance, advice, reading lists, and alcohol-fuelled rants, I could never have written this—first as a dissertation, and then again as a book. Thank you to his wife Kelly and his beautiful babies, Duncan and Hugh, for letting me occupy so much of his time and attention. I also want to thank Stephen Cain, Art Redding, Richard Telekey, David Goldstein, and Craig Dworkin for reading this work in its first iteration and guiding it so generously and thoughtfully to its current state. I also thank Juliana Spahr, W. Mark Sutherland, and Jesse Cohn for responding to personal correspondences and talking words and anarchy with me.

I also owe a huge thank-you to my partner, Jesse, for reading through this work in its many forms and for tiptoeing through my office when he knew I was in writing mode. Thank you to early readers of the blog, Kate Siklosi, Matt Carrington, Caitlin O'Kelly, and Sean Braune, and to the generous and fabulous members of my writing workshop, Melissa Dalgliesh, Samantha Bernstein, Jonathan Vandor, and Thom Bryce. Thank you to the team at the Electronic Literature Organization and the Electronic Literature Directory, especially Dene Grigar, Davin Heckman, and Joseph Tabbi, for bringing me into the wonderful world of electronic literature. And, of course, a huge thank-you to my parents, Marie and Jerry, who paid for this book in more ways than I can count. I won't ever be able to repay you, but I will keep making books for the Green Room Archives, so maybe that's an okay trade?

I would also like to express my deep gratitude to Lesley Peterson, whose careful, creative, and political editing has made this a much better book. I am also grateful for the hard work and dedication shown by everyone at University of Alberta Press, especially Peter Midgley, Duncan Turner, and Monika Igali.

Thank you, also, to the authors and the authors' estates who granted me permission to reprint some of their work in this volume, including Jim Andrews, W. Mark Sutherland, Eleanor Nichol, and the estate of bpNichol. This work has been supported, in turns, by an Ontario Graduate Scholarship, and a Social Sciences and Humanities Research Grant. It is not every day that so many levels of government support an anarchist project, and I am grateful.

An earlier version of the introduction to this work appeared as "Postanarchist Literary Theory and the Experiment: Some Preliminary Notes," in the *Journal for the Study of Radicalism*, vol. 11, no. 1, 2017, pp. 83–111. Elements from the first chapter appeared in earlier versions in the essays "John Cage and the Comunis of Communication," in *Canadian Review of American Studies*, vol. 46, no. 1, April 2016, pp. 22–41, and "Freely Revised and Edited: Anarchist Authorship in Jackson Mac Low's *The Stein Poems*," in *ESC: English Studies in Canada*, vol. 41, no. 2–3, June/September 2015, pp. 91–108.

# Introduction

*Postanarchism, Experimental Poetry, and the Academy*

IN THE THREE DECADES that have passed since the term *postanarchism* was first coined by Hakim Bey, it has become clear that postanarchism lends itself well to political writing, and this book is not the first with the aim of incorporating postanarchism into the already politicized field of literary studies. However, earlier work of this kind (by Lewis Call, Allan Antliff, Sandra Jeppesen, and others) has consisted almost entirely of studies either of fiction or of explicitly political poetry. The purpose of this book is, instead, to demonstrate how postanarchism offers a useful theoretical context for poetry that is not explicitly political—for, specifically, the contemporary experimental poem with its characteristic challenges to subjectivity, representation, authorial power, and conventional constructions of the reader–text relationship. Insofar as the field of literary studies may concern itself with becoming more political, more in line with activist movements of all kinds, it would seem that postanarchism, in its desire to reframe and rethink our ontological and epistemological practices within and outside of the academy, has the potential to be a powerful addition to literary studies on the whole and to studies of the experimental poetic tradition in particular. As I hope to show, postanarchist literary theory is highly relevant to an analysis of the political significance of experimental poetry's traditional focus on producing indeterminacy through machine-writing. Moreover, it is equally valuable to a critical analysis of the political and ethical issues inherent in conceptualism, one of the most popular contemporary experimental poetic movements: an analysis that challenges us to look away from conceptualism toward electronic literature for experimental poetry with truly radical potentials. Ultimately, in order to situate the sixteen case studies that make up the four chapters that follow, I propose here a postanarchist literary theory that reframes the reading and writing of experimental poetry as activist practice.

The claim that postanarchism is an inherently activist practice is one that Süreyyya Evren and Duane Rouselle make explicitly in their introduction to *Post-Anarchism: A Reader* (2011). Here Evren and Rouselle argue compellingly that postanarchism's fundamental nature must be defined not simply as philosophy but rather as a "consequence of actual activist experiences" (3). Turning to deleuzian discourse, Evren and Rouselle further argue that poststructuralism invigorates classical anarchism with a new, rhizomatic activism, thereby creating a new current in radical politics (5, 15). This is an important argument, in which Evren and Rouselle offer a re-evaluation and reclamation of anarchism that brings anarchism's classical texts into contemporary relevance. Given classical anarchism's standing as a political philosophy, and one primarily concerned with government and resistance, it may be worth recalling that classical anarchism has long been concerned with artistic practice. There has been a long-standing and close relationship between anarchist thought and poetry in particular, especially experimental or avant-garde poetry. We need only look at the popularity of Herbert Read's *Anarchy & Order; Poetry & Anarchism* (1938), or recall André Breton's frequently quoted adage, "an anarchist world...a surrealist world: they are the same," to confirm this, though Breton himself was a self-proclaimed socialist and frequently had difficulty resolving his socialist politics with an otherwise individualist aesthetics (Weir 3).

The postanarchism that Evren and Rouselle theorize, then, works to catch anarchist philosophies up to the changing face of contemporary activism and activist art. My own work follows theirs in examining postanarchism as a theory of activism that offers the means to incorporate the processes of reading and writing experimental poetry into the realm of activist practice. As poststructuralism teaches us, new understandings of power, subjectivity, and authorship that poststructuralist philosophers have elucidated require that we experiment with new forms of resistance. If we understand that diffuse power operates at the level of ontology and epistemology (an argument made persistently by Foucault and his contemporaries), then surely the cultural artifact, the literary artifact especially, must come into play as an element of activist practice. Of course, art has historically played a role in anti-authoritarian struggles internationally, but postanarchism challenges us to make a distinction between *political art* and *art as political*; in the latter, the very form (and not simply the content) of the artifact and the process of its production are political experiments. Throughout this book, accordingly, I focus on the formally experimental poem as the most appropriate place to put postanarchism's potentials to the test.

It is my express hope that turning to literary theory will not depoliticize postanarchism. Whereas Stephen Collis, in his magisterial study of Susan Howe, plainly states that he does not want his anarcho-scholasticism to be read as a "theory" but rather as "a *praxis* embodied in the *form* of certain texts" (11, emphasis Collis's), I do want postanarchism to be viewed as literary theory. In my view, postanarchism is not a property of certain texts so much as a property of certain readings. Texts are not postanarchic in and of themselves; rather, they do—or do not—lend themselves well to postanarchist reading practices. From this perspective, treating postanarchism as literary theory is a move to politicize reading and not a move to depoliticize postanarchism. This, I would argue, is just the kind of postanarchism called for by Saul Newman, who advocates in *The Politics of Postanarchism* (2010) for the merger of classical anarchism and poststructuralism as a way to reinvigorate new anarchist-activist practices. While Newman maintains that postanarchism is a response to the postmodern condition (140), marked by "a skepticism towards metanarratives," an abandonment of essential identities, and a new view of discourse and constitutive power (à la Foucault), he demonstrates how these philosophical ideas can move into activist practice (141). Arguing that the political is the "constitutive space *between* society and the state" (196, emphasis Newman's), Newman draws on postanarchism to contest borders and border control (172), to advocate non-authoritarian forms of political organization (177), and to develop a productive disjuncture between politics and ethics (139). For Newman, postanarchism is, at its core, not "tactical" (169)—that is, not an expression of the thought that precedes action—but rather, a celebration of heretical (anti)politics (180).

Alongside Newman, whose emphasis on the practical activist nature of postanarchism is so central to my work, I place David Graeber, whose "Anarchism, Academia, and the Avant-Garde" poses this important question: what would an anarchist academic *do* (107)? As Graeber argues, the anarchist academic occupies a precarious position because these two terms are often understood to be incommensurate; anarchists and academics hold entirely different and often contradictory values (104). Nonetheless, Graeber positions the anarchist intellectual as exemplar, a model that can "provide a potential role for the radical, non-vanguardist intellectual" (111). Classical anarchism, despite its vocal repudiation of vanguardist ideals, often implicitly believed in vanguardism;[1] in fact, as Roger Farr points out, numerous anarchist publications explicitly used the term "vanguard."[2] For this reason, Graeber's anti-vanguardist position is distinctly postanarchist: rejecting such avant-garde literary and artistic movements as dadaism and futurism (and in one fell swoop also dismissing the anarchism often attributed to them), Graeber breaks with classical anarchism to argue that the anarchist intellectual must be interested in exploring alternatives, not in setting a vanguard (109).

The anarchist academic's task is difficult, then, but not doomed. "Untwining social theory from vanguardist habits might seem a particularly difficult task," as Graeber writes, "because historically modern social theory and the idea of the vanguard were born more or less together" (108). Yet the role of the anarchist academic is to develop methods of reading, writing, and understanding, not as a "vanguard leading the way to a future society," but as a way of "exploring new and less alienated modes of life" (109). Postanarchist literary theory gives me hope that it is indeed possible to study avant-garde literature as an academic without necessarily falling victim to a vanguardism myself. Through its multiple strategies of defamiliarization, the formally experimental poem offers one way of doing just this.

### Hakim Bey and the Temporary Autonomous Zone

In 1985, when Hakim Bey published *The Temporary Autonomous Zone; Ontological Anarchy; Poetic Terrorism,* he did so, at least in part, out of frustration with an anarchist-activist movement that had stalled, a movement that he believed to be suffering from an unidimensional and unidirectional approach that failed to account for a society in which power is diffuse and pervasive. In this foundational book, he proposes *postanarchism* (61), a poststructuralist anarchism that is not oedipal (to borrow a term from Gilles Deleuze and Félix Guattari, as Bey is wont to do) but band-like, carnivalesque, and psychically nomadic (95–97). Bey's *postanarchism* is not a temporal term, not an *after anarchism* that picks up where a failed movement leaves off, but an anarchism that always contains within it the lessons learned from poststructuralist conceptions of power and the State, as well as its own revolutionary potentials. With this concept, he believed he was offering "a perfect tactic for an era in which the State is omnipresent and all-powerful and yet simultaneously riddled with cracks and vacancies" (93): a tactic for achieving the *ontological anarchy* identified in the title of his book.

The feature that makes Bey's postanarchism most obviously of interest to literary studies, and one of the key features that differentiate Bey's postanarchism from the anarchism that preceded it, is its prioritization of art—often poetry specifically—as a revolutionary activist practice. Lamenting what he sees as an authoritarian regime that no longer regards art and literature as threats, Bey insists that poetry must become more radical (although he does not specify *how*) and that other facets of resistance movements must take on the revolutionary potentials of poetic language: "If rulers refuse to consider poems as crimes, then someone must commit crimes that serve the function of poetry, or texts that possess the resonance of terrorism" (27). However, Bey never fully develops this concept of (political, corporeal) radical poetics. Instead, what he means by "poems as crimes" remains unspecified. Even his own poetry leaves this poetics underdeveloped and unclear. He maintains in it the mysticism, the politics, and the visceral appeal of his political writing—see, for example, his *Opium Dens I Have Known* (2009)—but because so much of his creative work recalls or even works within the confines of the lyrical tradition, it is difficult to see where or how these poems engage with the criminal potentials of language. Bey thus provides us with more of a tantalizing poetic theory than an effective poetic practice. This is not to say that his poetry lacks force irredeemably, but rather that his concept of *poetic terrorism* (again, introduced in the title of his book) can, and should, be taken further than he himself takes it in his creative work. Accordingly, I set out in this book to interrogate the poetic theory nascent in Bey's work and to develop this into a post-anarchist literary theory that shows us not only how to create texts that are crimes against poetry (texts that defamiliarize the modes of poetic production, in other words) but also how to make the reading and writing of these poems activism on the level of ontological anarchy.

Central to the poetic theory Bey proposes is his concept of the Temporary Autonomous Zone (hereafter referred to as the TAZ). The TAZ, as he explains it, is a philosophical thought experiment that also can be, should be, and often is realized materially. Infinitely variable in longevity, type, and size, TAZs range from an individual moment of refusal to the widespread "Occupy" movements popularized in 2012. Bey goes to great lengths not to define the TAZ, but he does note that it is a moment when artistic and activist practices convene in an "uprising that doesn't engage directly with the State, a guerrilla operation which liberates an area (of land, of time, of imagination) and then dissolves itself to re-form elsewhere/elsewhen" (92). The TAZ is the site of acts Bey refers to as Poetic Terrorism, which he refuses to define prescriptively. Instead, he does so indirectly through such examples as this: "Pick someone at random & convince them they're the heir to an enormous, useless & amazing fortune—say 5000 square miles of Antarctica....Later they will come to realize that for a few moments they believed in something extraordinary, & will perhaps be driven as a result to seek out some more intense mode of existence" (14). While still obscure and eccentric, this definition by example reveals the hallmark of the TAZ: it defamiliarizes by moving the quotidian into the extraordinary and, in this example especially, does so by calling into question the taken-for-granted principles of capitalism and statism. The sudden acquisition of Antarctic territory may have the effect of bringing to the fore assumptions of ownership as economic, as state-sanctioned, and as socially recognized. The TAZ asks: how does government, in its many forms, limit our ability to believe in and embrace the "extraordinary"? Eruptions of TAZs infringe on the laws of State and logic, patriarchy and normativity, grammar and propriety. These regulating and codifying effects produce, as poststructuralism insists, the political subject, and TAZs can help to liberate the individual from these effects.

While Bey's TAZ is a concept that is central to postanarchism, and central as well to the postanarchist literary theory I propose, it is worth noting that the TAZ, and with it Bey's postanarchism in general, has been widely critiqued by many anarchist authors who believe that the diffuse, dreamlike nature of the TAZ is an ineffectual thought exercise at best, and at worst a narcissistic impediment to real activist labour. Murray Bookchin is the most vocal of these critics: the title of his 1995 monograph, *Social Anarchism or Lifestyle Anarchism: An Unbridgeable Chasm,* challenges readers to choose between two incompatible options; and his argument in this work condemns Bey as a mere "lifestyle anarchist" whose work is "so absurd as to seemingly parody a self-absorbed and self-absorbing ideology" (20). Much of the postanarchist appeal of the TAZ is that it relies heavily on the dreams, imagination, and magic of the individual creativity while at the same time calling for the social dissolution of closed subjectivities; Bookchin, however, who views this concept through the lens of the classical anarchism he inherited, sees Bey's prioritization of the self as incompatible with collective resistance and social responsibility. Bookchin also condemns the transient, temporary nature of the insurgency Bey associates with the TAZ; indeed, he sees this as its greatest weakness. The TAZ's transience, according to Bookchin, makes it "conspicuously powerless in its capacity to leave any imprint on the individual's personality, subjectivity, and even self-formation, still less on shaping events and reality" (*Social Anarchism* 24). It is, in the end, a "flight from all meaningful social activism" (*Social Anarchism* 25). Clearly, Bookchin does not mince words. My debt to Bookchin's work will be evident at many points in the following chapters, and I do not mean to dismiss his importance. Nevertheless, the postanarchist literary theory I propose here takes the TAZ as a metaphor for momentary insurgencies in authorship and readership in poetry; as such, its transience is important in revealing a similar transience of meaning, interpretation, and reading.

There are, of course, problems with the TAZ beyond Bookchin's inability to believe that the briefly imagined or the dreamlike may have real, lasting effects on individuals. Most notably, the liberatory *anything goes* attitude of the TAZ has led many, including Bey, to use it to justify harmful or abusive behaviour. Bey, who outside of his writing lives as Peter Lamborn Wilson, is a documented contributor to many pedophilia-apologist journals and newsletters, including NAMBLA's.[3] As Robert P. Helms notes in his exposé of Bey, it is not only that the TAZ provides a metaphorical refuge for abusers; it is that "many of Hakim Bey's best-known anarchist pitches first saw print as pedophile apologies" (np). For example, NAMBLA published his "Association for Ontological Anarchism, communiqué #2" in 1986, and the journal *Gayme* ran "A Temporary Autonomous Zone" and "Pirate Utopias" in issues of 1993–95 (Helms np). The potential to misuse the liberatory potentials of postanarchism is clear; moreover, such abuses go for all kinds of insurgent tactics. It is thus important that postanarchist literary theory stress the common and the communal responsibility of the TAZ. Such communal responsibility not only deprives Bey and others of their potential justifications for abusive behaviour, but also highlights the practical lessons and social responsibility of postanarchism's communal poetics.

## Experimenting with Poetry in the Common

Throughout this project I have opted for the term *experimental* in preference to *avant-garde* for a number of reasons, not least of which is the military connotations of the latter. I also share Graeber's skepticism about vanguardism.[4] It is worth noting that anarchist movements have found it necessary, historically, to distance themselves from avant-garde movements in poetry and art that frequently touted their anarchist sympathies. As Jesse Cohn details, while anarchist political and social groups have often appreciated the challenges that avant-garde movements made to power structures, traditional form, and normativity, they have typically understood the avant-garde as self-serving, levelling against it criticisms not unlike Bookchin's charges of lifestyle anarchism. Cohn explains:

> the anarchist movement, which refused to nullify social commitments in the name of the autonomous individual, was not on the whole welcoming toward these experimenters, whose work they often saw as willfully obscure at best, more suited to the narcissistic enjoyment of a self-appointed élite than to the needs of working class people in struggle. (80)

The anarchist point here, which presents avant-garde poetic movements as essentially anathema to effectual political engagement in literature, is well taken. Experimental art, however, while sharing many of the same aesthetic and formal concerns as the avant-garde, actively works against the linear narratives of influence and closed, filiative communities upheld by vanguardism.

In this project I define the experimental, first and foremost, as a matter of formal innovation. The experimental text does not discount or ignore innovation in terms of content, but rather ties innovative content to the creation of new, alternative forms of expression. The experimental verse I focus on, furthermore, is of a kind that resists the vanguardism that marks many of the movements of the literary avant-garde. These texts avoid vanguardism's hierarchical nature in favour of a more egalitarian relationship between the reader and the writer—and between texts themselves—in two ways: they complicate the role of the author (through the use of machines in the writing process at times, but also through chance or indeterminate operations, "plagiarism" or copying, and direct or collaborative engagement with the reader), and they demonstrate an interest in the commonality of language. In light of this, any definition of the experiment is nebulous, a compendium of ideas that forms a collaborative series of suggestions rather than a prescriptive map of what the experimental poem *should be*. I include these criteria only to gesture toward a theory of the poetic experiment.

**Artifice:** The experimental text is concerned with exposing and/or foregrounding artifice. As Charles Bernstein argues, a poem's meaning is located in a "complex" (9), wherein the artifice opposes the realism and mimesis often attributed to conventional texts (and especially to the lyrical poem). Artifice, which also includes "nonsemantic" effects (11), is part of any poem's meaning. This is to say that a poem's form is *meaningful* in and of itself, rather than simply re-enforcing the meaning of the poem's content (10). However, the difference between the artifice of radical experimental forms and traditional forms is that in experimental poetry artifice negates, undermines, or complicates semantic meaning rather than contributing to it (15).

**Openness:** The experimental text is never exhausted or exhaustive, and its production is a constant revisionary practice. As Lyn Hejinian famously argues, the experimental text refuses the "smug pretension of universality and its tendency to cast the poet as guardian to Truth" (2). Closed texts, for Hejinian, maintain a stratified system that enforces certain interpretations while disallowing others and shutting out readers from the process of making meaning. An experimental text, by contrast, radically resists closure and leaves itself open to multiple readings—even welcomes contradictory readings—because of gaps in the text left to be filled by readers.

**Chance:** Experimental authors leave themselves and their work open to the intervening forces of chance, indeterminacy, improvisation, and spontaneity. This includes collaborative inclusion of machine, code, or digital media, the direct engagement of the reader or other participants, and uncreative or Oulipian modes of writing that leave the writing process (in part or whole) up to external procedures. This element recalls the scientific meaning of the term "experiment," wherein the parameters of the project are set, but the ability of the initiator to determine the end result is severely limited.[5] Jackson Mac Low argues that leaving ourselves open to chance writing is an anarchic political decision; it reproduces an anarchic "state of society wherein there is no frozen power structure, where all persons may make significant initiatory choices in regard to matters affecting their own lives" ("Some Remarks" 384). In other words, the initiators of these procedures anarchically refuse authoritative control over the process and thus relinquish power over the products.

**Politics:** The experimental text is political. Bernstein, Hejinian, and Mac Low all argue that formal manipulation in poetry is a political (anti-traditional, anti-authoritarian) act that disturbs the organizing and limiting principles of language. This is made most apparent in John Cage's frequent references "to N[orman] O. Brown's remark that syntax is the arrangement of the army" and Cage's subsequent devotion "to nonsyntactical 'demilitarized' language" (*Writing Through Finnegans Wake* 1). For Cage, the experimental poem is a way out of this militarization, a way not to resist, but to refuse; as he asserts in *Silence*, we need new language in order to have new ideas (203).

Moreover, the experimental text may be as difficult to pin down as Bey's TAZ, for it must also be defined by what it *does not* do. For my purposes, the only concern here is that the experimental text not reify, rely on, or relish the individual as author. This principle contradicts John Ashbery's definition of the experimental avant-garde, as stated in his 1968 Yale lecture, "The Invisible Avant-Garde." Here, Ashbery argues that the very existence of his lecture proves that the avant-garde has become "stratified" (394), and he insists that the primacy of anti-traditionalism in the avant-garde has created yet another tradition that eventually subsumes the individual prowess of the author. In the end, he tellingly laments: "has tradition finally managed to absorb the individual talent?" (397). Recalling Eliot's famous treatise on the subject, Ashbery maintains that the *real* avant-garde is the individual; it is not a school, genre, or group, but rather a personal refusal. While I do not question that Ashbery's privileging of the individual, monadic author is one marker of the avant-garde, I would nevertheless argue that it is antithetical to the most radical kind of experiment: a process that embraces the influence of the literary community (contemporary and historical), the mutability of the writing subject, and the collaborative nature of the processes of reading and writing.

Even with all of the above principles established, however, some difficulties remain to be addressed. The distance between Ashbery's "individual" and the author of the experimental text is a useful theoretical distinction, but it does not help us much to recognize or theorize the real people who author experimental works, even when they do so in collaboration with human and non-human entities. Another difficulty is that of reconciling the seeming contradiction between postanarchist literary theory's anti-traditionalism, as outlined above, and its embracing of poetic community. In essence, postanarchist literary theory makes a distinction between two understandings of the concept of "tradition": one is a common, a community, an assemblage of writers working with and from each other; the other is a lineage, a line of tradition that uses normative reading practices to govern reader experience. Postanarchist literary theory may oppose the latter understanding of tradition, but it does not necessarily pretend that authors (least of all experimental authors) write in vacuums. As Stephen Voyce points out, "To suggest that one is simply an individual writer without allegiance to a tradition is to abjure the influences and ideological principles that frame all aesthetic activity; it is to ignore the community of those who enable one's own creativity" (*Poetic Community* 254). Indeed, as Cohn notes, anarchist writing itself (in poetry and other genres) has a long and rich tradition, and anarchist writers have always noted this influence.[6] However, anarchist writers typically understand tradition as rhizomatic rather than linear, and as a site of rewriting, of revision, and of an essential refusal of inheritance. The distinction between these two conceptions of influence is, at its core, a distinction between two conceptions of subjectivity, about which postanarchist literary theory displays a similar ambivalence. In acknowledgement of these issues, I argue for a postanarchist literary theory that positions the individual authorial subject in a history of writers who have themselves established a tradition of diffusing authorial power, who understand this movement from self to dissolution as central to the poetic common. This theory of postanarchist subjectivity recognizes the importance of the self in building community but also maintains that a true common (of which literary community is just one example) requires the disruption and dissolution of precisely the self that it also requires. This postanarchist subjectivity is ambivalent and procedural—sometimes even paradoxical.

For these very reasons, this postanarchist subjectivity is also an artistic and cultural construct that conflicts to at least some extent with the necessities of lived experience. Nevertheless, I do not consider this conflict to detract from the anarchist-activist potentials of postanarchist literary practice. In recognizing anarchism's power as a cultural or artistic ideology rather than a coherent political philosophy, I follow David Weir, who argues that the eventual disavowal of anarchism as a viable political practice is what led directly to its viability as a guiding cultural and artistic practice. While anarchist philosophy has permeated many different kinds of artistic practice, as detailed in such studies as Weir's and Cohn's, it often, as both scholars observe, has been used to justify vanguardist and individualist practices, particularly in poetic and visual arts (Cohn 79, Weir 2–3). As Weir puts it, anarchism "as a form of individualist politics is perfectly suited to the type of individualist poetics" that such avant-garde writers and artists as surrealists, dadaists, and others practised (3). It is with this history in mind that I assert postanarchism's efficacy as a literary theory that mirrors anarchism's political and social concerns, but with one essential difference: postanarchist literary theory replaces the individualist politics and poetics of classical anarchism and its vanguardist counterparts with a politics and a poetics of the *common*.

## "Poetry is radically communal"

This poetics of the common is articulated clearly and explicitly in Robert Duncan's poetry. Consider, for instance, the following, part of the late series "Dante Études":

> Go, my songs, then in zealous
> liberality,   no longer mine,
> but now the friendship of the
> Reader's heart and mind (*Ground Work* 126)

In offering his "songs...in zealous / liberality" to "the / Reader's heart and mind," Duncan creates the kind of space that postanarchist theory recognizes as a TAZ. This shared linguistic space is central to Duncan's poetic and political theories, as Collis argues; for Duncan, "language is the commons: we all have equal rights to enter there—permission to return to the common source....Poetry is a gift of the *givenness* of language and no poet holds property rights over it....Poetry is radically communal" (np). The poetic experiment emphasizes the importance of understanding language, and poetic language especially, as a major feature of the *common*, and it does so through indeterminacy, engagement of a reading community, anarchic themes of attentiveness and interconnectivity, and a politics of responsibility. Such attentiveness and interconnectivity is termed *love* by Michael Hardt and Antonio Negri, who provocatively argue for love as a central political concept and a resistance tactic: "Every act of love is an ontological event in that it marks a rupture with existing being and creates new being....To say that love is ontologically constitutive then, simply means that it produces the common" (181). The traditional prioritization and valorization of the author figure, in its privileging of a single voice and its subsequent resistance to conversation and collaboration, is, we might say, unloving: it fails to produce the common.

This approach to understanding the common may well lead us to conclude that Duncan's notion of the communal nature of language is, to an extent, naive. Many critical theorists have argued that language (through its game of giving and receiving information, its substitutive process) is in itself inequitable, predicated on the exclusion of others for its expression. Furthermore, as Hardt and Negri note, language, although a part of the common, is becoming increasingly privatized (ix). For this reason Hardt and Negri propose a common that is not, as Duncan's work may suggest, a purely public space, but rather one that seeks alternatives to the binary: "neither private nor public, neither capitalist nor socialist," such a common "opens a new space for politics" (ix). This insightful argument, which has deep roots in the classical anarchist tradition, posits a common predicated on embracing the mutability of human nature and individual subjectivity. The common, understood in this way, shows us that "human nature" is always in flux (353). Consequently, the best way to experiment with (and against) closed subjectivity is to embrace this flux as process, and to compose "in the common the singular subjectivities that result from this process" (x). While the language here is deleuzian, the concept is straightforward; in essence, postanarchism understands the self as procedural and, thus, understands the common produced by a self that is "in flux" as markedly different from one produced by shared but "privatized" codes that necessarily become restrictive or oppressive.

The dissolution of subjectivity achieved through an experimental disruption of authorship, is, to be sure, just one of the goals important to postanarchist activism. As Hardt and Negri maintain, a revolutionary politics cannot exist solely through the refusal of identity. And after all, as Susan Howe states, the complete refusal of authorship and identity is "alluring—but problematic," and it is especially so "for women writing/reading poems" (qtd. in Guthrie np). Instead of falling prey to this allure, as Hardt and Negri argue, "revolutionary politics has to start from identity but cannot end there" (xi). Nevertheless, "identity," normally "a weapon of the republic of property,...can be turned against it" (ix). This process begins with an attack on invisibility, a reclamation of the means of production of subjectivity, and, ultimately, a shift from stratified identity to a singularity in flux (327–33). In language, this shift can occur only when the text refuses representation because representation, as Hardt and Negri argue persuasively, turns singularities into concrete identities (346). Accordingly, Hardt and Negri propose a production of the common that relies not on *anti-globalization* but rather on what they term *alter-globalization*, a process that moves beyond opposition and resistance into creative experimentation (102–04). Understood in this way, the common is the production of a revolutionary politics that relies on collective social expression, and here we return to the importance of love. For Hardt and Negri, love is the productivity *of* and *in* the common (xii). It is a physical force and a political action, but it is one that embraces flux, seeks alternatives, disrupts representation, and engages the social in collective responsibility within and to itself. It is responsible to, and part of, the common.

My own approach to postanarchism does not make a central concept of *love*, as such; nevertheless, I note its importance to several of the poets who are the focus of this study, Duncan and Howe in particular; more generally, my analysis of the postanarchist subject is influenced and supported by Hardt and Negri's insights into the binarism of individual and society, of self and other, and the value of embracing the varied connections between individuals that exist exclusively in flux. I would argue, in fact, that Hardt and Negri's "love" is synonymous with experimentation as postanarchist literary theory defines it. What they term love is simply the (supportive, anti-hierarchical) relationship between subjectivities as process. It is the relationship between postanarchist subjectivities that disrupts the understanding of self and community as a binary, instead seeing these two terms as mutually dependent, constitutive, and disruptive. The postanarchist subjectivity is ambivalent in this way, both required for communal interaction and an impediment to it, which is why subjectivities manifest in experimental poetry as transient and fleeting, solidifying and dissolving, as they are continually removed and re-inserted.

## The Crisis of Identification

In its approach to subjectivity, postanarchist literary theory necessarily critiques representation. Yet despite this fact, the only scholar who has developed an explicitly anarchist literary theory is Cohn, whose *Underground Passages* I cite above. An earlier work of his, *Anarchism and the Crisis of Representation* (2006), is also important to my theoretical project, as here Cohn "calls into question the relationships between our concepts and the truths they mean to denote, our images and the realities they are supposed to depict" (11). In efforts to create unifying and clearly expressionist systems of meaning-making (on the level of language, but also on the levels of genre, canon, tradition, etc.), these representative systems, in essence, speak to (and thus *for*) the multitude, and in turn silence its multiplicity (12). Cohn insists quite sensibly that writers and readers cannot reject all representation—it is, after all, requisite for signification—but he also argues that an anarchist literary theory necessitates viewing representation as a relationship of power (13). For this reason, Cohn's work privileges prose texts with "decentered, polyphonic, or rhizomatic" narratives that present "a collage of juxtaposed multiple voices rather than the single controlling perspective of a narrator" (172). These criteria have strongly influenced my own choice of texts for the case studies that follow, although of course they are all works of poetry, not prose.

What really sets Cohn's work apart is his assertion that an anarchist literary theory must always be understood as a dialectic between identification and disidentification (177). That is, Cohn suggests a reading and writing strategy that begins with identification and subjectivity and then turns that strategy against the text and its representation, in order to embrace both unity and multiplicity. In proposing this move Cohn pre-empts Hardt and Negri, who would propose understanding identity as a part of a process that turns against identification in *Commonwealth* some three years after Cohn. Cohn asserts that we can, and must, read identitarian subjectivities as products of coalition rather than hegemony (244). Poststructuralism and postmodernism destabilized subjectivity and did away with some universalisms and claims about "human nature," but, as Cohn notes, poststructuralism "has all too often produced...unity in the form of unstable alliances and single-issue reformist activism" (242). Postanarchism's response is to produce singularity in the form of radical difference. Embracing singularity, Cohn's anarchist society is a series of networked communities characterized by extreme regionalism and by affiliation rather than filiation (253). This translates directly to his anarchist reading and writing practices, which entail a "representational politics of duration and difference, motion and multiplicity" (256). Cohn's argument in *Anarchism and the Crisis of Representation*, despite its explicit concern with anarchist politics and aesthetics, shies away from developing a literary theory out of anarchism, but just such a theory follows in "What Is Anarchist Literary Theory?" published the following year (2007). The theory that Cohn proposes here, with its "aim of determining what kind of relationships the text offers to bring about between ourselves and one another, between ourselves and the world," reflects anarchist ethics (3).

What is particularly important to my project is the way Cohn's theory articulates these ethics in terms of the relationship between text and reader:

> An ethical approach to the text cannot simply mean a receptive or empathetic reading, in which we merely submit to its terms, nor can it mean a purely active reading, reading as the "use" or violent "appropriation" of the text; instead of positing ourselves as the slaves or the masters of texts, we ought to place ourselves into a dynamic relation with them, to see each encounter with them as a dialogue fraught with risk and promise. ("What is" 7)

The anarchist literary theory Cohn develops here, with its emphasis on "dynamic" relations and "dialogue," recalls poststructuralist thinking about readers and moves toward Craig Dworkin's production of new forms of reading and writing about *illegible* poetry (*Reading* 13). What Cohn ignores in this early formulation is the role of the authorial presence in the production of the literary artifact, a presence that postanarchism sees as absolutely essential to the reader. Notwithstanding this omission, however, Cohn's critique of representation, concern with the collective, and interest in liberating language from the substitutive function make his work invaluable to postanarchist literary theory. Certainly his work has helped to shape my approach in this book, in that I seek to prioritize the intersectionality of all that contribute to the linguistic process: the author, whom the postanarchist reader must confront; the reader, whose intrusive, annotative ways perform this confrontation; and the material media and technology, which are used to produce and disseminate the work. To this mix I would also add the author-function, which, as I explain below, reflects and illuminates the text's social context.

## Digital Media and Machine-Writing

Postanarchist literary theory sees all poetry as containing both the potentials and the limitations that have been attributed to digital poetry. This may seem to some readers as a very controversial argument, but it draws on a large body of digital poetry studies. For instance, according to C.T. Funkhouser, it is not only useful to understand that digital poetry has its roots in a history of the avant-garde; it is equally useful to consider that all poetry written in the last half-century—especially, but not exclusively, experimental poetry—is influenced by the radical potentials and McLuhanian obsolescences of technology and the technologization of poetics. Digital poetry, as Funkhouser demonstrates, was "mechanically and conceptually built in the decades *before* personal computers" (1). With roots in Dada, Oulipo, Black Mountain, projective verse, concretism, imagism, Futurism, and high modernism, digital poetry cannot be understood as separate from the print-based tradition. Conversely, we must also consider the extent to which writing *anything* in the last fifty years has necessarily been influenced by the technologization of this practice, as it has moved from the typewriter to the personal computer to the current ubiquity of networked computing. For these reasons, the tendency in scholarship of digital poetics to look back on precursors and influences should work both ways; it would be incomplete to study any of the texts that feature in this book without also considering them as a part of the network of digital poetry. Throughout this book, accordingly, my approach is to maintain a sustained focus on the material and technological conditions of production, which is often though not always digital in nature. At the same time, I would like to make explicit the need for a postanarchist literary theory that pays attention to the digital and networked elements of all poetry, *especially* print-based (read: not born-digital) poetry.

Digital poetry explicitly works toward a depersonalization of poetry and a de-individualization of the author by virtue of its networked nature and the often indeterminate or machine-driven elements of its production. This is because "Digital poems," as Funkhouser notes, "are more inclined toward abstraction and are largely depersonalized, especially as the media used in composition has become hybridized" (17). As my postanarchist readings in the chapters that follow will show, print-based media also see this inclination enacted by means of palimpsestic rewriting and intertextuality. While these effects are not exclusive to digital poems, the processes of "Randomization, patterning, and repetition of words, along with discursive leaps and quirky, unusual semantic connections, are almost always found in digital poetry, though sometimes these effects are so amplified that the poems would not be considered poetry by someone using traditional definitions" (Funkhouser 18). Additionally, digital poems are marked by instability and flux, a characteristic that should recall the ephemerality and transience of the postanarchist TAZ (and Bookchin's critiques of this very ephemerality). "Digital poems do not exist in a fixed state," as Funkhouser has also pointed out, and thus "Any work that exists in digital form is temporary" (21). Furthermore, "Longevity is not one of the genre's defining characteristics" (21). While recent curatorial work by such digital humanities scholars as Dene Grigar[7] and the growing popularity of the field of media archaeology are changing the way we view the ephemerality of the digital text, nonetheless this ephemerality is a hallmark of it. Postanarchist literary theory challenges us to be informed by this transience rather than bemoan it; accordingly, I treat the fleeting nature of meaning inherent in the print-based media I consider in this project as a reflection of the temporariness of the digital poem and an implied critique of the archive as theoretical concept.

One of the most important features of digital poetry from a postanarchist perspective is that it is marked by a rhizomatic linking, through hypertext and also through a radical intertextuality that both directs to other texts (either digital or print-based) and conditions itself to generate new poems or replicate itself (or both). For Funkhouser (and this position is affirmed by the scholarship of many other digital humanities scholars studying electronic literature, including Florian Cramer, Brian Kim Stefans, and Sandy Baldwin), "Digital poetry is not a fixed object," and "its circuitry perpetuates a conversation" (18). Insofar as it embraces the conversation and discursivity inherent in the common, digital poetry makes it apparent that "Poetry is a socially constructed art form, always situated within other texts (not limited only to poems) and extended by readers" (18). The poetry I study in the chapters that follow embraces the hypertextuality Funkhouser describes, whether in print or in new media.

The other important issue to highlight in this context is that the digital takes over some of the more laborious elements of the writing process; as digital and networked technologies have taken over menial or unspecialized labour in many other industries, they also absorb the menial work of experimental poetics, affording poets more time, energy, and opportunity to pursue more radical, elaborate, and thoughtful poetic projects. Bookchin points to the value of these affordances for anarchism in his early and influential *Post-Scarcity Anarchism*, even though, writing in 1971, Bookchin could only imagine the "surfeit" of poetic goods provided by the twenty-first-century digital (152). Its immediate access to nearly infinite information, its ability to data-mine, to transform and manipulate, and to link indefinitely to other texts points to new modes of poetic authorship afforded by this new media.

I do not mean by any of this to suggest that postanarchist literary theory is better suited to the study of experimental digital poetry than it is to other art forms. Instead, I argue that any political and literary theory is bound to its sociohistorical context, and thus postanarchist theory must embrace the digital in a way that Bey could never have envisioned when he coined the term. When postanarchist literary theory does address the radical potentials of the digital, the result is a collapse of the distinction between it and the classical or traditional anarchists that the term was originally meant to usurp. As Saint Schmidt argues, such a distinction is not only unhelpful but also runs counter to the postanarchist desire to replace epistemological and ontological binarisms with openness and commonality: "I...do not believe that it is desirable or even possible to pigeonhole unique individuals into two distinctly labelled boxes, namely 'classical anarchist' or 'traditionalist' and 'postanarchist,'" he asserts, because "the postanarchist attitude is characterized by the endless interrogation of the reality of these very boxes" (np). If Schmidt is right that postanarchism is predicated on "the assumption that power is a pervasive, multinodal phenomenon which is both creative and destructive in its operation" (np), which I would not dispute, then the digital offers postanarchism a way to address and appropriate power that works against its potentially destructive capacities and toward its more creative ones.

Yet it would be disingenuous to suggest that digital humanities and digital poetics are inherently postanarchist, or even inherently political. Accordingly, I have no interest in claiming for my digital humanities practice a superiority to other projects that appear to be much more traditional. Instead, I would argue that *any* digital intervention into humanities scholarship—a historically print-dominated medium—has the potential to be disruptive, but it need not be (and often is not). What I would like to insist upon, however, is that all postanarchist projects *must* in some form or another pay attention to the potentials of the digitally networked world to create many and multiple TAZs and to connect disparate and unique individuals into a common in which a greater diversity of voices can be accessed. This is not to suggest that the internet is a postanarchist utopia where all humans are created and treated equally, but rather that postanarchism must insist on creating moments of digital art in which radical freedom and relative autonomy can erupt more easily and more accessibly thanks to the connective potentials of the digital.

Postanarchist literary theory proposes an understanding of the digital as one manifestation of the assemblage of humans with machines. Machine-writing, too, is only one manifestation of the many potential versions of this assemblage. By machine-writing, I mean not simply to refer to any literary production in which hardware is used as a tool for the writing process, but rather to productions in which the machine plays a significant and agential role in the writing process, so that some of the onus of meaning-making is placed on the machine itself.

Furthermore, despite the frequent turns in this book to deleuzian terminology, the machine I invoke here is quite different from the machines (desiring- and war-) that Deleuze and Guattari theorize in *A Thousand Plateaus*. For Deleuze and Guattari, the machine that produces noise for artistic or poetic purposes is ineffectual; it "ends up reproducing nothing but a scribble effacing all lines, a scramble effacing all sounds" (344). They even go so far as to argue that material that is "too rich" in noise ends up being too "territorialized" because what results is only inconsistency, with no way for reader or audience to identify the disparate objects being synthesized. By contrast, postanarchist literary theory prizes illegibility, inconsistency, and noise; in my view, the closer we get to a machine-writing in which the disparate elements are indistinguishable and inseparable, the closer we get to pure communication freed from signification. I admit that if even Deleuze considers an experiment ineffectual, we have to start seriously considering the practicality of the project. But, as the case studies in this book demonstrate, there is a real practicality to the noise-filled text that these claims overlook: anyone can write it, anyone can read it, and no one is beholden to it.

## How Do We Read the Illegible?

Part of what digital or machine intervention in experimental poetics points to is new, variant forms of legibility and new ways of reading what might be termed illegible. This concern with illegibility is brought to the fore in Dworkin's *Reading the Illegible* (2003), a meditation on the author-function in formally experimental poetic texts. In this work,

Dworkin argues that poetics of machine, "plagiarism," indeterminacy, and collaboration all refuse to validate the Author and, instead, privilege a *détournement*, Guy Debord's concept of the defamiliarization of the quotidian. Dworkin explains:

> The antithesis of quotation, which marks and reinscribes authority, détournement pursues a poetics of plagiarism in the tradition of Lautréamont, whose infamous syllogism declares: "*Les idées s'améliorent. Le sens des mots y participe. Le plagiat est nécessaire, le progrès l'implique* [Ideas improve. The meaning of words plays a part in this development. Plagiarism is necessary. Progress implies it]." (13)

While I do not adopt Dworkin's (and Lautréamont's) progressivist rhetoric, what is most important to note here is that *Reading the Illegible* does not dwell on authorship. Instead, Dworkin cites Lautréamont's syllogism as if to justify accepting all radical forms of authorship without reservation, and then moves on. The rest of his text examines the reader and the reading processes of formally experimental, "illegible," or semantically nonsensical poetic texts, with an approach that consistently refuses prescriptive ways of reading. As he explains in his introduction, "In short, the basic thesis of this book is [redacted]" (xviii). This blacked-out line frustrates the authorial power of the scholar, a power that depends on authoritative reading; in *Reading the Illegible*, Dworkin consistently avoids offering definitive readings of the texts he considers, stating rather that he hopes "to establish," through his "book's many close readings,... an alternative strategy of reading itself" (xviii). This alternative strategy embraces the artifice, openness, indeterminacy, and politics that I consider integral to the experimental text, and I hope my own close readings that follow show the influence of this strategy.

The experimental poem is, then, to be read but not authoritatively interpreted. In Dworkin's words, "If I have, at times, abjured interpretation in the following pages, it has only been to give onto *reading*" (xxiv, emphasis Dworkin's). He argues that experimental, illegible texts complicate both representation[8] and denotation; their "active language," that is, their language that does not languish in the denotative realm, demonstrates that "when language exceeds its communicative authority—in those moments when its familiar and overworked utility stutters to reveal its 'fundamentally strange and foreign' nature—one catches a glimpse of 'the insubordination of words'" (11). Of course, complicating semantics and denotation is central to all poetry, and it has long been a hallmark of formalist poetics. Consider, for example, Ludwig Wittgenstein's now infamous note in *Zettel*: "Do not forget that a poem, although it is composed in the language of information, is not used in the language game of giving information" (§106). Dworkin's project suggests a way of reading (and perhaps, too, a way of writing) where communication is achieved without subordinating language to the limiting, denotative process of Wittgenstein's language game of information.

Of particular relevance to postanarchist literary theory is Dworkin's understanding of the reading process as, necessarily, a communal practice born out of communication. He first makes this point implicitly in his reading of Susan Howe's *Eikon Basilike*, where he notes "the repetition and emphasis of 'common' ('in common,' communism,' and twice with 'common-wealth')," which "gesture toward 'communication' through the Latin *comunis* from which they all directly descend" (*Reading* 45). This may seem, on its own, unremarkable, until we understand that Dworkin reads Howe's work as "noise"—that is, nonsemantic communication. In striking contrast to Deleuze and Guattari, Dworkin contends that "noise proliferates hand in hand with an increase in the terms of communication" (*Reading* 45). On this reading, then, the proliferation of noise produces the *common*. Experimental, illegible texts produce in readers a *commonality*, a community based on the ethical, political dimensions of reading and engaging with the formally experimental text. Dworkin makes this political element explicit at the very end of *Reading the Illegible*, when he invokes Bey:

> Whatever the value of the claims I have made in this book...the mere fact of that hermeneutic activity...should suggest an ethics of the illegible and remind us that the unreadable text is a *temporary autonomous zone*: one which refuses the permanence of its own constitution, and which calls on its readers to account for the semantic drives that they cannot, in the end, resist—and for which we must learn, as readers, to take responsibility. (155, emphasis mine)

In light of such passages as this, I consider Dworkin's work relevant and helpful to articulating a postanarchist literary theory. All of the elements Dworkin values—the proliferation of noise, the act of communication, the inevitable "hermeneutic activity" amidst the attempted resisting of "semantic drive," and the "responsibility" that readers must "take"—produce a postanarchist literary theory that is, at its core, a theory of poetry as inherently communal. It is a theory of new activist reading practices that re-envision the production and reading of experimental texts as producing the *common*.

The theory of new, activist reading practices that I have argued for in this introduction is, in the chapters that follow, tested in sixteen case studies—sixteen experiments, I might say—that read texts through the lens of postanarchist theory, and often read these texts quite closely, but only sparingly interpret them. Looking first at writers whose machine-writing practices function retrospectively as precursors to the digital (Jackson Mac Low, John Cage, Robert Duncan, and bpNichol), my first chapter draws on postanarchist literary theory to place emphasis on the readerly freedom afforded by the process by which machine-writing substitutes for authorial intention. This same process is explicitly gendered in my second chapter, where I extend these earlier findings and translate them into a study of how the machine (which quickly becomes the computer) opens identity politics for effective feminist ends in the works of women writers who engage with machine-writing methods (Susan Howe, Erín Moure [Erin Mouré], Juliana Spahr, and Harryette Mullen). My third chapter offers a critique of conceptualism based on the new radical potentials revealed in the first two chapters, with reference to contrasting works by four prominent conceptual authors (Kenneth Goldsmith, Vanessa Place, Christian Bök, and Darren Wershler); here postanarchist literary theory points to the ways in which conceptualism purports to use technology to achieve political ends and to resist signification, but more often reifies the Author and authorial intention. In my fourth and final chapter I apply postanarchism and its considerations of the machine to a varied selection of important figures in the fields of e-lit and digital poetics (Jim Andrews, W. Mark Sutherland, Brian Kim Stefans, Andy Campbell, and Mez Breeze). Through this study of more recent forays into digital poetics I show that electronic literature has the radical potential to use the digital interface to engage with intervening and agential readerships, to reveal the ways that traditional authorship governs a text, and to resist such authorial power.

Ultimately, in this book I present an argument for the potential of a postanarchist literary theory of the experiment to encourage greater advances in digital literature in North America, advances that engage with readers and allow for greater reader freedom. To do so, I must perform acts of both theorizing and close reading, and in the midst of these practices I must perform acts of interpretation. In some ways, this practice contrasts with its stated goals. But if I can make manifest the material conditions of writing and researching this book (the practice of many of the authors I study here), I can perhaps fracture to at least some extent the authorial power afforded to the writer and especially to the critic. The aim is to encourage reading practices that allow greater freedom to the reader, greater reader intervention, and greater reliance on machines, codes, and other non-human material to do the writing itself. If Dworkin can proclaim his basic thesis to be a blacked-out line relinquishing legibility, my thesis instead would be ____________________. A blank. A line to fill in. A clear and inviting space for the reader. Write yourself, reader, onto that line, between these lines, and throughout the margins of this book. Intervene where you will.

# 1 Precursors to Digital Writing

THE MACHINE, in its various forms, has been used historically in North American avant-garde circles to mediate, suppress, and reduce the power that the author has over the reader. In this chapter I look at some early examples of machine-writing to identify foundational methods through which four poets writing between the years 1968 and 2003 experimented with systemic methods and methods of manipulating source texts written by other authors in order to reduce the power that authors of poetry have over their readers. I refer to these works as precursors to digital writing because they pioneer many of the interventions in authorship that later born-digital and transmedial writings would take up decades later.[1] In my selections here, I work across national boundaries and between genres and even across a rather large historical period in order to demonstrate the primary features of these early machine-writings while at the same time demonstrating the ways in which the incorporation of the machine into the writing process works politically to break down boundaries (of, for instance, genre, nation, and subjectivity). In doing so, I claim for machine-writing four foundational features that, together, make it the ideal focus of a postanarchist literary theory: that it is anarchist in its reduction of power; that it is "noise" in its refusal of semantic, logical sense; that it is communal in its revelation of the many voices that have always gone into authorship; and, finally, that it is occupied with engaging its readers on a level that the traditionally composed and print-based (frequently lyric) poem simply cannot be. In other words, my primary focus here is readership, the core of the postanarchist project.

To demonstrate each of these four primary features of a postanarchist reading and writing practice, I look to four diverse poets linked by their turn to machines that play a significant role in textual production. First, I discuss the American poet Jackson Mac Low, who used the Diastex program to write systematically through the prose and poetry of modernist icon Gertrude Stein. The resulting *Stein Poems* (1998-2003) appear late in Mac Low's career and represent the results of his grappling with the best way to reduce the ego of the poet in the writing process and to make room for readers to make their own choices and their own meanings. As a result of this reduction of the ego, the poems become anarchist analogies for free communities. Similarly, self-identified anarchist poet and composer John Cage, also American, invents a systemic rule for *writing through* books owned and written by his partner, the dancer and choreographer Merce Cunningham, in order to produce poems he terms *mesostics*. In the process, he queers and demilitarizes language to make room for nonsense and noise. Suppressing syntax, sense, and meaning, Cage's "62 Mesostics Re Merce Cunningham" (1973) leave room for readers to take what they wish from the text. Next, not wanting to include only texts that employ obviously indeterminate methods, I apply postanarchist reading practices to the work of American poet Robert Duncan, who does not engage with machines in the same way as Cage and Mac Low but instead turns to a tapestry metaphor to depict a writing that is more about compilation than anything else. In his *Passages* series of poems (1968-87), Duncan represents himself as a weaver of various sources together, an authorial practice that is communal rather than expressive. Finally, I consider the work of Canadian experimental poet bpNichol, whose poetry in *First Screening* (1983) extends the concern with the typewriter evident in his earlier poetry and translates these pre-digital poetics into the digital realm. While *First Screening* is born-digital, I discuss it here as a precursor to digital poetics because it so clearly acts as a bridge between print-based experimentalism and later digital projects, specifically in advancing Nichol's desire to incorporate the personal but remove the expressive, lyric potentials of the writing subject.

What all four of these poets demonstrate is that these four primary concerns of the (literally or metaphorically) machine-written text render the text itself unusually open to its readers. By refusing the expression and subjectivity of the lyric subject, who has dominated mainstream poetry for centuries, these writers envision a readership that is able to engage with the poems on a meaningful level. Whether this engagement is literal, as in *First Screening* where Nichol hides poems, or as an instruction to read extensively elsewhere, as in *Passages* where Duncan's quotations serve as directions outward, these works are all explicitly concerned with presenting themselves to an autonomous, agential reader who plays an important and frequently collaborative role in the meaning-making of the text. It is also worth noting, as preamble to these case studies, that Mac Low, Cage, and Duncan all engaged in anarchist debate on a political level, writing for journals like *Direct Action* or carrying out some direct action of their own.[2] Nichol, by contrast, devoted a lot of energy to small presses, art-based psychotherapeutic practice, and communal living, but was never an active, explicit anarchist in the way that the other three were.

## Jackson Mac Low Is Something Something

In my discussion of Jackson Mac Low, I look not to his early poems in which he pushes the limits of chance, spontaneity, improvisation, deterministic methods, and computer systems designed to produce diastic poems,[3] but to his poetic sequence *The Stein Poems*, composed between 1998 to 2003, ending just a year before Mac Low's death. Among some of the last poems Mac Low ever wrote, *The Stein Poems* represent the culmination of a lifetime of experimentation with indeterminacy and chance. As Mac Low himself asserted in the cover letter that accompanied a submission of some of these poems for journal publication: "I returned to using a deterministic procedure in April 1998, when I began writing the poems in the Stein series, but now I always, to some extent, modify the results of the procedure, making personal decisions of different kinds. My writingways [*sic*] came together" (*Thing of Beauty* 376). In *The Stein Poems*, then, Mac Low returns to deterministic methods of writing, which he had more or less abandoned, only to adapt these chance-based procedures by making clear the moments in which his individual judgement intervened in, or added to, the deterministic process.

Also quite clear from Mac Low's publication history is that it was his writing about fellow poet Cage's chance-based poetry that led him to write *The Stein Poems* in this way. Mac Low's essay, "Something About the Writings of John Cage," first published in 1993, examines the role of taste and authorial intent in Cage's chance-based work. In 2001 Mac Low published a revised and expanded version of this article as "Cage's Writings up to the Late 1980s"; at the same time as he was revising this essay, however, he was also writing *154 Forties*, poems written according to a more traditional compositional method, with an emphasis on prosody and caesural spaces. Chance thus served as one writingway, and the traditional composition of *154 Forties* the other, eventually coming together in *The Stein Poems*. In 1998, between the two Cage essays, Mac Low "returned," as he says, to deterministic methods, but with the concession that these methods were not without ego: both the decision to return and the new attitude toward ego were triggered in part by his work on Cage, in which he rails against those who wrongly believe Cage to have eliminated the author's ego through indeterminacy. For Cage, Mac Low insists, "Chance was always constrained, to a greater or lesser extent, by his intentions" ("Cage's Writings" 231). Moreover, "He knew very well that if he did anything at all, it would be done by or through his ego" ("Cage's Writings" 232). For Mac Low, then, the complete removal of the ego, even in a chance-based text, is impossible. "The point is not whether" Cage "ever entirely evaded his individual ego and its predilections," Mac Low writes, "but that he diminished to some extent the value-judging activity of the ego that excludes possibilities, and that he thereby let in, to some extent, 'the rest of creation'" ("Cage's Writings" 227). For Cage as for Mac Low, the goal was never to remove the author but always to make room for something greater.

Mac Low was probably always convinced of the egoism involved in chance-based and deterministic writing methods, if we may judge by his two seminal writings on poetics, "Statement" (1974) and "Some Remarks to the Dancers" (1974), for in both he touches briefly on the role of choice in chance-based texts. In "Statement," he asserts that the author is not a dictator over a text, but is nevertheless a co-initiator of action, and for this reason is able to produce, even (or especially) by means outside of the author's control, "absolutely unique situations" (385). In "Some Remarks to the Dancers," he notes that although he relied on "chance" to create the poems in his acclaimed sequence *The Pronouns*, by way of a filing card system he devised, some "crucial features" were matters of free choice (390–91). These brief pieces demonstrate that by 1973 Mac Low had already begun to think about the relationship between chance and authorship, but it was not until after Cage's death in 1992, and his subsequent work on Cage's use of chance, that Mac Low had the hindsight to re-evaluate his own views on indeterminacy. This re-evaluation is demonstrated most clearly in "Making Poetry 'Otherwise'" (2001), where he asserts "that the choices he [Cage] and many of us made when we devised systems would be egoist in the very absolute Zen sense" (np). Here Mac Low's language is stronger than ever in his assertion that "many" chance-based operations were carried out by and through the ego.

Reflecting the development of Mac Low's views, *The Stein Poems* stand at a mediatory position between chance and choice, between nonintentional and intentional writing.[4] Mac Low's discussions of authorship in Cage's chance-based poetry forced him to re-evaluate what constitutes a nonintentional text or a deterministic text, and led him to conclude that the two terms actually refer to different qualities of chance operations. He notes that, sparked by a discussion with his son, he realized that though his systemic reading-through text-selection procedures were "nonintentional"—in that he "cannot predict to any extent what will be brought into a text through using them" ("Cage's Writings" 224)—they are also "deterministic" in that "If followed out to the letter, they must find, and bring into the work being written, the same linguistic units in the source texts each time" (225). "Nonintentional" thus refers to the lack of authorial control in the procedure, and "deterministic" to the reproducibility of the textual experiment, as in the scientific connotations of the term "experiment" itself. The element of chance is a third term, introduced into the procedures by way of "human errors (and when these methods are automated, computer errors)," which "provide an unlooked-for but inevitable element of chance" (225). While the author has relative control over the procedures, then, and while this process is necessarily egoic, the element of chance also destabilizes the writing subject.

Indeed, destabilizing subjectivity is central to Mac Low's work, as Tyrus Miller observes. With focus on the ways in which subjectivity is defined and constituted by language, Miller argues that by accepting the inability of a poem to be completely devoid of ego, of an Author, Mac Low gives his work the opportunity to expand the field of play of authorship within and outside of chance-based methods. In other words,

> the different instances of the subject in language (grammatical, intentional, incarnational) are still operative, in part at least, in Mac Low's acrostic-chance poems, but relate to one another asymmetrically, making the hypostasis of a single thinking/ speaking/ acting self impossible. (Miller 51)

Similarly, in his discussions of Mac Low's *Stanzas for Iris Lezak*, poems composed in 1960 and identified by Mac Low as his "first deterministic yet nonintentional system" (*Thing of Beauty* 49), Miller makes the important argument that "The self is not so much absent from this text as it is ascetically chastened" (61). While politically charged, Mac Low's decision to disrupt authorship in this way is, at the same time, aesthetic. Simply put, Mac Low enjoyed the computer's output for what it was, and "felt that whatever was given should be accepted" ("Making Poetry" np). The ascetic limitation of the writing self thus opens space for the aesthetic pleasure of what the computer has written. Accordingly, his later nondeterministic writings, such as *154 Forties*, and the merging of these two ways of writing in *The Stein Poems*, demonstrate "a real change" in which he "started thinking that what was made by the systems was not necessarily better" ("Making Poetry" np). Mac Low's interventions in the systemic processes thus mark his own desire to make the products of these systems "better."

This desire for betterment is tied to Mac Low's eventual decision that there can be no writing truly outside of sense. That he believes all writing to be, to some degree, sensical is best demonstrated, too, in his writings on Cage, in which he takes Cage to task for his use of the term "nonsyntactical." Cage sought to free language from conventional, normative syntax, Mac Low asserts: to free it "from 'the arrangements of an army,' which Norman O. Brown told him [Cage] was the original meaning of 'syntax'" ("Cage's Writings" 212). Mac Low, by contrast, preferred the term *asyntactical*: "There is some question, of course, as to whether any arrangement of language elements, no matter how different from normative syntax, doesn't in itself constitute a new, non-normative syntax. (For this reason I never use Cage's term 'nonsyntactical')" ("Cage's Writings" 212). As an extension of this reasoning, Mac Low came to believe that there was no such thing as complete randomness, especially not in deterministic or computer-based systems of textual production: "There's no randomness if it's computer generated....No, I never like randomness. I want specific things" ("Making Poetry" np). Finally accepting that a nonsyntactical, entirely random, and authorless text was impossible, Mac Low produced *The Stein Poems* as the culmination of a lifetime of experimentation with sense, chance, and ego.

This acceptance helps to explain why the brief explanatory endnotes included after each poem in the *Stein* series include detailed accounts of how Mac Low altered the products of the systemic procedures. Ranging in level of intervention, some poems, such as "Stein 15," get "accepted" as they are produced (*Thing of Beauty* 382). "Stein 11–13" are included with "minimal subsequent editing" (379–81). "Stein 32" is published after having been "revised a number of times" (397). And "Stein 53" gets included after having been "freely revised and edited" (400). Some of the explanatory notes are extremely vague, but even these suggest a good deal of editing, revision, and authorial intention, such as the note that follows "Stein 76," where Mac Low writes that the poem was produced by "'mining' what remained of the output of this procedure and producing normative sentences from the words elicited thereby" (402). Taken together, these late poems and the notes describing Mac Low's interventions constitute an invitation to a postanarchist reading practice: an invitation that downplays authorship and, instead, relies on Stein and the computer to bring readers into a freer, more autonomous engagement with the poems.

Mac Low's desire to see political effect in his art is loosely related to his inclusion in the Fluxus School of the avant-garde in that, in keeping with Dick Higgins's views of Fluxus,[5] Mac Low wanted the artistic practice to include "a good deal of ordinary life," not just "everyday" art but art that is analogous to life rather than a metaphor for it (Mac Low, "Interview" 266). This artistic value lays the groundwork for a critical approach that reads Mac Low's poetry as embodying and enacting meaning, rather than encoding and decoding messages. Mac Low was always open about the activist or political elements of his work, arguing often that his attempts to produce texts that are "minimally egoic" (Tardos xviii) oppose the closed subjectivity of social institutions. In "Poetry and Pleasure," for instance, he writes that "The kinds of pain that people suffer in present day societies are often due to clumsy social, economic, and political arrangements that simply need not be so clumsy, so slovenly" (xxvii). And again, "So many artists and experiencers of art believe that the point of art is to change these slovenly, pain-causing—and boredom-causing—arrangements" (xxviii). Mac Low sets out to alter these painful arrangements on two levels: first, on the author's part by arranging for the readers to be initiators of and collaborators with the text; second, on the readers' part by arranging for them to have greater freedom in reading the text. Thus, the playfulness that characterizes his *Stein Poems* is in itself political. By subjecting Stein's work to machinic operations, Mac Low produces poems that do not really make sense, even though they still recall Stein's dedication to the quotidian and banal. Consider, for example, the first few lines of the series' first poem: "Little lingering father little regular simple. // Little long length there louder happening deepening. / Beginning and little way singing neat cooked" (377). By avoiding the limitations of a syntactical text that needs to be received and interpreted on an exegetical level, the text opens itself up to a playfulness that could not be available otherwise.

Besides the variety of readings that *The Stein Poems*, in their virtual illegibility, open up, the text also serves as a politically effective anarchist-activist text in that it acts as an analogy of a free community rather than offering a description of one. In "Poetry and Pleasure," Mac Low writes that he shares the belief of many other political or activist authors who have argued that "speaking differently changes a culture and...different ways of speaking are most prevalent in poetry" (xxxiii). However, he also notes that this process works both positively and negatively; it can open up potentialities just as easily as it can close them off. For Mac Low, any text that is politically prescriptive—that instructs its readers about better, freer ways of living—actually enforces an opposing politic by limiting the reading process. According to Mac Low, then, his poetry has an effective anarchist politic specifically *because* it does not prescribe a change in thought or speech. Rather, it engages with systemic operations in order to leave itself more open for its readers. In this sense, Mac Low's poetry acts like a microcosm for anarchism and reveals his dream of a utopian anarchist community, albeit one that even he admits is still imperfect.

As I have mentioned, Mac Low preferred to think of his work as producing analogies rather than paradigms of anarchic communities. He made this view explicit in an interview with Gil Ott, who posed the following question: "When one of your works is being performed...is that a model political community?" (Mac Low, "Dialog" 21). I quote Mac Low's response at length because he summarizes what I have been trying to say about his work for some time:

> Although performers are not directly regulated by a central authority, eventually they are, since I as the composer am giving them the materials, procedures, rules, etc. (This is why I usually say these days that such performances are "analogies" rather than

"paradigms" of free communities). Nevertheless, they're exercising their own initiative within the situation, the *given* materials being analogies of the real-life conditions provided by nature and society. (Mac Low, "Dialog" 21)

Bearing in mind the role of "initiative" as Mac Low here describes it, we may conclude in the case of *The Stein Poems* that the reader, as a collaborator on the level of meaning-making, can choose, momentarily, to refuse some of the regulatory aspects of a larger system of limitation: to refuse the "clumsy,...slovenly" categories that limit the initiatory choices we are able to make in our lives; to choose, instead, spontaneity. Nevertheless, this choice is incomplete and imperfect, as Mac Low also acknowledges here, and it is important for those who encounter Mac Low's work to realize how and when certain choices are made for them.

Consistent with his interest in the politics of choice, Mac Low's asyntactical texts also reflect an egalitarian interest in the intrinsic significance of all sounds. In "Making Poetry 'Otherwise,'" he asserts his belief that "there's something significant in any sound made by a sentient being" (np). Arguing that, for example, animal noises convey meaning or significance without the encoding and decoding of a linguistic message, Mac Low asserts that the meaning (or meanings) of a sound are intrinsic to, or a part of, the sound itself. In making this claim he directly opposes Ferdinand de Saussure, who asserts in his *Course in General Linguistics* that the relationship between signifier and signified is arbitrary and that semiotic meaning does not significantly correspond to the visual or aural properties of the signified itself. Mac Low, elsewhere, directly acknowledges that his viewpoint is anti-Saussurian:

> I believe (despite Saussure and his followers) that there's an intrinsic connection between sound and meaning....However, each word has a number of different meanings connected with it, and these multiple meanings may be combined in an infinitely large number of ways, so that perceivers of work such as mine may find (or "enact") for themselves many different meanings. (Mac Low, "Interview" 257)

What this means in the context of the present argument is that while some may understand a refusal of the arbitrary relationship between signifier and signified as a gesture toward essentialized meaning, for Mac Low such a refusal need not lead to that conclusion. To understand that each phoneme, intentional or nonintentional, semantic or otherwise, is the vehicle for infinite possible meanings is to open up the reading process in ways that traditional semiotics does not and cannot.

Rather than understanding the materiality of language as essentially meaningless, Mac Low revels in the limitless potentials of meaningful sounds. As he exclaims in an interview with Nicholas Zurbrugg, "I am convinced that meaning abounds" (Mac Low, "Interview" 270). In poetry, as he further explains, this understanding places the responsibility of meaning-making not on the poet who composes the piece, but rather on the reader who performs meaning-making at the level of experience or perception:

> All words in poems are meaningful, whether they intentionally convey messages or not and whether they're brought into the poems intentionally or through nonintentional methods. The perceivers of the poems enact meanings, at the end of the day, whether the poets intend to convey meanings or not. (Mac Low, "Interview" 271)

This process of enacting meaning, he argues, frees language from the weight of the communicative message, allowing the linguistic elements to speak themselves, and freeing the reader to engage with the piece unburdened by semantics. The goal of this writing "is to let what's there *be*; especially letting words, linguistic units, be, not make them carry a burden of my thoughts, my feelings, whatever" ("Making Poetry" np). What Mac Low proposes here is, in effect, a postanarchist reading practice in which expression is refused in favour of a more productive engagement with the text at hand. This view of readership opens up asyntactical texts like *The Stein Poems* to infinite unique readings. "Each person who hears or reads this kind of work produces something new," he tells Zurbrugg, "whether one wishes to call it 'meaning' or something else" (Mac Low, "Interview" 271). The result is a reading practice that is communal and anarchic, because authorial intent is deferred through the use of the systemic, diastic method.

I say "anarchic" here because by placing the responsibility of meaning-making on the reader as performer, Mac Low refuses the potential authority of the composer/author role. This has long been a concern of his work, as his widow Anne Tardos recognizes in her foreword to his selected poems, *Thing of Beauty* (2008), where she quotes the now unavailable "Instructions" for his "Music for Gathas": "'He [the composer] values freedom—everybody's freedom with this composer-performer community. He is neither the dictator nor...the primary soloist'" (xvi). Ever the realist, Mac Low never claims that these moments of free meaning-making are purely anarchic. Rather, a reading of Mac Low's poetry is like a TAZ, which is what the poet himself suggests when he states that the pieces are "'analogies' rather than 'paradigms' of free communities." By creating a TAZ, a performative analogy of an anarchist, free community, Mac Low helps his readers recognize how sign systems and their concomitant limitations reinforce the organizing, ruling, and inhibiting effects of larger social institutions, and gives them momentary freedom from such limitations. Much of this freedom is afforded to the reader because Mac Low, as author, diminishes himself by way of the inclusion of Stein as source text and by way, of course, of the computer that he used to select these lines.

These key features of *The Stein Poems* are exemplified by "Time That Something Something (Stein 18)," a poem that not only invites and embraces the potentials of multiple meanings but also relies heavily on aurality (on rhythm, silence, and repetition, elements that Mac Low retained from the Stein source texts). This emphasis on aurality foregrounds the reading of this poem as a performance, and the excessive use of blank space to denote silence acts as a reminder for the reader to meditate on the potentials of the language in the poem. The poem begins, following the vague but inviting title, with the following lines, making up the first "sentence":

That
being,
This,
One and one is is,
The. (383)

The specificity of the singular demonstrative adjectives or pronouns "That" and "This," and of the definite article "The," stands in stark contrast to the extremely vague "Something Something" of the title and to the emphasis on the multiple inherent in "One and One is is," which is repeated throughout the poem, identically at first, but then in variations, such as "If is one one," as "One, / and one is, / is one," and as "One and one, / is ís then there" (383). The multiple variations of the line, as well as its repeated suggestion that the multiple ("one and one") cohere incompletely, invite the reader to become aware that the individual linguistic unit carries with it multiple potential readings. When the line is repeated with an added emphasis on the second "ís" (via a stressor accent), the poem reminds its reader that the message, the object of the verb "to be," is not encoded in the poem. Instead of the burden of syntactical meaning, the poem presents its reader with an emphasized but emptied "ís."

The rest of the poem is similarly filled with pronouns without antecedents, definite articles without clarifying nouns, progressive verbs without clear acting subjects, and the almost frustrating repetition of vague pronouns such as "something" (four times) and "anything" (three times). The final four lines of the poem dramatize the potential frustrations of a reader seeking expression, unaware that the poem requires that readers take the role of meaning-maker in the text. It ends:

Talking,
seeing,
expressing,
discovering something something. (383)

While readers may hope to interpret and thus "discover" something previously "covered" by the text, they are met with illogic and anticlimax. As the implied acting subject of these progressive verbs, each reader fills in the emptiness of the words, accepts the potentials of their meaning, and, in so doing, performs the piece. The reader enacts—and becomes—something something.

## John Cage Making Excessive Noise

Despite the rise in critical attention paid to John Cage's work over the past two decades, his poetic sequence "62 Mesostics Re Merce Cunningham" has garnered little critical attention. The sequence is a difficult one to deal with in scholarship: its unique typography makes quotation cumbersome (see Figures 1 and 2); it is semantically nonsensical and often visually indecipherable; furthermore, it invites readers into dangerous biographical exegesis because Cage dedicates the piece to his partner, Merce Cunningham. Yet these very problems make it an important work: the primary concern of the Cunningham mesostics is to engage the reader not in narrative or even logical sense, but rather in a communal attention to language. Any discussion of authorship in the Cunningham mesostics is extremely difficult, and must be at the very least tentative, because, in the conventional sense, Cage has not written these poems. In terms of content, the "syllables and words" found in the poem were, as Cage writes in the foreword, "obtained from Merce Cunningham's *Changes: Notes on Choreography* and from thirty-two other books most used by Cunningham in relation to his work" (ii). Even the order in which the words appear was decided, not by poetic diction, but by chance. Cage subjected the source texts to *I Ching* chance operations, "a process which brought about in some cases syllable exchange between two or more of them" (Foreword ii). These exchanges produced a multiplicity of new words and meanings in excess of the original source texts. The form of the poems is also largely outside of Cage's control. Cage decided on the mesostic form (a mesostic is like an acrostic poem, but the spine is in the centre rather than left-aligned) and on Cunningham's name as the poems' "spines," but the poems are composed in "over seven hundred different type faces and sizes available in Letraset and, of course, subjected...to *I Ching* chance operations" (Foreword ii). With this deference to chance and indeterminacy, the image of the author, even in abstract or experimental art, gets critically complicated. There is little correlation between Cage's approach of subjecting Cunningham's books and Letraset typefaces to chance operations and the more traditional aims of poetic production (*sprezzatura*, Romantic inspiration, lyrical subjectivity, etc.).

Nevertheless, as Mac Low makes clear, it would be inaccurate to claim that Cage's use of the *I Ching*, or of chance more generally, was designed to eradicate the role of the author. While chance is certainly one of the most often studied aspects of Cage's work, it is also, as Constance Lewallen writes, the most often misunderstood: "misunderstood because it is often mistakenly believed that Cage used chance to avoid making choices" (235). Of course, Cage made many choices in the production of the Cunningham mesostics, not only selecting the source texts but selecting them based on the intimately personal criterion of those "books most used by Cunningham." In this way, Cage's use of chance is not a way to avoid making decisions about the poems he is writing, but rather a way to change the kind of choices the author makes and to see what happens as a result. In Lewallen's terms, he "used chance as a discipline... to circumvent personal taste and memory so that he would be more open to outside experiences" (236). Cage identifies this misunderstanding himself in an interview: "Most people who believe that I'm interested in chance don't realize that I use chance as a discipline. They think I use it—I don't know—as a way of giving up making choices. But my choices consist in choosing what questions to ask" (Kostelanetz 17). In this way, Cage's role as author of these poems becomes not eliminated but destabilized. Unlike traditionally authored poems, these are written by a collective involving Cage, who asks the questions; Cunningham, whose work dictates the source texts Cage chooses from; the specific books he ultimately chooses; and the *I Ching* and the Letraset typefaces, all working in concert. The authors of the source texts, too, play a role in this collaboration, albeit without their consent. Most importantly, a postanarchist reading of the poems includes the reader in this collaborative view of the poems' production. As readers enter in the *comunis* of communication with the texts and take value from the noise produced in the asyntactical poems, they engage in this production in a manner that Cage as author can neither control nor predict. Language becomes a gift we give each other in the common, for no other reason save that we can. Thus, Cage produces the Cunningham mesostics to avoid reinforcing the ego of the Author as arbiter of this gift exchange.

Cage achieves this strategic avoidance by way of experiment, although he works here with a definition of the experiment that is somewhat unconventional. A helpful analysis of this definition has been carried out by William Brooks, who contrasts Cage's discussions of the artistic experiment with those of Cage's contemporary, composer Lejaren Hiller. While Brooks discusses Cage's music specifically, the definition of the experiment he arrives at is equally relevant to a discussion of Cage's poetry. Cage and Hiller both published articles defining the artistic experiment in the late 1960s, but they define it in different ways; Brooks summarizes this difference by way of a hypothetical anecdote, which may be paraphrased as follows:

> Let's say, then, that I am bicycling home from work, and notice a different route I could take. Taking this new route is my experiment. If I follow Hiller's definition, I pose a hypothesis: this route will get me home faster. I take the route, and end up home much later than usual. My hypothesis is incorrect, but I learn about the new route's value upon my arrival. If, instead, I follow Cage's definition, and ask, "What will I encounter if I take this alternate route?" I cannot fail. I see a new coffee shop, a park, and a market I would like to visit later. I do not gain any "use value." I do not prove or disprove a hypothesis. I merely make observations.[6]

In Cage's words, most succinctly: "What is the nature of an experimental action? It is simply an action the outcome of which is not foreseen"

("History" 69). As experimental texts according to Cage's definition, the Cunningham mesostics encourage readers to pay attention, to make observations about the language rather than to interpret a message (or in a more passive conception of the reading practice, to read and decode an encoded message).

This turn in reading practice provoked by the Cunningham mesostics is even more striking once we learn that, as "experiments," the mesostics have failed. That is, Cage writes that he originally planned to print the poems so that the various-sized letters would touch both horizontally and vertically; the vertical touching would give the poem "a spine," and thus each poem could "resemble Cunningham himself, the dancer" (Foreword i). Despite the fact that this desired outcome did not come to fruition—that instead, the poems more closely resemble "waterfalls" or "ideograms"—he nevertheless notes that "this is how they came to be made" (ii). Eschewing the conventional kind of scientific "experiment," Cage begins with a semblance of a hypothesis, but then, when *that* fails him, what he uncovers is a greater gift in its refusal to provide answers. Cage's inclusion of the failed experiment in his publications demonstrates both his interest in observation *and* the egalitarian potentials of a lack of purpose. The mesostics gesture beyond use-value, privilege noise above semantic function, and thus express a deep discomfort with language systems.

Cage's discomfort with language is well-documented. We only need to consider how frequently he echoes Brown's views on syntax (views that, as we have seen, also exerted a strong influence on Mac Low). "Syntax," Cage insists, "is the arrangement of the army. As we move away from it, we demilitarize language" (Foreword ii). But in the "62 Mesostics Re Merce Cunningham," Cage tries to mediate this discomfort. In its form, this sequence is made up of sixty-two mesostic poems that repeat Cage's partner's first and last names throughout; nonetheless, the poems are illegible, constituted by nonce or nonsensical words arranged according to the name-spine. While some words contained in the poems are fairly clear, they do not form cohesive sentences or even phrases: even when the text can be read, a reader cannot make sense of it. Because of this the Cunningham mesostic sequence is, above all else, a metapoetic series that strongly resists exegesis, hermeneutics, and the limitations of semantic language. The poems seek pure communication rather than the limited expression of militarized language.

In the Cunningham mesostics, this discomfort with language is represented most clearly by the nonce word "sicductor," which appears as the second line of the very first mesostic, shown below (Fig. 1). "Sic," the Latin adverb meaning "so" or "thus," first appears as an English word meaning "intentionally so written" in the mid-1800s and is subsequently used, as academics are so used to seeing, to denote an error reproduced in a quotation ("sic, *adv.*"). But it is pronounced just like the word *sick*. "Ductor," in Latin "one who leads," refers to, in a printing press, "A roller which conveys the ink from the ink-fountain to the distributing-rollers" ("ductor, *n.*"). It is responsible, in part, for getting the ink onto the page, and thus metonymically represents the materiality of language. When these two words are joined, "sicductor" suggests that the ductor is sick, that the use of language in the Cunningham mesostics fails because Cage's experiment seeks to represent, to literally present Cunningham's body in the poems. "Sicductor," then, also hints that Cage's work demonstrates an awareness of these errors. Yet at the same time, by recalling the Latin meaning of "sic," Cage's nonce term "sicductor" suggests a movement beyond the limitations of representation and exegesis, a *thus* from which Cage's experimental work follows. It encourages Cage's readers to look beyond interpretive reading, beyond use-value. In this way, Cage's work points us to Steve McCaffrey's adaptation of Georges Bataille's theory of general economy. For McCaffrey, "meaning...is staged as the telos and destination of the de-materialization of writing," which is to say that "the physical act of speaking or writing must withdraw so that what has been said or written can appear meaningful" (204). Yet the chance appearance of "sicductor" in the first mesostic establishes the sequence as one of material waste and excess. We can thus understand Cage's prioritization of the physical act of the text's production as a refusal to withdraw. The Cunningham mesostics do not make meaning or satisfy a logical

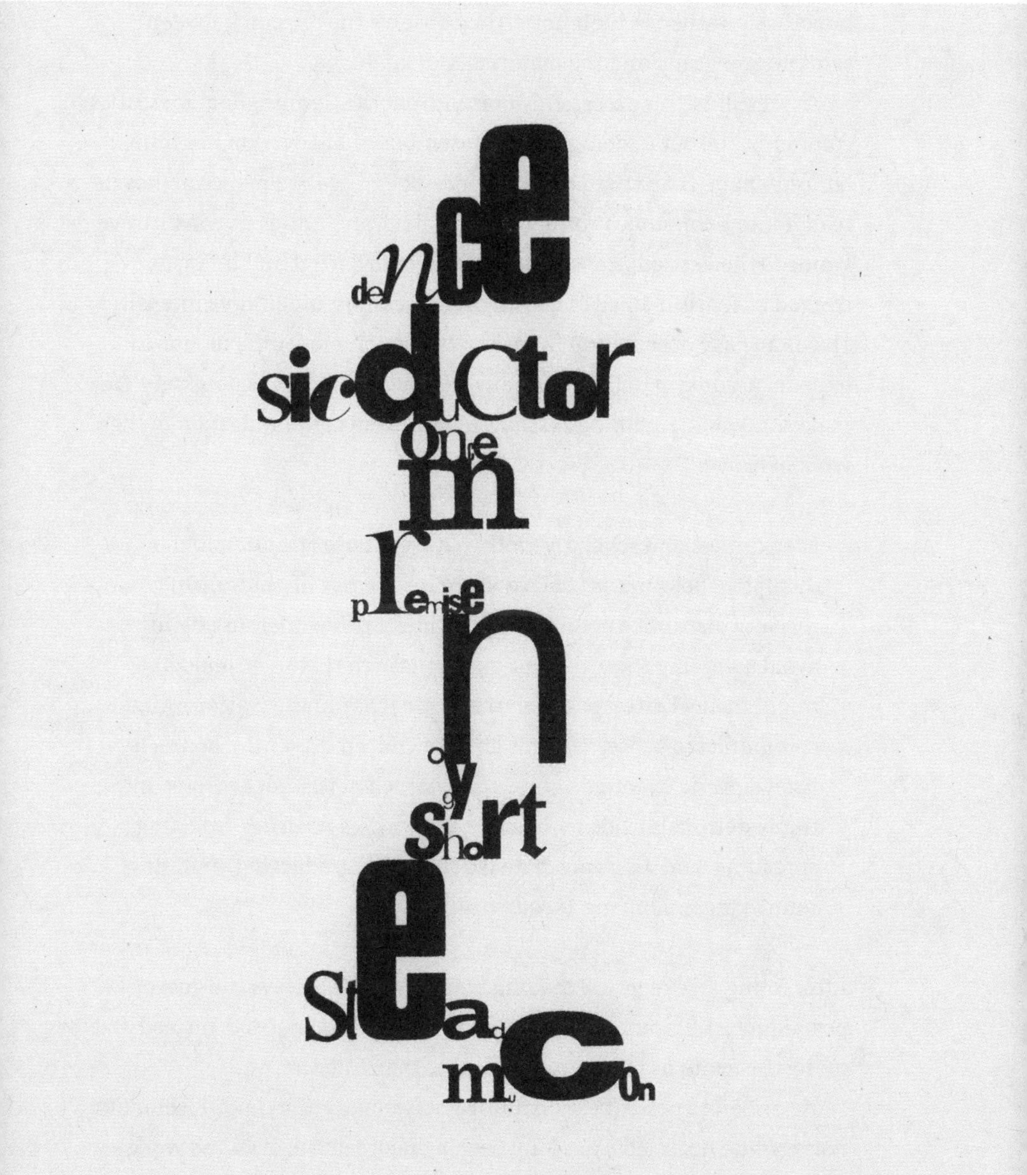

FIGURE 1. John Cage, "Mesostic 1," from "62 Mesostics Re Merce Cunningham."

hypothesis; rather, in their noise, they observe the tension between semantic meaning and the materiality of language.

The result of this excess, this noise, is that the Cunningham mesostics communicate, but in doing so they resemble what Dworkin has termed *parasites* more than coded semantic messages. Cage's sequence invites its reader into a *comunis*, a communicative field, and brings its constitutive words to the very edge of semantics, conveying affect and intensity instead of sense. Instead of quantitative meaning, qualitative intensity.[7] This is an easy observation to make, but a much more difficult one to explain. According to Dworkin, however, such difficulty is necessary. He makes this claim in his discussions of noise and communication in the work of Howe:

> Even critical and scholarly work that pays close attention to the disruptive possibilities of it [noise] runs the risk of neutralizing the very disruptive potential it identifies. Such work must try to avoid co-opting those disruptions for its own rhetorical ends, and might instead attempt to communicate noise in the way one might communicate a disease....This chapter, indeed this entire book—is itself a prime example of the way in which noises get accepted into the system, get inside us, become, in short, *les parasites*: infecting, spreading, and disabling, but also structuring, adapting, mutating, mimicking, colonizing. (*Reading* 49)

Attempting an exegetical reading of Cage's noise betrays the goal of a postanarchist literary theory, as Dworkin here articulates it. Instead, the mesostics invite us to be attentive rather than interpretive.

Attention to noise (be it disruptive noise, background noise, semantic noise, white noise, etc.) has long been a major feature of Cage's work musically. He makes this clear in *Silence*: "Wherever we are, what we hear is mostly noise. When we ignore it, it disturbs us. When we listen to it, we find it fascinating" (54). Cage's use of noise is, then, political; it defamiliarizes our relationship with noise, as it allows us to pay particular attention to those sounds that make up music. This noise translates to linguistic (rather than semantic) noise in the Cunningham mesostics in part as a result of the visual form of the poems, wherein each letter is given a unique typeface and size, which at times obscures the letters themselves. As Cage himself notes in an instalment of his "Diary" series of poems, placing emphasis on each letter invites the reader into a particularly attentive reading process:

> *To raise language's*
> *temperature we not only remove syntax: we*
> *give each letter undivided attention,*
> *setting it in unique face and size;*
> to read *becomes the verb* to sing. (107)

In this attentive reading process, the reader is invited into affective relationships with the words, letters, phonemes, and morphemes that make up the mesostics. The poems become notations for a reading public,[8] who perform the piece (who "sing" it) as they read. For Cage, this distinction between text as notation and reading as performance is one that adds an additional level of chance or indeterminacy to the production of textual meaning. That is, "Composition becomes distinct from performance. One cannot determine exactly what effect the notation causes—thus, indeterminacy" ("Form is a Language" 135). Consequently, the chance-determined form of the poem plays a role in the chance-determined effect of the text, functioning much like the unbiased coin-toss of the *I Ching* chance operation. The various-sized letters perform their noise-function, disturbing exegetical or interpretive reading habits, but remaining fascinating all the while.

"Inging" is Cage's cheeky neologism that appears in "Mesostic 19" ("62 Mesostics" 82). While semantically nonsensical—there is, of course, no *Oxford English Dictionary* entry for "inging"—the word functions in Cage's context as a sort of *ur*-verb that implies a perpetual *doing*, on the one hand, and on the other, a pure linguistic transience: a *mis en abîme* verb that folds in on itself, repeats itself, means itself. A feedback loop of noise. Repetition is one means of robbing a signifier of its semantic

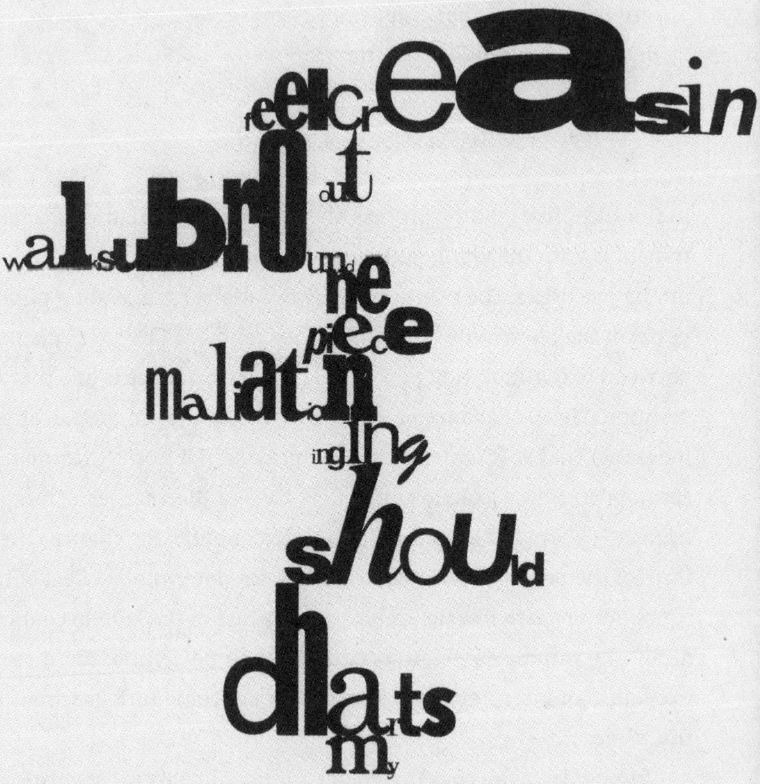


FIGURE 2. John Cage, "Mesostic 19," from "62 Mesostics Re Merce Cunningham."

meaning; a word gets repeated so many times that, in Saussurian terms, the arbitrary relationship between signifier and signified gets pulled apart. "Inging" is indefinite repetition. It sits in the mesostic as a fulcrum: toward the centre of Cunningham's name, the first "g" holds it in place (see Fig. 2). The letters themselves increase in size; the first "ing" is much smaller than the second, suggesting that the noise of "inging" gets louder, more disturbing, as it continues. Interestingly, the final "g" is written in a cursive typeface (the only cursive on the page), signifying both interconnectivity between letters and an expected continuation. The lack of another letter after the final "g" suggests emptiness, invites a rereading of the word. This emptiness is especially striking in light of the sheer size of other letters in the poem; the "ea" in the first line, the "bro" in the third, the "hou" in the eighth, and what appears to be an overlapping "d" and "h" in line nine, are all enormous, demanding the reader's attention away from the blank space, and the otherwise unassuming "inging."

Indeterminacy notwithstanding, the mesostic advocates this communal authorship with repeated references throughout the series to collection and combination: "mix" (23), "crossing" (29) and "cross" (154), "sum" (39), "inter" (136), "series" (139), "between" (148), and "we" twice (9, 71). At times in this series, the words themselves even intermingle due to the varying sizes of the characters, making it difficult to separate characters from each other or to tell which letter belongs to which "word." In one poem, for example, the "h," "i," and "n" in the word "(behind" blend so there is no space on either side of the "i" (150, no close parenthesis). Further down this poem, a "g" is so attached to a hyphen and a comma that the three appear to make one unique character together. In the poem just following this, "Mesostic 20," an enormous "o" takes up two full lines, and it would be unclear which line the "o" was meant to belong to were it not for the fact that both lines consist of actual English words: "people" and "other" (151). Through such means, form and content support a collaborative authorship that destabilizes the understanding of the expressive self as artist.

The romantic, anarchic, and experimental reasons why Cage would structure his poems in this way are certainly seductive, but the practical elements that inform these decisions are also worth noting, especially because they provide additional readings to a work that already provokes multifarious readings. Cage's work is not often discussed in terms of issues of practicality, yet the elements of ease and practicality necessarily influence the writing of the Cunningham mesostics, and is therefore central to the poems themselves. I am speaking here specifically about the length of Cunningham's name. According to Cage's account, he initially "tried to write syntactically" as he had "in the case of the *Mesostics Re and Not Re Marcel Duchamp*, but the length of Cunningham's name proved an obstacle" (i). Instead, he wrote the poems using chance operations and avoided standard syntax. Moreover, the decision to have letters touch one another, which I have read as a symbol of the common, was also made out of practicality, a decision whereby Cage could turn the length of Cunningham's name, as he puts it, "from obstacle to utility" (Foreword i). In discussing the practicality in this way, and especially in using the term *utility*, Cage brings the focus away from purely aesthetic readings. He aims to encourage the reader to engage in the production of the poems on a real, material level.

It is perhaps not very interesting, even potentially mundane, to note such practicalities, but the issue of the length of Cunningham's name is of great importance to any study of the work; more generally, the issue of practicality is very important to Cage's poetics. In fact, when asked in an interview what his "greatest legacy to future generations" would be, Cage replied in his characteristically axiomatic way: "Having shown the practicality of making works of art nonintentionally" (Kostelanetz 26). In view of the painstaking, laborious process of subjecting so many books to *I Ching* operations and then subjecting each letter in the poem to these operations to decide the typeface, the idea that this process is practical may seem laughable. But I would argue that the practicality here is not in the production of the poems so much as in the poems that are produced, and in how these poems could come to be read. Cage has succeeded in writing poetry that is practical to write, easy to read (in the sense that there is no singular interpretation toward which we must work), and excessive in the multiple reading processes it evokes. Without the power over both reader and writer innate in expression (however abstract), the militarized language of syntax, or even the limitations of pre-existing words, Cage creates a poem that is indefinitely multiple in the ways it can be read and by whom. The goal of creating literature that can be read by anyone (although he remains unclear about who *anyone* would encompass) was always a major concern of his. As Cage said in an interview in 1971, the same year the Cunningham mesostics were first published, "I am hoping to find a language [that] people can read in their own way, no matter where they come from" (Kostelanetz 143). Nonsense is one way of approaching an open reading public, a *comunis* into which all readers can gain entry.

### Robert Duncan Plagiarizing

Robert Duncan's *Passages* is a series of poems that punctuates his well-known collection, *Bending the Bow* (1968), and both volumes of his final work, *Ground Work* (1971). Unlike the cases of Cage and Mac Low discussed above, or that of Nichol discussed below, Duncan's use of the machine is not quite literal. That is, the poems in *Passages* are produced not *by* a machine but with the author writing *as* a machine, in a process whereby lyrical subjectivity and self-expression are usurped by a process of gathering references to and quotations (cited or otherwise) from various source texts, a process that Duncan terms "communal." Throughout *Passages* Duncan uses a metaphor of writing compared to tapestry or loom, which bring the machine-like elements of *Passages* to the fore; in this way he produces a poetic common where he is not author but rather compiler or mixer. Duncan understands writing poetry as reading; writing poetry thus inextricably links the practices of reading and writing, rather than considering them as separate or as having a cause-and-effect relationship. To position the author as first reader of the text rather than as governing authority over it, then, Duncan extracts the author from a position of privilege, producing a poetic common rather than a linear power structure. Through the incessant and intrusive use of quotations, borrowings, and expropriations that often verge on plagiarism, with which he litters *Passages*, Duncan suggests that texts are singularities that exist in rhizomatic bonds with each other and that by this shared existence they demonstrate the same communality and public love and trust that he articulates in his politics.

*Passages* offers a particularly good example of Duncan's politics of borrowing, of anarchism, of active readership, of a refusal of integration, and of a politics and ethics of communal love. I say this especially because the series is, as Michael Palmer claims in his introduction to *Ground Work*, "perhaps the most radical example of his poetics" (x), most notably regarding Duncan's use of allusion and intertext. Clément Oudart's description of the *Passages* poems as "palimpsestic" is especially apt, with the term's connotations of rewriting, re-visioning, and expanding (np). Many of the other poems Duncan wrote throughout his career contain similar allusions and quotations, but the *Passages* poems stand apart from the rest because of the distinctly revisionist nature of the serial poems themselves. Duncan saw *Passages* as distinctive:

> In *Passages* verses may be articulated into phrases or tesserae of utterances and silences leading to a series of possible sentences. As *Passages* themselves are but passages of a poem beyond that calls itself *Passages* and that is manifest only in the course of the books in which it appears...phrases have both their own meaning and yet belong to the unfolding revelation of a Sentence beyond the work. ("Some Notes" 5)

The similarities between this poetic series and the singularities praised by postanarchism are clear; in each case, the singularities (poems or persons) "have their own meaning" and yet at the same time belong to a greater commonality. It is the same politics of the common, of what Hardt and Negri call love, that unites everyone in Duncan's politics and that unites the poems of the *Passages* series. For him, the individual elements, as well as the connections that join them, are just as important as the assemblage as a whole because the individual elements are manifestations of the whole. This means that the only way to approach the whole is through the individual part, but it also means that Duncan is not concerned with an end product that would present a misleading image of wholeness. Consequently, his interest shifts to process.

In terms of the *Passages* poems, this process is most clearly evident in the process of reading through a vast array of original or source texts, or reading-writing, evident in the poems, which Oudart insists we should read as emblems of a process rather than end products: "The published poems," he writes, "ought...to be read as notebooks, as a groundwork for an illusory Book to come" (np). An example of the reading-writing process is "The Concert, Passages 31 (Tribunals)" (*Ground Work* 15–31), a poem whose title puns on two important themes in the series: it is at once a public performance by many artists and a suggestion of harmony or agreement. The performers in this concert are evoked by the various allusions Duncan makes throughout, beginning almost immediately with his reworking of the concepts of Jakob Boehme. Duncan's use of Boehme is extensive and varied; it starts with an allusion in line four to Boehme's concept of "Salitter" (the essence of God), continues with a quotation in lines eight to eleven, and culminates in Duncan's referencing Boehme directly in line twenty-eight. As readers, we may be thankful for the fact that Duncan cites Boehme so we do not confuse the two voices, saving us from Oudart's warning that "unwary critics" may "quote him when they are in fact unwittingly quoting Duncan quoting" someone else (np). Instead of their two voices merging in a confusing way, Duncan and Boehme write in concert.

Nevertheless, "The Concert" does have its share of unquoted borrowings. For instance, "MUST MUST MUST" (line 56) and "MOVE, / INSTANTER, ON ANOTHER!" (lines 58–59) are both from Charles Olson's "Projective Verse." While uncredited, these borrowings are easily identifiable due to Olson's characteristic capitalization and the reverence with which Duncan attributes these words to "the Poet" (line 57). By contrast, the two quotations from Rudolf Bultmann's *Theology of the New Testament* (1955) are more difficult to identify. Bultmann's name does not appear anywhere in the poem, and Duncan's choice to refer to him as "the scholar" does little to make clear the allusion (line 66). What is perhaps more interesting about Duncan's use of Bultmann, however, is how Duncan rewrites the source text. The changes are minimal: where the original text reads "songs and especially ecstatic speaking in tongues" (Bultmann 161), Duncan changes "songs" to the singular "song"; and where Duncan places an ellipsis between "prayers" and "song," only one word is actually removed, and this is the word "and." This kind of disrespect for the original source copy may, at first, be interpreted as irreverence, but it is precisely his politics of the commonality of language that enables Duncan to work so freely with his source texts. If his reading-writing is valued as equal to its source text, if language is valued as common and thus never owned, then the manipulation of the source text, however minimal, is an act of love. The collage consists of quotations and references in concert, a "concerting" of multiples to eventually form a kind of whole (namely the poem, *Passages*, that larger Book that Duncan imagines but cannot complete). Furthermore, the definite article in the poem's title signals a link to his spiritual beliefs. "*The* Concert [emphasis mine]," as opposed to *a* concert, suggests a "Grand Collage" or, as quoted above, a "Sentence beyond the work," of which this poem is only one manifestation.

In "Transmissions (Passages 33)" (*Ground Work* 23), the quotations become even more difficult to decipher as polyvocality shifts to multilingualism. While a reader may be tempted to dismiss these quotations, when we attempt to follow these "intertextual clues"—as Oudart called them—the quotations' content proves integral both to the individual poems and to the serial project as a whole. "Transmissions" begins with two lines of Greek, "όνομα βίος / έργον δέ θάνατος," both uncredited and untranslated. The Greek, translated, is the oft-quoted line from Heraclitus, "Its name is life, its work is death" (§48). In the original language, as translator T.M. Robinson notes, the phrase is a play on words, where the "it" in question is a bow (as in bow and arrow), the Greek word for which is "βιός," remarkably close to the term for life, "βίος." The only difference is the accent on the "o" (111). Here, then, we may see that the word for life needs only an accent to become a symbol of death, and the ease with which these words and meanings shift reveals the arbitrary nature of the signifier, the mutability of the signified, and the importance of connection and context. Duncan does not include these uncredited and untranslated passages in an elitist manner. Rather, as a quotation from Dante suggests in "Before the Judgment (Passages 35)," the reader is told "*Guarda, guarda,*" that is, "Watch, watch" (*Ground Work* 32). The importance of detail recurs in "Transmissions," when Duncan quotes Philo's *On the Creation of the World*:

*"Under the graver's hand*
    *the minutest seal     takes in*
*the contours of colossal figures"*
(*Ground Work* 25–26, emphasis Duncan's)

It is not a test of literary history; Duncan writes for a reader to pay attention, and for himself to pay attention, too. The poems make manifest connections between and within texts that we (or he) may miss without careful attention to detail. And throughout his work, this attention to detail is closely aligned with his commitment to the common, a deleuzian multiplicity made up of singularities.

Images of singularities that form assemblages abound in the *Passages* poems. In "The Concert," Duncan writes that

                the stars also
are and remain     severe and distinct,
each being of the universe     free to itself
    having its own law (*Ground Work* 15)

The lawless, anarchic stars are "distinct" from each other, yet are bound by sameness in the universe. Thus, it is not surprising that when the ego of the speaker encroaches on this image at the end of the poem, his attempts to own or to take the magnificence of the stars is doomed. The speaker bemoans how "man's share of the stars' // majesty" is "thwarted" (*Ground Work* 17). Similarly, "Transmissions" is filled with references to singularities and multitudes, as the following lines exemplify:

Not one        but many energies shape the field.
It is a vortex.    It is a compost. (*Ground Work* 27)

The reappearance of the common Black Mountain term "field" here is important because this field of Duncan's is shaped by those singular "energies" that inhabit it; even the field is only an assemblage, reducible to parts but never really able to be disassembled. Similarly, the reference to Ezra Pound and Wyndham Lewis via Vorticism ("a vortex") brings another reading of the "field" into play and forges another connection.[9] It should come as no surprise that the ego in "Transmissions" suffers the same pitfalls as the ego in "The Concert"; it attempts an appearance when Duncan writes of "the 'I' passing into sIght" (*Ground Work* 24), but the personal pronoun loses stability as it is reduced to a singularity in the assemblage of "sIght." Moreover, the word "sight" transforms the uppercase "I" into the "eye," which can see the singular only as a part of a larger field of multiplicity. We might consider this turn to quotation as a return to a lyric sensibility, but it is precisely via the idiosyncratic and fragmented way that texts are treated like singularities in a multiplicity that the lyrical subject is dis-integrated in *Passages*.

In my discussion of Duncan's work here, I have tried to mimic Duncan's persistent use of quotation and polyvocality in his poetry by incorporating many quotations from a variety of interviews with Duncan, all of which are collected in the volume *A Poet's Mind* (2012). My goal in so doing is to foreground the various dis-integrated versions of the poet that have appeared over time. I do not want this turn to the poet's interview responses to reify his position as author or to assign to him a clearly-defined "voice." Indeed, Duncan was always anarchically resistant to the idea of owning language, presenting his poems as revisions or expansions that were almost blindly working toward a greater "Book," or "Sentence," which he could neither envision nor articulate. He clearly expresses this concept in "Transmissions":

–no one
nor poet

nor writer of words
can contrive to do justice to the beauty of that
  design he designs from
          We pretend to speak.   The language is not ours
and we move upward beyond our powers into
        words again   beyond us   unsure measures
      the poetry of the cosmos (*Ground Work* 25)

Duncan's work never does "contrive" to do such a "justice"—he acknowledges throughout his body of work that this is impossible. Instead, he tries in *Passages* to capture this mystical whole in parts, to stress connection throughout, and to value (or love) each incarnation equally. The serial poem is, for Duncan, an act of love, both poetic and political. Its guiding principle is that we can only understand the world through its bits and pieces, and so we must value those pieces. Duncan's reading-writing, rewriting, misquotation, and borrowing show that his poetry works in just this way: he can only understand and communicate this greater poem in these small parts, so each deserves inclusion.[10]

When I write about Duncan's assertion that the poems in the *Passages* series "are but passages of a poem beyond that calls itself *Passages*" and that they ultimately "belong to the unfolding revelation of a Sentence beyond the work" ("Some Notes" 5), I do not mean to suggest that these poems, while dispersed throughout *Ground Work* and *Bending the Bow*, unite into a larger textual whole. In fact, to suggest such a thing would be to do a disservice to Duncan's poetics in terms of both authorial subjectivity and textual production; Duncan was vehemently opposed to such visions of unity or integration. He makes this clear in many interviews, for example when he explains that his interest in the multiple is rooted in this discomfort with integration and unity: "since I'm quite the opposite of what would be called an integrated personality (I dislike personality and I dislike integration), I tend to cultivate—not a disintegration, because that's a part of the same subject as integration—call it a multiphasic possibility" (*A Poet's Mind* 9). He weaves this opposition to an integrated or unified personality (or subjectivity) with an opposition to a unified or integrated text by arguing that when a poem is produced in a manner that leaves it open to the multiple, we (as writers and as readers) "disappear in the poem" (*A Poet's Mind* 51). For Duncan, then, the unintegrated or multiphasic text is necessarily political in its desire to "disappear" (but not to "disintegrate") the individualized self as well as the monadic text. What all of this means is that when Duncan refers to his work as a part of a larger "Sentence" or an external Book called "*Passages*," he refers to a larger project that he can never even articulate, let alone complete. The implication is that Duncan's work is a part of a larger whole, that "Grand Collage" of literature of which his entire oeuvre is only one small part. To his mind, the *Passages* poems seem to exist elsewhere and come into being by way of an apparently infinite process of reading, writing, rereading, and recontextualizing insofar as he re-presents what he has already read. He also suggests that there is a grand theory of poetry that all writing will never exhaust or capture in its entirety: "I do feel I'm working on a very large poetic and that it never gets stated" (*A Poet's Mind* 20). The *Passages* poems exemplify Duncan's exploration of this larger poetics.

He discusses this sequence most candidly in an interview with Howard Mesch, arguing that *Passages* serves as a "test point" for this larger poetics "in which, theoretically, everything can coexist. It doesn't have any boundaries supposedly" (*A Poet's Mind* 86). To explain this theory, Duncan in this same interview describes the process of writing a *Passages* poem as entering into the field[11] of *Passages* by way of writing, which, for him, is an entirely unplanned experience: "when I return to 'Passages' I find out what's going on in it. The poem's dependent, in the first place, on a particular tone from which I recognize that 'Passages' is 'on.' I don't sit down and say, 'Now I'm going to write a Passage'" (91). The spontaneous quality of the production of a *Passages* poem signals two important things about the series: first, that the poems gesture toward a much larger work ("the poem beyond" or the "Sentence beyond the work"); second, that they cannot possibly complete it. What they share in their relationship to each other is tonal (and thus formal) rather than thematic. Duncan's understanding of what these poems do have in common can provoke a reader to ask, as interviewer Howard Mesch does, why the poems are not united, at least, into their own collection. Duncan's response to Mesch summarizes the discussion effectively: "But they're not in a book of their own any more than I'm in a world of my own....they're not part of a great poem at all. They're part of a tapestry" (91–92).

Given such a claim, it is entirely fitting that the second poem of *Passages* takes up this image of the tapestry in such a way as to align the poet with the weaver at his loom. In "At the Loom (Passages 2)" (*Bending* 11–13), the image of the tapestry serves as a metapoetic device; here the poet as weaver is more concerned with the loom itself, and the process of the weaving, than with the image constructed. While Duncan does take a moment at the beginning of the poem to note the "luminous soft threads," the poem is, for the most part, concerned with the "back of the images, the few cords that bind / meaning in the word-flow" (*Bending* 11). Later in the poem, Duncan foregrounds this interest in process rather than end product:

> art shall never be free of that forge,
>     that loom, that lyre— (*Bending* 11)

For Duncan, these tools are more central than "the fire, the images, the voice" (*Bending* 11), which are secondary conduits, although ones that are necessary to bridge the gap between art's meaning and its form. Tapestry, thus understood, refuses integration in the way that other media, for example, painting, do not.[12]

The image of the tapestry is brought to the fore in this poem by way of Duncan's allusion to George Gascoigne's 1575 poem "The Complaint of the Green Knight." Duncan's intertext spans three lines: "'*O weaver, weaver work no more,*' / Gascoyne is quoted: / '*thy warp hath done me wrong*'" (*Bending* 12, emphasis Duncan's). The lines describe a scene in Gascoigne's original, in which the Green Knight bemoans his fate in the form of fabric:

The fatal sisters three which spun my slender twine
Knew well how rotten was the yarn from whence they drew their line
...
Yet must I wrap always therein my bones and body both,
And wear it out at length, which lasteth but too long.
O weaver, weaver, work no more; thy warp hath done me wrong. (109)

The "warp" (the threads that form the basic structure or netting on which the tapestry is woven), the "threads twisted for strength" to which Duncan refers, is blamed for the "wrongness" of the "tapestry" of the Green Knight's life (*Bending* 12). For Duncan, the warp is the underlying structural element that allows for the joining together of the separate threads of a tapestry. As the etymological lists he includes indicate, "warp, *wearp, varp*: *'cast of a net, a laying of eggs'* / from **warp 'to throw'*" (*Bending* 12), the warp is also a netting that is designed to collect and to gather. The poem begins, in line three, with a direct reference to Pound, and to the *Cantos* specifically, as a similar kind of netting or warp, the "twisted sinews underlying the work," with Duncan functioning as a "shuttle among / set strings of the music" (*Bending* 11). Duncan relishes the sound of the shuttle's movement:

        the clack of the shuttle flying
forward and back    forward and
                back (*Bending* 12)

The sound has a musicality that makes his work transient, in contrast to the timeless tome Pound envisioned for his *Cantos*. In *Passages*, the process of "reading to ourselves" or "reading aloud / sounding the music" (*Bending* 11) destabilizes "the stuff" that eventually "vanishes upon the air, / line after line thrown" (*Bending* 12). This process is, then, a way of dis-integrating the tight netting of Pound, allowing Duncan to be able to include and use Pound's work despite those elements of Pound's work that he found problematic.

It is also significant, in light of this dis-integration, that "At the Loom" ends with the characterization of wholeness as mixed rather than coherent: here Duncan imagines a "nation / one body [that must] not be broken," but then qualifies this image of wholeness with the comment, "Yet, it is all, we know, a mêlée / a medley of mistaken themes" (*Bending* 12-13). This characterization of the nation as "mêlée" is loaded, denoting at once the violence of close combat and the mixture of types, or "medley," that fits in squarely with this theme of unintegration ("medley *n.* and *adj.*"). The term "mêlée" can also refer to "A confusion, jumble; a medley, a mixture" ("mêlée, *n.*"). Moreover, an obsolete meaning for the word "medley" is "A type of cloth made of wools dyed (freq. in different shades or colours) and mixed before being spun" ("medley, *n.* and *adj.*"): a definition that echoes the language of the tapestry. For Duncan, then, writing is both a weaving, a gathering together of disparate parts, and a confusion, a medley of jumbled distinct elements. Ultimately, *Passages* critiques the possibility of organization. The question of integration in these texts becomes, in the end, a question of whole and of part. Duncan's preoccupation with dis-integration and the singular suggests, above all, that we cannot and should not attempt to experience the whole (the "Sentence," the "Book to come"). Instead, we act as weavers, moving our singular stories through the warp threads of a much larger loom than we could ever envision.

### bpNichol for the Curious Viewer/Reader

It might seem strange that I include a discussion of bpNichol's early forays into digital poetics, *First Screening* (1984), in a chapter on precursors to digital poetics. But I would argue that, while this small collection of a dozen kinetic visual poems is now considered a foundational text of digital poetry, in *First Screening* Nichol develops the concerns of his concrete and typewriter poetics that are well established in the wealth of scholarship surrounding his work, and therefore these poems can more accurately be understood as constituting a transitional text (between

Nichol's earlier concrete and typewriter poetry and the electronic literature that would come) rather than as born-digital explorations. Although *First Screening* does deserve to be recognized as a prototypical work, Nichol has the computer screen somewhat resemble the page in print-based poetry while also resembling the screen in film. In reading *First Screening* as a precursor to, rather than a vital part of, digital poetry I do not mean to downplay the importance or influence of Nichol's work on the digital poetics that would be developed in the decades after it. Instead, I want to use *First Screening* to explore Nichol's relationship as a poet with the machine. *First Screening*, I argue, demonstrates that this relationship is that of craftsman and tool, but it is also an attempt to diminish some of the power of the authorial subject through the use of digital tools. That being said, it is still important to identify the primacy of *First Screening* in the field of digital poetics. As Geof Huth notes, "These poems appeared so early in the development of digital poetry that Nichol felt justified in including 'FIRST' in the title to these, but primarily these were screenings, movies of words" (np). In many ways, Nichol's work in *First Screening* extends the authorial disruption already characteristic of a poetics concerned with formal and material experimentation into a new medium (the digital), in which he continues seeking means to connect authorial disruption with an invitation to readers to be more autonomous in their engagement with the text.

Because so much of the scholarship on Nichol has looked to the author's biography to contextualize his poetry, a lot is known about how Nichol came to work in the digital medium so late in his life. As Frank Davey details in his critical biography, Nichol purchased an Apple IIe in 1983 and began learning BASIC programming language. By 1984, he had completed the diskettes (5.25" floppies) of what would become *First Screening* and sent them to Underwhich Editions, who would produce a very small run of a hundred numbered copies (245–46). Later in the year he revised these disks and sent them to Red Deer College Press for wider publication (280). But, because they had been programmed on the Apple IIe, the poems' technology was already trending toward obsolescence. Red Deer did not publish *First Screening* until 1993, when a graduate student at the University of Calgary translated the code to Macintosh HyperText (319n1); the "translation" was written on HyperCard, and it too obsolesced about ten years later.

Because of the popularity of media archaeology in digital humanities and the study of electronic literature, we know a lot about the transitions the work took from form to form. As Erkki Huhtamo and Jussi Parikka demonstrate in *Media Archaeology* (2011), and as such scholars as Dene Grigar of the Electronic Literature Organization likewise demonstrate in their curatorial work, the study of earlier formats of these works is integral to the scholarship and the critical reception of electronic literature. Each version of *First Screening* offers the reader a different way of encountering and engaging with the text, and much has been made in the surrounding scholarship of the various versions of *First Screening* we have access to, just as, for example, Early Modern scholars get excited about the discovery of new folios or editions. And it is true that, as Lori Emerson demonstrates in her blog post for the *Media Archaeology Lab,* Lionel Kearns's donation of two "manuscript floppies" that contained the code for Nichol's digital poems in Apple BASIC for an Apple IIe changed the study of this work substantially ("From Apple BASIC" np). Nevertheless, while such work as Emerson's is welcome and valuable, we should also note Katherine Wooler's warnings against equating these early floppies to "manuscript" versions; in her view, we should not apply singular and print-based understandings of authorship to the digital text, instead considering the so-called "manuscript floppies" to be the poems in "beta-phase" (56). Rather than highlighting the preliminary state of the works for the author, Wooler's approach highlights the poems' role as "tests" for readers.

On a more practical note, the case remains that, because we do not all have access to these "beta-phase" diskettes or Apple IIe computers, the vast majority of readers who encounter *First Screening* do so via Jim Andrews's website, www.vispo.com. According to Andrews's introductory comments (co-written with Huth alongside Kearns, Marko Niemi, and Dan Waber), *Vispo* contains the following:

1. The original DSK file of the 1984 edition, which can be opened with an Apple IIe emulator, along with the Apple BASIC source code as a text file, and scanned images of the printed matter published with the 5.25" floppy disks it was distributed in.
2. A video-captured documentation of the emulated version playing in Quicktime format.
3. The 1993 HyperCard version, ported by J.B. Hohm, along with the printed matter of that published edition.
4. A JavaScript version of *First Screening* ported by Marko Niemi and Jim Andrews. (np)

A quick look at the numerous authors involved in presenting the introductory comments and in the programming, emulating, curating, and disseminating of *First Screening* demonstrates what scholars of electronic literature since N. Katherine Hayles have argued: the authorship of the electronic text is never singular. On one level, this is true of all texts; Duncan's reading-writing may remind us of that. What is nonetheless significant about the digital text is that it explicitly reveals the collaborative and communal nature of authorship. As Kate Eichhorn observes, "*First Screening* may have been created by Nichol, but today the work—or the ghosts of the work originally produced by Nichol—points to a much larger collaborative effort, one that exceeds the author's original intentions and any media that Nichol encountered in his lifetime" (518). For the most part, my discussions of *First Screening* here use the Apple IIe emulator on Andrews's site to look at Nichol's "original" presentation of the work, but Eichhorn's point remains valid.[13]

Studying *First Screening* in various formats allows us to see the vital role that the technological medium plays in the reception, engagement, and critical study of these works. I follow Wooler in my own argument that we must read and situate Nichol's work in *First Screening* not as a reinvention but rather as a kind of "remediation." I take this term from a long history of digital humanities and electronic literature scholars; Parikka, in the aforementioned collection, recycles the term from foundational media archaeologists Jay David Bolter and Richard Gruisin, who argue that all new media, in some form or another, remediate old media. It is an understanding of new media technology as old as Marshall McLuhan's discussion of extensions in *Understanding Media* (1964). For Wooler, "The concept of remediation encourages the examination of media history from the perspective of any particular media development and is another reason that media should not be studied in a strictly linear way" (63). Emerson, too, identifies the intermediate position of *First Screening* in her entry on the piece for the *Electronic Literature Directory*, noting that "Because the twelve poems in *First Screening* move soundlessly across a black computer screen, the work positions itself halfway between film and sound/concrete poetry and self-consciously (mis-)uses the filmic medium to create poetry" ("*First Screening*" np). In other words, *First Screening* remediates a number of media, some traditionally considered appropriate for poetry, others not. The effect Nichol achieves with this remediation is, in some useful and radical ways, to minimize the role of the author in these works and thereby to allow greater room for the reader.

Most of the scholarly or critical discussions of this work focus on the radical role of the author, and frequently do so to counter the argument that scholars of print-based or more traditionally authored literature might be expected to make about digital, computer-generated, or machine-written works: that the poems use technology as novelty, kitsch, or crutch. Instead, as Kerry Doran argues, "While Nichol eagerly began experimenting with the capabilities of the Apple IIe upon its release, the novelty of the tool was not necessarily the allure, though that is the story often told with new media practices" (np). For Nichol, as Doran convincingly argues, BASIC code served rather as a "tool [that] enables the practice and, in turn, the form" (np). Because of this understanding of code and computer as form, *First Screening* encourages a reading of the poem and its authorship as process, in ways not unlike what we have already observed in the works of the three poets I consider above. Ultimately, "This emphasis on process is what made the computer such a suitable environment for Nichol's work, and—given the fact that this process was partly enacted by the computer—what makes it so inseparable from its original technological context" (Doran np). Part of my work in this section on *First Screening* is, accordingly, to read the text as inseparable from its technological context, particularly where that context requires a manipulation of the role of the author to make room for interventionary readers.

In order to accomplish this goal, it is important to identify the ways in which *First Screening* extends the work of Nichol's print-based explorations of the typewriter and the grid, as found for example in *Konfessions of an Elizabethan Fan Dancer* (1967). As Doran observes:

> The poems in *First Screening* have many similarities to poems Nichol made before he experimented with digital poetry: repetition, permutation, and movement. Letters, words, and phrases are treated as both linguistic and aesthetic elements of a composition, with the "page" serving as a dynamic space for fluid forms. With a careful, sparse selection of words, Nichol gives the same amount of importance to the words themselves as the way they appear on the page, or move across the screen. Programming enabled Nichol to employ these properties to their fullest, so that his computer poems are more effective than those in print: Motion isn't implied, as it would be in print; instead, it is actively happening. (np)

Because of these "many similarities," a study of *First Screening* is also a study of translation into new media; the digital poems in *First Screening* do not simply remediate the understandings of language and the grid in Nichol's earlier works. In some cases, they recreate earlier poems. For example:

> Two of the poems in *First Screening* existed prior to 1984 in print form: "Letter" (as "The Evening's Ritual") and "After the Storm" (composed as "This is the Sentence the Wind Blew Here" in Fall 1973 and later published in *Truth: A Book of Fictions*, 1993). The print and digital versions of these two poems have the *exact same content*, just different formats based on the media used to present them. (Wooler 67, emphasis mine)

Although Wooler is here referring to "content" as the poems' language (somehow distinct from its form), it is clear that the poems published in *Truth* are, because of their "different formats," markedly different from their later appearance in *First Screening*. I would argue, therefore, that the inextricability of content from form (in the visual avant-garde on print or screen) means that these poems do not have the "exact same content" but are instead remediations. Much as Duncan's *Passages* series presented the author as first reader of other works, the position of *First Screening* as a remediation of Nichol's print-based work in typewriter and concrete poetry renders Nichol's authorial position as that of first reader of his *own* work, too.

Still, this complicated authorship intervenes in a far less radical way than we have seen in Mac Low, Cage, or Duncan. Nichol is certainly interested in opening up the authorial process and limiting some of the authorial power, but he does not deny the importance of the personal, of the literal person behind the authorial subjectivity. Instead, Nichol here manipulates lyric subjectivity rather than simply opposing it. As Gregory Betts observes in "I Object," Nichol's work in digital *and* print-based poetics has always had a complicated relationship with the persona of the author (47–48). While studies like Davey's have always looked to the confessional, autobiographical, and lyrical traces of "Barrie Phillip Nichol" in the poetry, Betts is satisfied to observe a lyrical subjectivity that is present but always incomplete and always critical of the ability to ever really present subjectivity with a few pronouns. "Nichol," Betts observes, "uncovered a kind of poetry that obliterates the coherence of such a collection of empty abstract nouns....Although Nichol of course never stopped writing lyrics....What do you write if not yourself? It almost seems unfathomable" (48). Indeed, as I hope to show, Nichol identifies the problem with the lyrical subject and the power over the reader that this affords the author. But as Betts also points out, "Nichol wants to but cannot reject the pre-revolutionary authorial model and so calls forth this commitment to his preferred revolution to acknowledge his frustration at the semantic trap. The language revolution functions as a vestige of hope for the reclamation of the human, the liberated human" (54). He simply

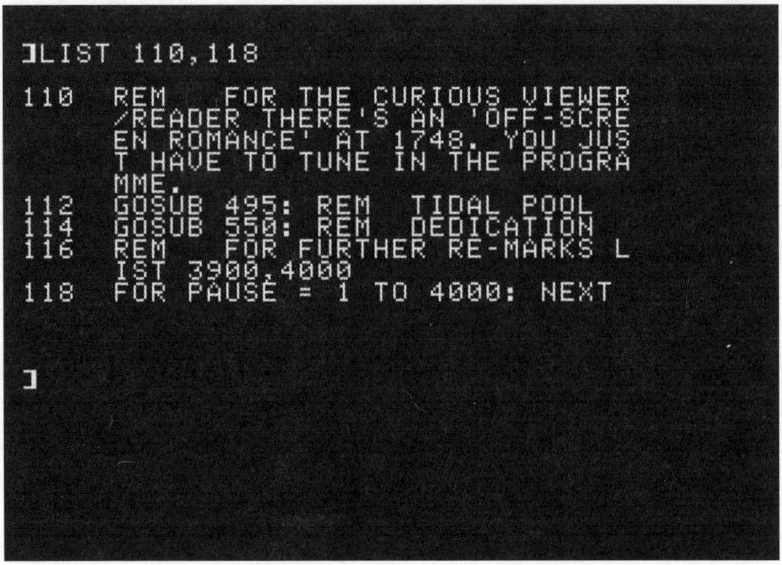


FIGURE 3. bpNichol, "REM FOR THE CURIOUS VIEWER," from *First Screening*.

cannot envision an authorship that is not, to some degree, driven by the feelings, desires, and thoughts of the human who writes.

Nichol's "hope" and his "frustration" are both evident in his poem "Off-Screen Romance," which hides like an Easter Egg in the original Apple IIe version.

In the Apple IIe emulator, as in the original version, entering the "LIST" command for line 110 provides the reader with the following prompt: "REM FOR THE CURIOUS VIEWER/READER THERE'S AN 'OFF-SCREEN ROMANCE' AT 1748. YOU JUST HAVE TO TUNE IN TO THE PROGRAMME" (see Fig. 3). While acknowledging the filmic elements of the text—the "viewer" can "tune in"[14]—Nichol also encourages his readers to intervene in the text if they are "curious" enough to do so. It is interesting to note that though working in the digital format, Nichol uses the rhetoric of network television, absolutely normative at the time he was writing. Entering the "RUN" or "GOSUB" command at this point starts a "hidden" kinetic poem, "Off-Screen Romance," which is dedicated to Nichol's wife, Ellie (see Fig. 4). Because of this dedication and the intimacy implied

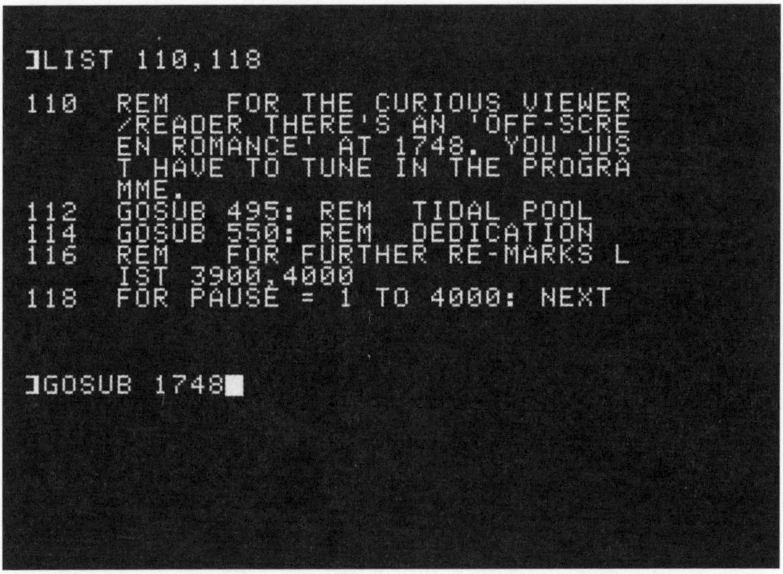


FIGURE 4. bpNichol, "GOSUB" command that starts "Off-Screen Romance," from *First Screening*.

FIGURE 5. bpNichol, "Off-Screen Romance," from *First Screening*.

by the poem's being "hidden" in *First Screening*'s original format, the poem reads as highly personal, almost confessional; yet the content of the poem is decidedly *not* about Nichol and Ellie, save perhaps in a more deeply intimate, metaphorical sense. The poem presents the words "FRED" and "GINGER" dancing a duet in their movement across the screen (see Fig. 5), an obvious reference to dancing film stars Ginger Rogers and Fred Astaire, who enjoyed many onscreen romances but were never partners off-screen (despite much speculation and rumour). As this poem plays out on the screen, the reader can start or stop the dancing at any time by pressing CTRL-S to stop the dancing and any key to restart it, although such engagement is not explicitly encouraged. In some ways, then, the poem is intensely personal, supporting Betts's argument that Nichol cannot seem to help but write himself into his work. At the same time, however, in the sparse presentation and the length of the movement of the dancing words, the work also invites the intervention of the reader who is, no doubt, just as "curious" as Nichol supposes.

The end result of this complication of the authorial persona is, as we have seen in the three poets discussed above, a remarkable gesture toward the readers, who are invited to interact and engage with the text in a way that is closed to readers of more traditionally lyrical print-based works. Part of this is because, while we may become enamoured with the immaterial and ephemeral potentials of the digital, electronic literature (in its best examples) continues to remind readers about the many real and material elements that go into the production and reception of a born-digital work. As Wooler points out, "*First Screening* is made visible to readers because its code has a specified place and function within an operating system that is comprised of physical parts and depends on the spatial organizing of all electronic content" (59). Part of this reminder of the materiality, the physicality of the born-digital work, is lost when I read *First Screening* on an emulator; I lose the engagement with the original text that comes from removing the floppy (or eventually the compact disc) from its case, perusing the print matter that comes with it, inserting the disk into my computer, and commanding it to run. "This is," Wooler observes, "probably the furthest point that every user's experience could be guaranteed to be the same," because the very fact of its digitalness makes *First Screening* "an interactive text" (54). Even if the reader does not look behind the scenes at either the source code or the list command described above, the format of the work allows for reader intervention in the piece, making it markedly different from a film despite the comparisons to film that I, or Emerson, have made. "The user can," as Wooler notes, "pause the movement on the screen and choose to resume with the press of any key, allowing infinite viewing variations and speeds. It is not as straightforward as picking up a book and having a limited amount of options for interaction" (54). Moreover, stopping and starting the text is only one way that the reader is invited to engage with it.

Looking behind the scenes at the text file of Nichol's code reveals even more potential for engagement with the reader. As Wooler also notes, the text file on *Vispo* of Nichol's original BASIC programming language "reveals that Nichol imbedded a bonus poem in the programming language. This poem cannot be run as a subroutine using the correct GOSUB command but can only be viewed as part of the code" (66). The embedded bonus poem Wooler refers to here is a poem written in the code itself, perhaps the first codework poem documented. Line 116 of the code reads: "116 REM FOR FURTHER RE-MARKS LIST 3900,4000." Entering the "LIST" command for lines 3,900–4,000 results in the image shown below. This is a concrete poem, embedded in the code itself, about Noah's ark, the flood, and the rainbow that would follow (see Fig. 6). The poem reduces the Judeo-Christian deluge myth into its constituent parts, as the REM commands transform Noah's ark into the rainbow's arc using Nichol's characteristic breaking down of words into their syllabic components. REM commands become individual REM-arks, and hidden, too, within this codework is a reference to French poet Arthur Rimbaud (REM-BOAT), whose "The Drunken Boat" is a poem that likens the speaker to a ship at sea during a storm. The effect of the singular parts of this codework poem commingling is lost, to some degree, in this screen capture, as the words should appear one-by-one, mimicking the disorienting visual of raindrops falling in a storm.

These "FURTHER RE-MARKS" of Nichol's set the example for a long line of digital poets who would include similar asides and hidden gems in their code. Andrews, a renowned digital poet and web artist in his own right, hides jokes, directives, and secret poems in the source code of his non-codework pieces as well, a clear homage to Nichol, which I will discuss further in chapter four. Such poems, I would argue, invite reader engagement by encouraging a physical engagement of our bodies with the poem, not just through entering commands and starting and stopping the work, but also by following subtle clues for engagement throughout. As Emerson points out, "Any of Your Lip," another one of the poems included in *First Screening*, is a good example of this aspect of Nichol's work, in that it encourages readers to mouth the words, thereby producing a "silent" sound poem that each reader enacts individually: even though the "poem is perhaps silent because of the technological limitations of Nichol's time...it is noticeable how this paradoxical silent sound poem draws attention to its silence at the same time as it enacts and perhaps even encourages readerly interactivity" (Emerson, "*First Screening*" np). Here Emerson refers particularly to the repeated flashing of the suffix "-ing" at the poem's end, which, she argues, "invites readers to sound out or to 'mouth' the words at the same time as they also try to make sense of the connections between the words as they flash across the screen" ("*First Screening*" np; see Fig. 7). With this astute analysis, Emerson contributes further reason for us to conclude that even though these poems "are not interactive in the sense that we've been accustomed to, they show us another iteration of an expanded sense of interactivity" ("*First Screening*" np). Whether asking his readers to insert a disk, run a program, or silently mouth sounds, Nichol uses his poetry to engage them on a physical level, encouraging them to perform his work as sound poets as well as readers.

*First Screening* is dated and obsolesced, but it is also way ahead of its time, for example in the way it prioritizes scrolling rather than clicking. As Doran observes, "unlike hypertext narrative, which necessitates clicking, Nichol's poems scroll in a predetermined way," and I agree with Doran that this feature actually "feels very contemporary" (np). In its

FIGURE 6. bpNichol, "FURTHER RE-MARKS," from *First Screening*.

FIGURE 7. bpNichol, from "Any of Your Lip," *First Screening*.

engagement of the reader and its use of codework, *First Screening* has, in every version, "served as the interface that needs to be activated, mediating 'between writer and text as well as between writer and reader.' You sat down to write the poem; the poem sat down to write you" (Doran np). Doran refers here to the poem "Letter," one of the most simple of the poems in *First Screening*. The poem first reads, "SAT DOWN TO WRITE YOU THIS POEM," but the line "moves" across the page so that the first word becomes the last. Next, "DOWN TO WRITE YOU THIS POEM SAT" reveals an awkwardly constructed sentence that, more or less, means the same thing as the first; the syntactic structure in this second iteration just appears somewhat archaic. But soon the poem reads instead, "THIS POEM SAT DOWN TO WRITE YOU," a gesture to the reader who is, rightly, constructed by the very presence of the poem itself (see Fig. 8). The digital poems in *First Screening*, much more than print poems, require an audience to initiate the sequence and engage with the output; in this way, the digital poem uses technology to create its reader. After the steady movement of the words in the line, the poem eventually reads, "POEM SAT DOWN TO WRITE YOU THIS" (see Fig. 9). This is a moment of explicit self-reflexivity which draws our attention to how much of the authorship of the poems in this sequence is taken up by machines, by code, and by collaboration. The very movement of the words in this poem suggests mutability and transience of meaning, and meaning is further destabilized by the pronoun "this," whose referent is unclear at first and is made all the more elusive as the poem carries out its movement. By all of these means, then, the constituent elements of the sentence (the poem, the process of writing, the reader) are all destabilized.

In fact, two of the concepts explicitly stated in Nichol's "Letter," that "this poem sat down to write you," and that "poem sat down to write you this," could adequately describe all four of the poetic projects discussed in this chapter. Cage, Mac Low, Duncan, and Nichol all write for a readership that is produced (via invitation to engage) by the work itself and from an authorship in which an external (machinic) force has done much of the work of the writing. The lack of the personal pronoun "I" in Nichol's "Letter" to his audience is thus telling. We never read, "I SAT

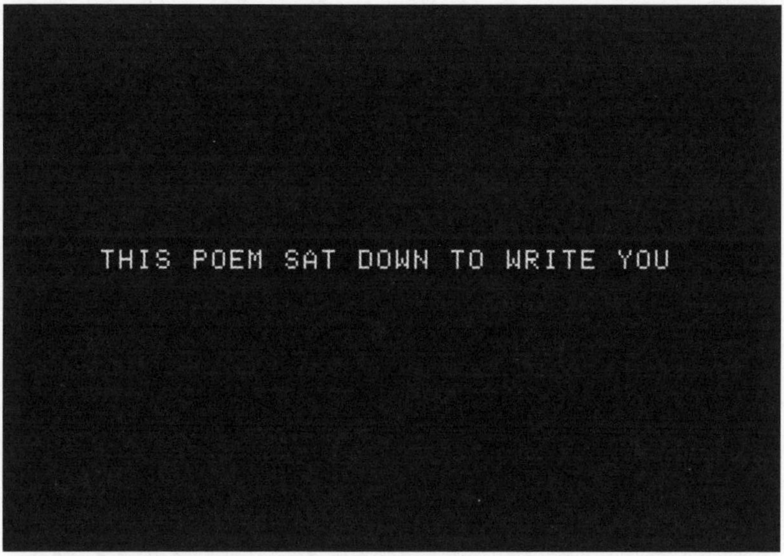


FIGURE 8. bpNichol, line 6 of "Letter," *First Screening*.

FIGURE 9. bpNichol, line 7 of "Letter," *First Screening*.

DOWN TO WRITE YOU THIS POEM." Nichol's omission of the first-person pronoun in this poem—his allowing the authorial presence to be implied but never articulated—is a refusal of the closed, monadic subjectivity typically ascribed to the lyric poet. As I will demonstrate in my second chapter, this refusal has significant precedent in avant-garde poetics by men, but it is a much more difficult or complex refusal when feminist writers and writers of colour work to refuse that same subject position.

# 2 Feminism, Print, Machines

THE EXPERIMENTS with authorship of predominantly male writers in the 1960s, 1970s, and early 1980s demonstrated unease with the power that the author held over his readers. In the late 1980s and into the early 2000s, such experimental works as those I discuss in the previous chapter gave way to work by feminist experimental poets who were also uncomfortable with the poet's interpretive and linguistic power over the reader. These feminist poets were, in large part, interested in using machines or machine-like impersonal structures to mediate the way language is used in poetry to engage with readers, but they also held that the unegoic, machine-written text was not an entirely helpful goal for minoritarian voices. Machine-writing did, for early practitioners, provide a way of queering meaning, making it particularly suitable for queer writers, such as Cage and Duncan; in many other studies of these two poets, scholars including myself have foregrounded the queer potentials of their forms of experimentation.[1] In this chapter, however, I would like to juxtapose those earlier engagements with machine-writing against later feminist re-imaginings.

White, heterosexual, and cis-gendered male poets have sometimes assumed that because majoritarian subjectivities like their own have significant precedent for being presented and represented in literature, the practice of breaking down or dissolving those very subjectivities is more easily accessible to them than to others. This sentiment is probably best summarized by Ron Silliman's frequently cited and often contested observation:

> Progressive poets who identify as members of groups that have been the subject of history...are apt to challenge all that is supposedly "natural" about the formation of their own subjectivity. That their writing today is apt to call into question, if not actually explode, such conventions as narrative, persona and even reference can hardly be surprising. At the other end of this spectrum are poets who do not identify as members of groups that have been the subject of history, for they instead have been its objects....These writers and readers—women, people of color, sexual minorities, the entire spectrum of the "marginal"—have a manifest political need to have their stories told. That their writing should often appear much more conventional, with the notable difference as to who is the subject of these conventions, illuminates the relationship between form and audience. (61)

Since the 1988 publication of this essay, Silliman's observations have been repeatedly attacked, first by Leslie Scalapino[2] and subsequently in criticism by Sianne Ngai, Nathaniel Mackey, and Timothy Yu.[3] The feminist poets discussed in this chapter similarly critique the kind of assumptions Silliman makes here; the breaking down of subjectivity is as central to women's writings as it is to men's, they argue, even though they also acknowledge that a complete withdrawal of subjectivity is not helpful.

Instead of attempting that complete withdrawal, these feminist poets incorporate machine-like or impersonal structures in a variety of ways and to varying degrees to demonstrate four primary concerns of the machine-written feminist text. First, these poets (along with others working in the same vein) demonstrate that it is still not only possible but imperative that the feminist poet continue the practice of limiting the power of the author over her readers and their interpretation of the poem. Second, they refuse to deny the role of the personal emotions and engagements of the literal poet-person (read: poet-woman) throughout the writing process. Instead they argue that, third, the feminist experimental poet inserts the intimacies of the personal into the impersonal structures of machine-writing *in order to* leave more power for the readers of her poetry. And, finally, they maintain that this process is an attack on the larger organizational structures of language, typically made manifest in their poetry in the figure of the archive. As Collis's anarcho-scholastic study of Howe attests, this multiplicitous approach to authorship reveals the archive as "riddled with" and "even defined by...its omissions, restrictions, repressions, and exclusions" (19). The reinsertion of an ambivalent subjectivity into the archive can serve to lay bare these repressions and reveal them instead as fissures, spaces for creative intervention; and postanarchist literary theory offers a useful approach to analyzing this process.

In this chapter I take just such an approach to four central feminist poets, all of whom critique the archive in their work (although writing in different schools, different countries, and at slightly different times), and I argue that, for all four poets, the process of inserting the intimate into the impersonal is a postanarchist practice that refuses to withdraw the telos of meaning-making, but also refuses to withdraw the subjectivity of the individual orchestrating the writing process. I look first at Howe's *A Bibliography of the King's Book; or, Eikon Basilike* (1989) to demonstrate the use of a complex of source texts and historical documents in generating aural and visual noise as a means of radically engaging with readers. I then look at Erín Moure's *Pillage Laud* (1999), where Moure collaborates with a computer program to produce indeterminate "lesbian sex poems." Alongside these more overt uses of machines in the writing process, I present two less obvious examples of the insertion of the intimate into the impersonal. Juliana Spahr, in her first collection of poetry, *Response* (1996), doctors source text and uses square brackets to invite the reader into an autonomous and agential engagement, while Harryette Mullen, in *Sleeping with the Dictionary* (2002), uses the indeterminate and machine-like methods of Oulipian poetry games to collapse the divide between the supposedly visual and material texts of the writerly avant-garde and the aural intimacies of the Black Arts Movement. All four of these poets insert the personal into the larger structures of the archive by intervening significantly in machinic writing practices; all four authors' works, as a result, invite reader engagement *with* an authorial presence rather than in place of one.

### Susan Howe Sleeping in the Library

My discussion of Susan Howe focuses on one of her most popular works, *Eikon Basilike*. This text has frequently been the subject of critical scholarship, but for the most part, scholarship on *Eikon Basilike* to date has stressed the visual, the historical, and the violent, as well as the ways in which these terms intersect. Howe's book works through *Eikon Basilike: The Pourtraicture of His Sacred Majestie in His Solitude and Sufferings* (a book of dubious authorship published in 1649, attributed to both Charles I and John Gauden, but probably produced by an amalgam of unidentified and unidentifiable authors), as well as Edward Almack's *A Bibliography of the King's Book; or, Eikon Basilike* (1896),[4] which tries in vain to establish clear authorship by Charles I for the 1649 text. Located on a complex and contested site of authorship, then, Howe's text negotiates sites of historical documentation, historical violence (by way of Charles I's execution), and the complex relationship between external "truth" and the visual markers of print.

Yet Howe refuses to withdraw subjectivity, the lyric "I," from her historical experiment, even as she works to dismantle the structures of language and authority that make the lyric subject possible. The autobiographical preface stands in stark contrast to the repurposed text that follows; the rest of *Eikon Basilike* is made up of lines, phrases, words, phonemes, and letters, all taken from the fraught source text or from one of several other supplemental texts (by such authors as More, Milton, and Dickens) and then redistributed. For the most part, then, Howe's repurposing functions *like* a machine in selecting from these source texts, but is driven still by an authorial subjectivity that never entirely disappears. Indeed, from the autobiographical anecdote that begins the text to the image of Ariadne's thread that weaves in and out of the long poem, a speaking subject—a storyteller—remains. Thus, *Eikon Basilike* demonstrates a discomfort with the ways in which language governs subjectivity, but it also refuses to withdraw that subjectivity. This is not to say that Howe is concerned with expressing the personal; rather, she reinserts the subject into the historical to show that the subject is produced and governed by text, *by language*. In this way her refusal to withdraw subjectivity warns against a world view in which the subject is not understood as a linguistic construct. For Uta Gossman, this reinsertion of the "I" entails in *Eikon Basilike* a working-backwards, a kind of anarcho-primitivist politic that resists what Howe sees as language's increasing ability to govern us as subjects: "Reversing the evolution of language also implies going back to a world less dissected, analyzed, and categorized by language than the increasing verbalization of culture has entailed over time" (105). I would argue, however, that this anti-evolutionary rhetoric mischaracterizes Howe's poetic project in *Eikon Basilike*. In my view Howe does not want to turn back an apparent "verbalization" of society but wants rather to insert herself into the structures of history and authority that are grounded in language. She refuses to be explained away by these structures; she would rather emphasize the subjective experience of constructing a text than let textual production dematerialize and pretend that language functions as a natural process. It is not enough, then, for Howe to remove herself from Gossman's "verbalization"; such a tactic would, on Howe's terms, be politically ineffectual or even damaging. Instead, she forces a very personal, very real writing self into the larger structures that "verbalization" normally sustains.

To demonstrate the importance of this writing self to Howe, I would like to look at the many manifestations of the first-person pronoun in *Eikon Basilike*. Howe's use of the first-person pronoun is significant in part because of her tenuous relationship to the LANGUAGE school of poetry, where the explicit Marxism of the movement encourages a large-scale refusal of the closed self of lyric subjectivity, replacing it with the multiple selves of LangPo. Yet, as Marjorie Perloff argues, Howe's work displays an approach to the authorial subject that is markedly different from the refusal called for by the LANGUAGE school; instead of refusing the lyric subject, Howe interweaves elements of memoir into the communal ("Language Poetry"). Perloff refers specifically to Howe's early work, but I would argue that, in *Eikon Basilike*, the lyric "I" is similarly present. In fact, "I" is everywhere: the lyric "I" appears on nearly every page of the text, most often in statements of identity or intent. For example, a pair of facing pages that are mirror images of each other include "I" twice each: "that I hide" and "I am weary of life" (56–57, see Fig. 11). They also contain the exclamatory "O make me / of Joy." Other appearances of the "I" include the following: "I go from a corruptible to an incorruptible Crown" (59); "Side of space I must cross" (69); "I am a seeker" (72); "Tell you my author / I knew his hand" (72); "Saying so I name nobody" (74); "I am afraid of him" (71); "I saw madness of the world" (82); "I feared the fall of my child" (82); and "Autobiography I saw" (82). Strikingly, these examples suggest an intent or an identity as well as an absence, a negativity, or an instability. For every "I" that speaks there is a "nobody," a "seeker," a "space" that must be "crossed." The personal pronoun also appears a number of times in the lengthy references to Charles Dickens's *David Copperfield* that Howe includes toward the end of *Eikon Basilike*: we read, first, "I Become Friendly with Mr. Dick" (77), and then "I" appears ten times in the Dickens quotation (88). Here, however, the authorial representation of the lyric subject is thwarted by the allusion, effectively adding another voice to the collaborative authorship of the text.

"I" also appears in various other, non-verbal instances; yet because Howe foregrounds the lyric "I" so insistently, I would argue that we must read even these appearances of the shape of the "I" as gestures toward an imposingly asserted subjectivity. Some of these appearances are as simple as the seemingly random appearance of the Roman numeral "I" in "Brazen Wall I" (54). Especially noteworthy is the "I" that appears over and over again in "Charles I," whose designation provides Howe with the ability to repeatedly insert a subjectivity into the text without relying on the lyric subject. Toward the end of the long poem Howe brings this king, the process of writing and producing bibliographies, and the construction of history together in the imposingly capitalized lines: "K CHARL | WORKS | VOL I / K CHARLE | WORKS | VOL II" (80). Because this passage contains both the capitalized "I" and the vertical bar—which is used in programming to denote the logical term "or"—the presence of the subject, the vertical "I," punctuates the incomplete names and titles. Rather than refusing subjectivity, Howe's *Eikon Basilike* in this way inserts the "I" repeatedly into a history made porous and unstable through language. The result is the production of a poetic subject that bridges the gap between the impersonality of history and of machine-writing and the fiction of the closed, lyrically expressive subject on the other.

Ultimately, Howe's reader is confronted with the task of reading without the traditional authorial subject to guide exegetical interpretation. Instead, Howe engages with her readers in what I call an *invitational* rather than an expressive way: she invites the reader into a collective (or a common) with the text. I am arguing, in other words, that *Eikon Basilike* is an anarchist text, for and by a popular and populist audience, that invites readers into an egalitarian, affective community. Nor am I the first to extend this kind of affinitive or invitational reading to Howe's work; for example, Norman Finkelstein's reading of *Eikon Basilike* as séance demonstrates the text's capacity to include its readers in its processes of reading and writing. For Finkelstein, "the reader of Howe's *Bibliography* is both witness to and participant in" the poetry (230). By staging the text as a séance in which the ghosts of authority are simultaneously summoned and banished, argues Finkelstein, Howe "exposes her readers to her daemon, which we discover to be our own" (233). Similarly, Miriam Marty Clark argues that Howe includes her readers in a continuum of authors and texts that transforms the typically sterile atmosphere of the library, the site of bibliography and scholarship, into an anarchic wild:

> In these recurrent figures—of the reader and the scholar as library cormorants, of thinking as telepathy, of prior voices as ghosts and vampires, of the library as wilderness—Howe establishes continuity between the singularity of texts and the ubiquity of

> information, between the materiality and temporality of the printed word and the virtuality and simultaneity of information. (380)

*Eikon Basilike* is not specifically the subject of Clark's discussion in this passage, but it does contain numerous passages in which Howe forges affect and ephemerality out of the preserving and stultifying tendencies of archivization (in libraries, museums, etc.). For example, trading cold logic for warm affect, Howe juxtaposes the "Driest facts / of bibliography" (64) with "This word *Remember*" (65). Appearing in the most lyric, readerly segments of *Eikon Basilike*, these contrasting lines suggest a movement from searching the archive for bibliographical information to finding instead the unquantifiable values of remembered emotion. Toward the poem's end, Howe gives up searching for an "original text" (47) that her introduction already told us could not exist, writing instead, "I am at home in the library / I will lie down to sleep" (75). Ultimately, Howe transforms the dry, sterile space of the archive into a home filled with comfort and security, via her misuse of the space.

By turning the library into a home for the already complicated lyric subject, Howe constructs a vision of texts as singularities within the multiplicitous continuum of textual discourse. In this way she encourages us to read *Eikon Basilike* as both populist in nature and anarchist in its assertions of the radical potentials of the people. Of course, the book that gives this poem its name could also be termed a book "of the people." As Howe notes in her introduction, "On the day of the execution,...*Eikon Basilike, The Pourtraicture of His Sacred Majestie in his Solitude and Sufferings*, was published and widely distributed throughout England, despite the best efforts of government censors to get rid of it" (47). As part of these efforts of the State, "Printers of the *Eikon Basilike* were hunted down and imprisoned. But in spite of many obstacles the little book was set in type again and again. During 1649 fresh editions appeared almost daily and sold out at once" (47). This history makes the 1649 *Eikon Basilike* itself a symbol of the proliferation of the common even under the strict eye of an anti-monarchical government. In its rapidly reproduced and constantly fluctuating identity, the *Eikon Basilike* of 1649 serves, despite its claim of royal lineage, as an anti-authoritarian symbol that refuses the closed structures of the library and its requirements of an Author in favour of the immateriality of the common. As Howe writes, "the material object has become immaterial" (50). It is thus unsurprising that in the very centre of the previously mentioned mirrored pages, Howe inserts "The People / Contemporary History" (56/57). Insofar as the text embodies a resistance to the bibliography and the archive, it becomes an anarchist pamphlet that invites its readers to sleep in the library beside it.

And yet, while the 1649 *Eikon Basilike* was indeed a "people's book" circulated against state regulation among the population, it was also a book meant to celebrate and deify a monarch, and it was meant to encourage the return of monarchical rule to England, a return that came about and a rule that has, in many ways, continued. We cannot read the text as purely anti-governmental if it is ultimately a text that supports the Divine Right of Kings and the reinstitution of monarchical rule, even if its subject is indeed a king beheaded. The king's execution, the literal deposing of a ruler, does suggest anarchy at the heart of the source text(s), but it is much more significant to this study that the voice of the king is presented rather than suppressed in Howe's text. The result is not reification but rather the addition of the king's voice into the irreducibility of the common. In Howe's treatment, then, the king's voice does not speak either for or to the people, but rather comes to speak as a part of the people. It is included in the communal narrative, along with Howe as the beheaded-Author-King, as just another subjectivity in the social authorship of the text's production. Read in this way, Howe's text does not support a monarchy despite the fact that her source text did: she includes the ghost of a king as one reader; she includes herself as another; and she makes all readers authors.

*Eikon Basilike* is bent on the destruction of larger structures and frequently depicts this as violence. Yet scholars of Howe's work often use terms of pleasure or positivity to describe these moments. Consider, for example, Kathleen Crown's note that characterizes Howe's work as "ecstasy" (488). While Crown does not pursue this line of argument, I would agree that *Eikon* functions as ecstatic insofar as it works to move outside of or beyond the gridlines of clearly delineated systems of logic, history, and legality. Dworkin also makes joking use of the term *ecstasy* in reference to Howe's visual disruptions, arguing that "With an ear attuned to the pleasures of noise, Howe writes from out of the static; ex-static indeed" (47). Dworkin does not elaborate on the term, but it is worth lingering over; "ex-static" conveys the radical potentials of a joyful movement that comes out of the static of the unmoving, out of the *stasis* of grid and structure, as well as a communication that comes out of static, in other words noise.

Here "ecstasy" results from the joyful acceptance of the multiplicity of a destabilized authorship, grounded in the disruption of monadic identity. Crown gestures toward this when she uses "ecstatic" to describe Howe's challenge to a linear view of history and its complicity with the supposed unity of the lyric subject (488). Crown sees the ecstasy in this text as tied to Howe's "stutter" (501): both ecstasy and stutter function as the "anti-telos" of Howe's work (486), which Crown foregrounds. Crown's analysis asserts, at its core, that these moments of anti-telos, of stutter and ecstasy, function as inarticulation or noise that serves to overwhelm rhetoric with what she terms the "somatic force" of language (499). A poetics of noise is necessarily a poetics of disruption and of breaking apart; nevertheless, it would, as Dworkin warns, be a misstep to suggest that a poetics of noise is necessarily an attempt to mimetically reproduce these disruptions. Rather, noise is primarily concerned with carrying out this disruption itself; noise poetry is a speech act. As I discuss in the introduction to this project, Dworkin sees in noise the potential to disrupt, "to unsettle the code of the status quo" (*Reading* 39). Rather than merely serving a communicative function, "noise proliferates hand in hand with an increase in the terms of communication" (*Reading* 45). Dworkin also reminds us that treating noise as representative or communicative—that is, reading it as hermeneutics—jeopardizes its disruptive potentials and "runs the risk of neutralizing the very disruptive potential it identifies" (*Reading* 49). However, I would argue that Dworkin's emphasis on the material and physical aspects of Howe's work, which he characterizes as "visual prosody," his interest in "poetry as a physical act" (*Reading* 31), tends to limit our appreciation of the radical potentials of noise in just the way he warns against. Even as Dworkin argues that Howe's abuses of language echo the historical dangers and violences of language, ultimately confronting "the illusion of the transparency of the printed page," his work reifies the static, fixing what is essentially ephemeral in the limitations of the material text (*Reading* 38, 41). To be sure, through her emphasis on the material conditions of the grapheme, "Howe reinvigorates a consideration of the material conditions of poetry," just as Dworkin asserts (*Reading* 43). But the anti-telos of *Eikon Basilike* suggests that a good deal more is happening in the literal intersections of these lines than a foregrounding of physicality.

Those points on the page where lines visually intersect are "visual prosody" and more, in that they severely disrupt how we would read the lines, either on the page or aloud. By disrupting both of these reading practices at the same time, Howe collapses the unhelpful divide between the aural and the visual. As a consequence, *Eikon Basilike* presents its discontinuities as inextricably both aural and written. In fact, the book functions as a radical activist text most effectively in the moments where the aural and visual disruptions work together to expose different and multiple radical and political readings. Each such intersection, therefore, becomes a point of activism, or what Paul Naylor calls a point of "intervention" (67) in the cognition and interpretation of its readers. We can categorize Howe's visual/aural interventions into three loose and necessarily interconnected categories: anti-regulation, anti-assurance, and anti-logic (all inherently linked to the anti-telos that Crown signals). They all speak out of static, and intervene in stasis.

### *Anti-regulation*

Howe's work as anarchic is concerned with a disruption of the regulatory potentials of language. By this I mean not simply that Howe understands language as regulating categorical or linguistic constructions, but that she also positions language as upholding the larger oppressive structures of government and property. As Naylor observes, "regulating nature's

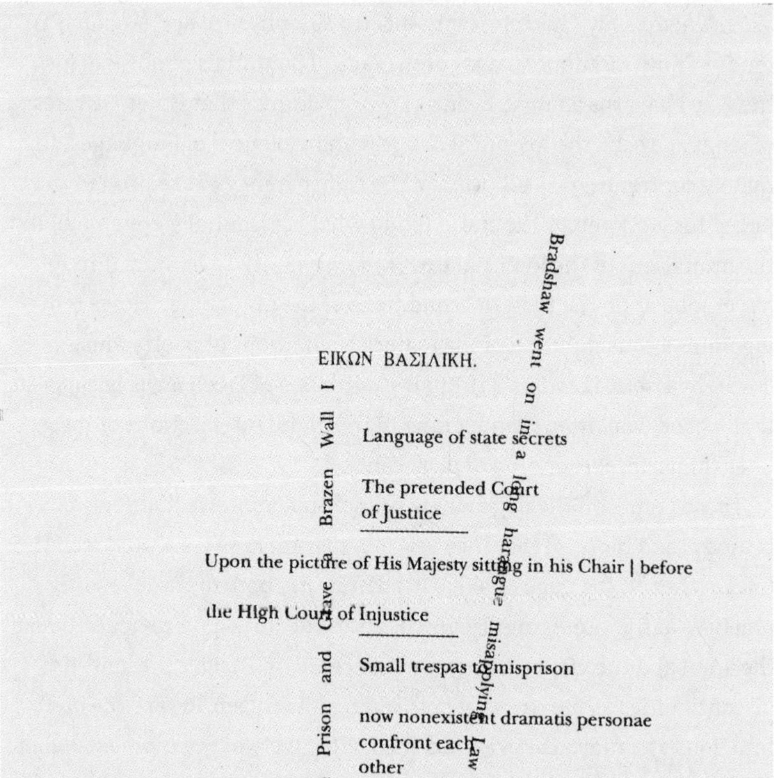

ΕΙΚΩΝ ΒΑΣΙΛΙΚΗ.

Steps between Prison and Grave a Brazen Wall I

Bradshaw went on in a long harangue misapplying Law and History

Language of state secrets

The pretended Court
of Justice

Upon the picture of His Majesty sitting in his Chair | before

the High Court of Injustice

Small trespas to misprison

now nonexistent dramatis personae
confront each
other

Heroic Virtue & Fame

54

FIGURE 10. Susan Howe, from *Eikon Basilike*, p. 54.

representation in language with the tools of grammar and spelling keeps the lines of ownership and mastery well defined and open to adjudication by the 'European grid' of property-rights law" (55–56). In *Eikon Basilike*, anti-regulatory interventions surface in the form of visual illegibilities that dismantle the emblems of government and law. At one point, for example, the words "misapplying Law" in a vertical line intersect with "misprison" and a "now nonexistent dramatic personae" (54). Here, Howe identifies the potential for those in power to manipulate repressive state apparati (Law, prison) for the purpose of stifling opposition (see Fig. 10). Yet in their intersection, the Law and the misapplication of it are also brought together with a "dramatis personae," the spectral actors in the scene of *Eikon Basilike*. As these two "confront each / other," Howe's illegibility shows the radical potentials of language to counteract such regulatory bodies.

A few pages later, in the aforementioned mirrored pages, the terms of the repressive state apparatus begin to disintegrate, as in the "s t e p s" toward execution from the "p r i s o n s" in which the anti-governmental voice (here paradoxically represented by Charles I[5]) slowly falls apart (56/57). Howe separates the letters of these terms to reveal the constructedness of both these structures and the authority that governs them. The revelation of this constructedness, this artificiality, encourages readers to confront government and incarceration as concepts. Both pages feature at their centre "A  p i v o t" (56/57). Just above this "pivot," the lines "The People / Contemporary History" and "Through populacy / through the populacy" appear connected as if by a fulcrum. In this way "History" is destabilized slightly—turned on its pivot—by virtue of its new constitution *by* and *through* the people rather than by monarchical powers. The fact that this visually disruptive poem is duplicated (albeit reversed) on the two facing pages also attests to the poems' exposition of the impossibility of an original text or a truthful documentation. Later, when the visual disruptions of *Eikon Basilike* become even more pronounced, these "s t e p s" and "p r i s o n s" as symbols of governmental repression and legality become even more illegible, until, eventually, the designations of illegality fall apart: upside-down and segmented, "a u l t e r e r" perhaps

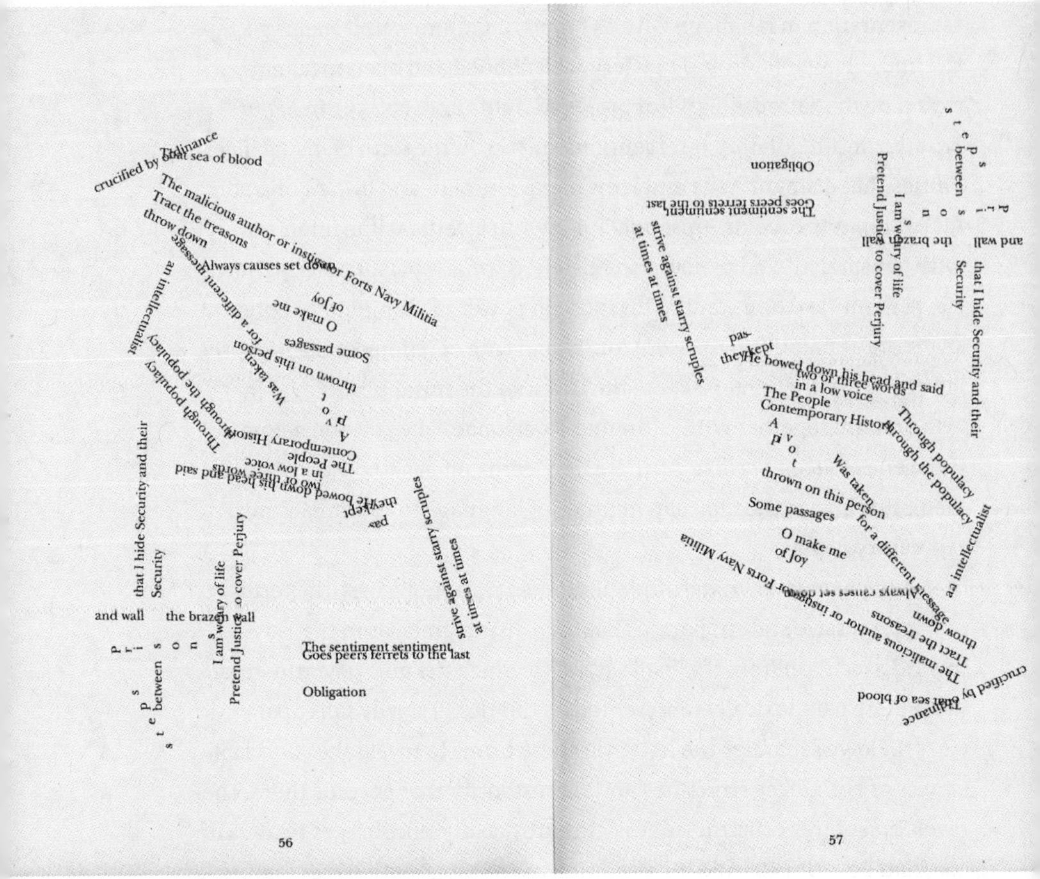


FIGURE 11. Susan Howe, from *Eikon Basilike*, pp. 56–57.

recalls "adulterer"; "P e r e r i a t i o n s" perhaps "perpetrations." We may also consider the aural resonance of "orator" and "perorations," associations that subtly connect these repressive state apparati to speech and rhetoric. Both visually compromised and aurally disrupted, these terms at this point contain only a trace of state-sanctioned repression. They become ex-static in that they mean nothing in and of themselves, yet their potential for multiple, excessive meanings is opened up even as the words are opened by the dramatic kerning.

The aural potentials for meaning are made manifold as the words are lengthened and the space for new and multiple sounds and meanings

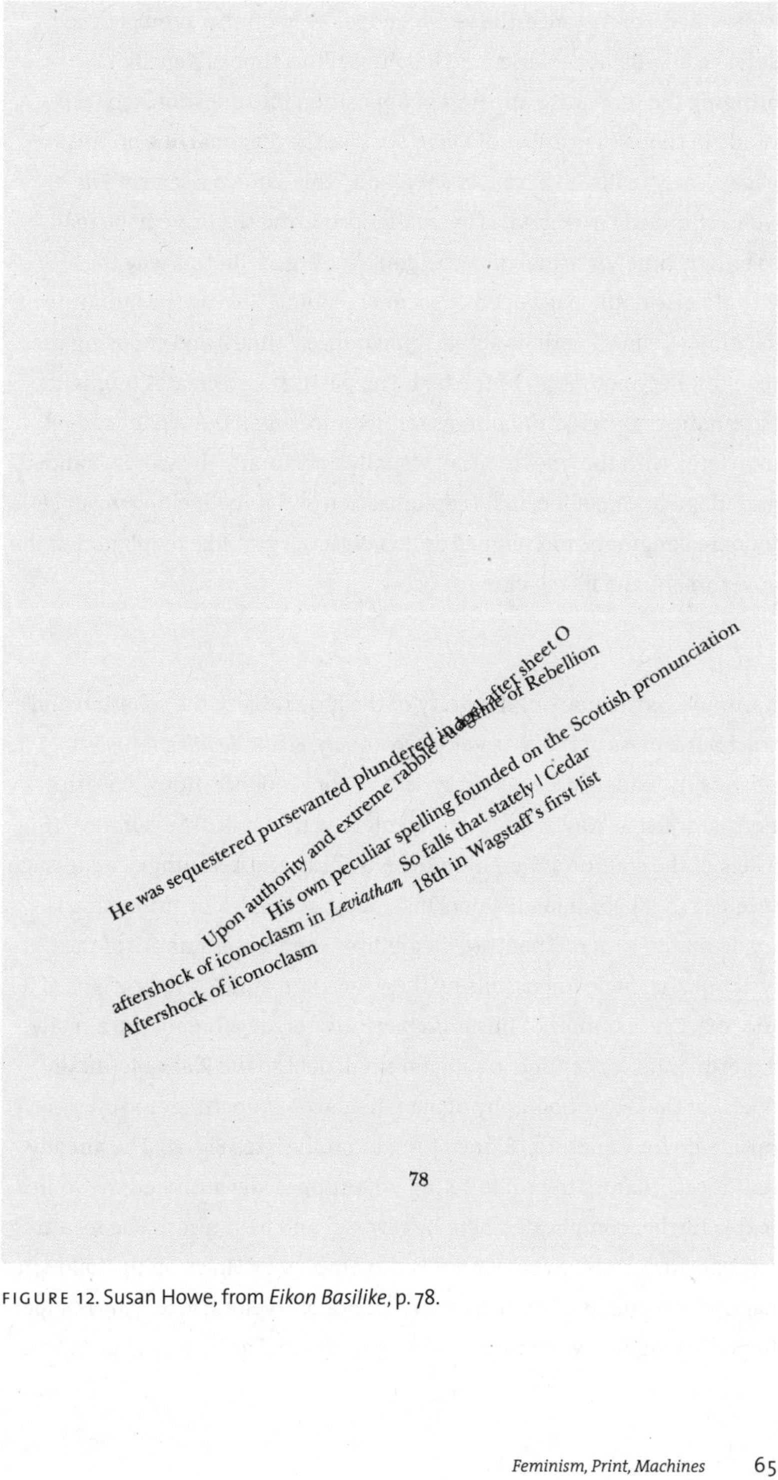
He was sequestered pursevanted plundered in [illegible] after sheet O
Upon authority and extreme rabble [illegible] of Rebellion
His own peculiar spelling founded on the Scottish pronunciation
aftershock of iconoclasm in *Leviathan* So falls that stately | Cedar
Aftershock of iconoclasm 18th in Wagstaff's first list

78

FIGURE 12. Susan Howe, from *Eikon Basilike*, p. 78.

is provided. For instance, the word "cudgel"—so often a symbol of self-defence or rebellion—obscures the phrase "in a time of Rebellion," bringing the repressive apparati of opposition into question, too (78). While in the 1989 printing of *Eikon Basilike* the diagonal line on this page clearly reads "in a time of Rebellion," this same passage in *The Nonconformist's Memorial* is in smaller print, and the line can be read as either "time" or "rime" of "Rebellion" (see Fig. 12). In this way the visual noise of the page opens up a new reading, linking the literature of Rebellion ("rime") with its actual appearance ("time") and exposing the revolutionary potentials of the text. The passage also creates moments of semantic nonsense or *noise*, as for instance when the "dg" of cudgel interferes with the "me" to recall visually and aurally the words "danger" and "dogma." Rebellion, in its capitalization and its cudgelling violence, is rendered dogmatic too, aligned as it is with the grid-like regulation of the government and its regicide.

### *Anti-assurance*

Assurance is the mark of the unity of the lyric subject, the cohesion and trustworthiness of the lyric voice. Obviously, *Eikon Basilike* refuses to provide its readers with such a lyric; as a consequence, Howe's disruptions are, just as Naylor suggests, all marked by a lack of "assurance" (61), a lack of the comfort inherent in the encoding and decoding of a message received in Jakobsonian fashion. Instead, the complex of authorship is made manifest in moments of illegibility when the assurance of the lyric voice is made impossible by the visual and aural complications of the text. One example of this is on page fifty-eight, wherein the already experimental conception (owing no small debt to the Black Mountain poets) of the "Historiography of open fields" has superimposed on it the upside-down signature, "Signed King in profile" (see Fig. 13). The already half-faced (that is, "in profile") King who supposedly authored the source text is further complicated here by reversal and palimpsest. The resulting struggle to decipher what we see is pre-empted by Howe on the following page where one line, "An intellectualist out of levelling love" (59), is superimposed diagonally over a prose-like paragraph. The historical facts here

A cleric's forgery
of a pseudo-biographical
apology

Finding the way full of People
Who had placed themselves upon the Theatre
To behold the Tragedy
He desired he might have *Room*
to the right
Speech came from his mouth
Historiography of open fields
Signed W. King in profile

Mend the Printers faults
T
The place name and field name
as thou doest them espy
Centuries of compulsion and forced holding
For the Author lies in Gaol
All the Civil War Authorities

and knows not why

58

FIGURE 13. Susan Howe, from *Eikon Basilike*, p. 58.

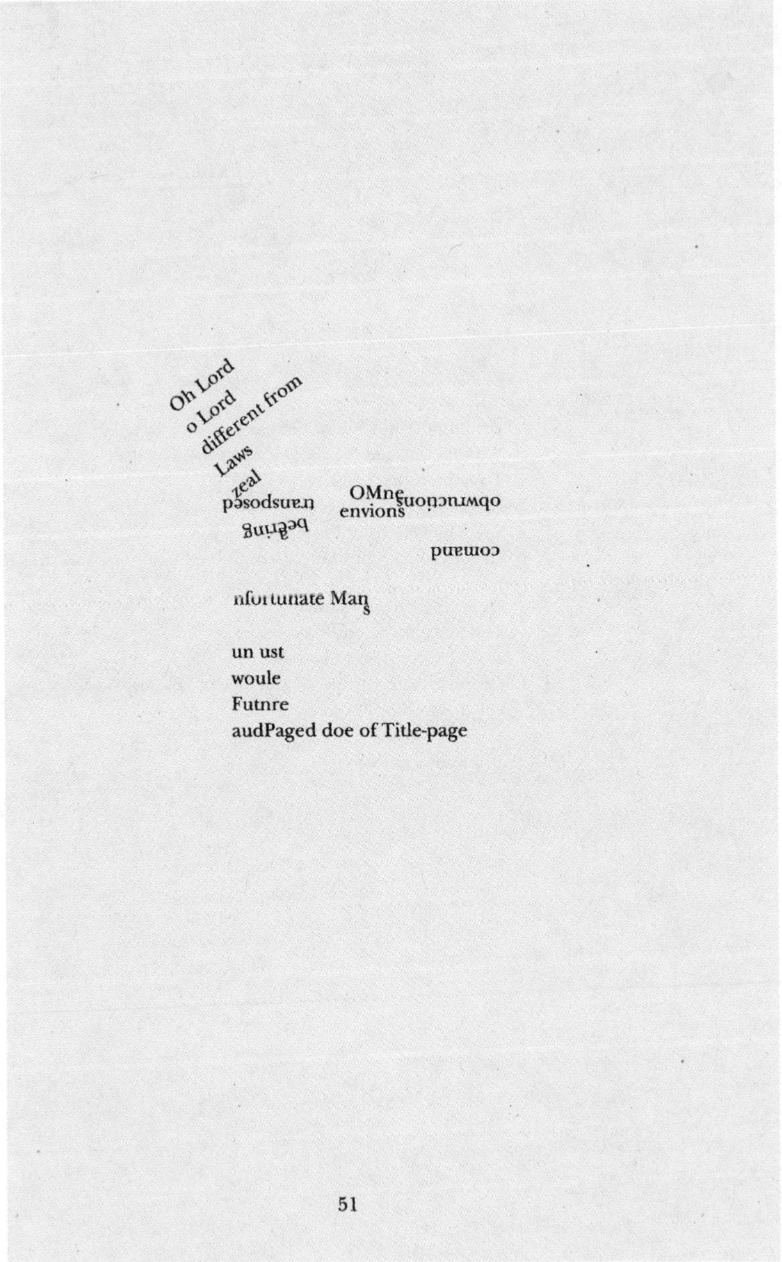


FIGURE 14. Susan Howe, epigraphic poem from *Eikon Basilike*, p. 51.

are already unclear, as details like "Tuesday *Jan.* 30," with "H T writings" on top, are made illegible (59). Thus, my desire as "intellectualist" to decipher the text is met with the "levelling" (or destructive) force of "love." Love is excessive and ex-static; it literally levels static structures as it produces illegible moments. Here is Hardt and Negri's love as flux, as a destabilizing force that complicates closed systems of selves, of meanings, of readings and interpretations. Toward the poem's end, the lines "in the ace of speechstone / Spelling surname" (76) criss-cross to remind us that assurance is withheld as a result of an impossible monadic identity.[6] And just a page later the words "ithuriel intent" (77) appear connected to an artificial centre by their "i"s. Here Howe not only foregrounds the artificiality of connecting an "author" with "intent," but she also suggests that "authorial" is "ethereal," the placing of the "I" into the ether. By withholding the assurance of authorship and intention in such ways as these, Howe destabilizes the reading process and opens it up to reading.

### *Anti-logic*

Howe's project, as she suggests herself throughout *Birth-Mark*, is one of "unsettling" history. As Naylor explains, "Howe's poetry seeks out a different logic, a logic she believes has been repressed rather than assured by the centuries" (61). It is this anti-logic that Crown hears in her stuttering, that Dworkin sees in her noise, and that Peter Nicholls observes in her "Stammering," which, he argues, "keeps us on the verge of intelligibility," where an "emphasis on sound is coupled with a habitual shattering of language into bits and pieces" (597). Such anti-logic is at work in the epigraphic poem (see Fig. 14), where the word "beering" (already upside down) contains above it the letter "a" hovering over the second "e." The word "beering" is a contemporary colloquialism for consuming alcohol, especially socially ("beer, *n.*"), but it also recalls "birring," a term for making a "whirring" sound ("birr, *v.*"). On the other hand, "bearing" suggests both a relevance or meaning (as in having or not having bearing on a case) *and* a movement or direction (as in a compass bearing). The meanings collide into one unpronounceable, unwritable word that refuses logical semantic inclusion. In its excess of

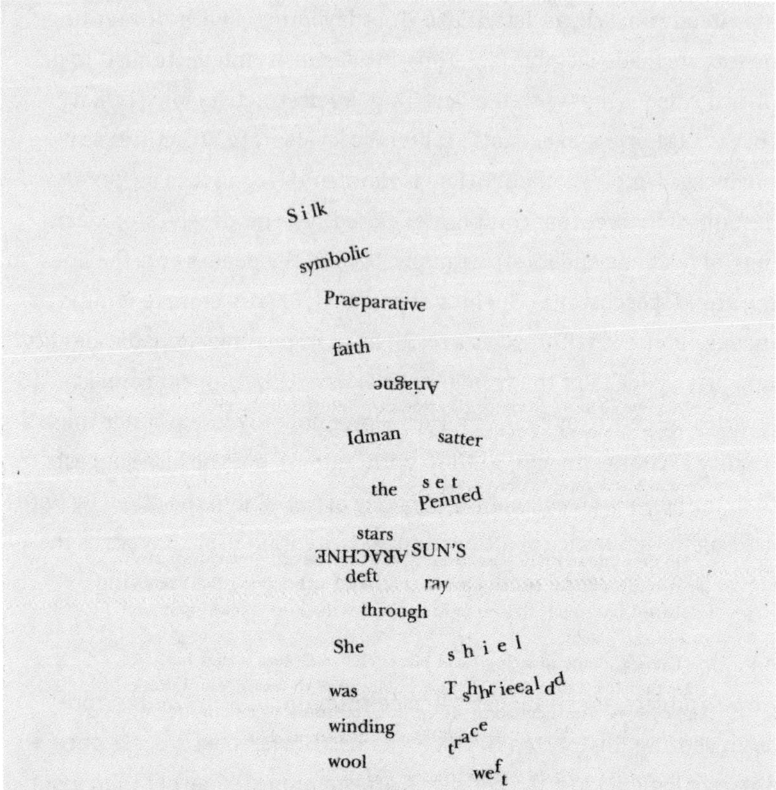
Silk

symbolic

Praeparative

faith

Ariagne

Idman satter

the set Penned

stars

ARACHNE SUN'S

deft ray

through

She shiel

was Tshhrieeald d

winding trace

wool weft

Cloud

soft

threada

twist

82

FIGURE 15. Susan Howe, from *Eikon Basilike*, p. 82.

meaning and its complicated aurality—this page actively resists reading aloud—this example too becomes ex-static in its illogic. This anti-logic is brought together with the themes of violence and authorship in the final page of the poem, where a disassembled "s h i e l" instructs us to remove the "s h i e l d" from "T s h h r i e e a l d d" (a nonce "word" that recalls "threshold"). Once the shield, the defensive posturing, is removed, we are left with "t h r e a d," a recollection of the various images of Ariadne and her art of weaving that are woven throughout (see Fig. 15). The poem risks disconnecting completely at its close: "t r a c e" works its disassembled way upwards, "w e f t" barely holds on in the bottom-right corner. By the poem's end, the "bearing" that is signalled in the epigraph is disintegrated, and we are left instead with the anti-logic of trace and weft, the spectral presence of meaning, the ecstasy of static noise between (and superimposed over) the lines of the grid.

### Erín Moure's Name in Quotation Marks

Issues of subjectivity, textual embodiment, and illegibility continue to be central in my discussion of Erín Moure's *Pillage Laud*.[7] Like *Eikon Basilike*, *Pillage Laud* flaunts its experimental approach to authorship, and thus the issues of authorship and subjectivity have not gone unnoticed by the few scholars who have discussed the book to date. To begin with, Moure's name appears on the cover of the 1999 Moveable Type edition of *Pillage Laud* as "Erin Mouré" in quotation marks, retaining the usual spelling of her name at the time but adding the distancing quotation marks, which signal the performativity of the authorial persona. Moure published as Erin Mouré until *Sheep's Vigil by a Fervent Person* (2001), where her "transelations" of Pessoa are attributed to Eirin Moure, but Erin Mouré is credited with the copyright. *O Cicadán* (2002) is another unique case, with Erín Moure named on the book cover and Erin Mouré named on the copyright page. Starting with *Little Theatres* (2005), however, both the covers and the copyright pages of all subsequent publications are attributed to Erín Moure. Finally, the Book*hug reprint of *Pillage Laud* (2011) reproduces the quotation marks of the 1999 edition but retains the typical spelling that Moure continues to use today, with the accent on the "í." Furthermore, the question of authorship that these changing and changeable names raise remains central throughout *Pillage Laud*, in which Moure constructs authorship as collaboration with an external force. The text, as its introductory note tells us, "selects from pages of computer-generated sentences to produce lesbian sex poems, by pulling through certain found vocabularies" (np). The jacket blurb of Book*hug's reprint details the particularities of its production; Moure has used "MacProse, freeware designed by American poet Charles O. Hartman as a generator of random sentences based on syntax and lexicon internal to the program" (np). Thus, *Pillage Laud* is produced by a social authorship.

One theorist whose work helpfully illuminates this element of *Pillage Laud* is Rachel Blau DuPlessis, who argues that our discussions of authorship must move beyond the poststructural insistence on the death of the Author, searching instead for ways to theorize authorship that recognize the impossibility of individual expression but still ascribe an agential role to the producer of a text. This theorizing is postanarchist, though DuPlessis never names it as such. "Authorship is neither dead nor singular," she argues; "neither all discursive mediumship nor all individual expression. Authorship occurs in being possessed, not mystically, not sublimely, but precisely by sociality as a part of a work's dissemination and reception" and "production" (987). This possession by the social, this inclusion of the author in social assemblage, is accounted for by neither an uncritical adoption of Foucauldian discursivity nor a utopian view of collaboration. Instead, DuPlessis presents a theory of authorship that revives Foucault's author-function from the dust of old poststructuralism:

> Far from denying agency, far from barring the possibility of social authorship in the production of literary texts, Foucault's somewhat quaint assumption of author-disappearance-and-death opens the space for a proposal of post-personal authorship and a discussion of the rhetorical modes that such authorship might choose to deploy. (988)

Moving beyond Foucault, DuPlessis wants us to envision the author as agential within an assemblage of subjectivity (990); moreover, we as readers can participate actively because social authorship has a "non-expressivist, not explicitly personal, goal for writing" (989). In this realm of social authorship, the author is not an *a priori* figure, not "the biographical person walking around in the world," but rather a figure produced by the text itself and by "what that [biographical] person 'announces' of her formal, ideological and discursive agency at the writing table" (990–91). Yet DuPlessis also acknowledges the utopian, communistic dangers of ascribing an essentially radical nature to social authorship. Accordingly, she cautions that "No form has any intrinsic content, any intrinsic politics" (997), and therefore social authorship is only radical because of the extant Author-god hegemony.

DuPlessis's arguments find strong support in *Pillage Laud*, filled as it is with passages in which the text refuses the subject position of the author, only to have that same subject position prove itself either unable or unwilling to come apart completely. At one point, for instance, we read, "My subject wouldn't split" (31). Yet later we find, "The writer orbits me. My line (article) has sighed" (52). Unlike other disruptions of authorship, then, *Pillage Laud* does not just admit the impossibility of the completely unegoic text; it admits this impossibility as a starting point for a more nuanced study of authorship. The writing "I" of the text, the "line (article)," is not rejected; rather, it sighs, opening itself to external forces, taking in the social, and embracing the extralinguistic possibilities for communication. In this way Moure represents authorship as an entrance into a field of interconnectivity with other texts rather than an individualized rethinking of semantics. Her construction of authorship constitutes a radical rethinking of subjectivity, as her destabilized but still necessarily present voice creeps into the computer's output, producing an "Erín Moure" by virtue of its enunciations. The speaker boasts: "my field had owned me" (24). In these terms, the speaker of this collection is an assemblage, a cyborg authorship that is produced by a rhizomatic field (a use of the term that should, again, recall the Black Mountain poets). This "field" encompasses the computer and its output, the human Moure, and the resulting text.

As a consequence, we arrive at a point where we must treat social authorship as something quite different from either the subjective authorship of the lyric or the Marxist abdication of the self in LANGUAGE poetry. This collaboration is also significantly different from the technological collaboration of Mac Low's interaction with his diastic output. Rather than treating the computer output as raw product with which the poet works to produce a text, Moure's collaboration with the computer in *Pillage Laud* privileges technology as co-producer insofar as the poet herself merges with the machine in order to place her own subjectivity in flux. The use of computer generation signals to Moure's readers that "the border of a name is not a straight line" and "has no final point" (Bergvall and Moure, 175). As Emerson argues, "Moure's poems are material objects devoid of authorial intention at the same time as they are material objects that reveal her intentions or the intentions to the programmer/writer" (48). The text therefore must constantly negotiate the relationship between machine and human, or between intentionality and "intentionlessness" (49): at its core, a relationship between material and intention that is not a binary (51).

I build on Emerson's analysis, then, in arguing that, if poststructuralist conceptions of the author do not account for the materiality of the text, then the materiality as manifestation of process in a computer-generated text must open us up to the consideration of intention, even where intention cannot unequivocally be found. That is, I can read the line quoted above—"The writer orbits me. My line (article) has sighed"—as indicative of social and agential authorship, even though the computer did not and cannot intend for me to read its cryptic "line (article)" as such. While Emerson and others maintain that issues of paratext will always be markers of interpretation,[8] I would argue that the collaborative nature of the text signals that these paratextual clues are merely signposts to guide rather than laneways to direct interpretation. Because certain paratextual notes advise readers that *Pillage Laud*'s intentionality is complicated by computer generation, other paratextual notes, such as the one that describes the book as "lesbian sex poems" (np), must be taken as tongue-in-cheek provocations. The book is indeed a collection of lesbian sex poems, but it also is distinctly *not* that—while the poems select from the lexicon of erotic poetry, none of the poems can be wholly or exclusively labelled a lesbian sex poem, largely *because* of the computer's role in the collaboration.

In reading *Pillage Laud* as collaboration with a machine I also follow a scholarly tradition of reading it as a collaboration between Moure and Hartman, creator of the MacProse program. rob mclennan invokes this view[9] in his review of the Book*hug reprint of *Pillage Laud* in 2011, which I quote here at length:

> [Is] *Pillage Laud* a collaboration between Hartman and Moure? And what does this have to do with language, how words mean? How does such a work alter the considerations we bring to poetry? I've heard arguments that poetry created through such processes... became negated as poems for their perceived lack of "authorial intent." Do we need to know what an author was thinking to read a single line, a single poem? I would hardly think so....Despite what some of the language poets might tell you, words can't help but *mean*, and the meanings emerge through how the words are combined. (np)

In mclennan's view, then, the text's meaning does not depend on "'authorial intent,'" and meaning-making is something the text "can't help but" do. While I agree with mclennan's analysis as far as it goes, it does not fully address the implications of the "collaboration between Hartman and Moure," for it does not account for the ways in which *Pillage Laud* questions *who* gets to mean and *how* this meaning can be attributed to a speaking voice. Whereas mclennan emphasizes words' inherent meaningfulness, Moure insists that there is no language without a speaking voice, even in the indeterminate, experimental text. In "In Tenebris, or *The Gate*," for instance, she keeps us from relishing the utopian radical potentials of the unegoic text, reminding us that, ultimately, "This is just a copped line from MacProse" (99). This is not to say that the speaking voice of the text should be considered inherent to, or even exclusively produced by, the text. Instead, *Pillage Laud* reflects Moure's understanding that any speaking voice of any text is necessarily produced by the complex interplay of the speaking subject and the reading voice of the audience, who must make sense of poetry even where no sense was intended. And all of this is further complicated by the fact that what we might term the speaking subject of the text is collaborative, social, and constantly in flux.

The obvious constructedness of Moure's authorship in *Pillage Laud* is just one demonstration of how our use of language—in reading and writing—is governed by larger, oppressive structures, for Moure's poetry, much like Howe's, is primarily concerned with confronting the structures that govern our use of language. In keeping with the postanarchist desire to engage with and confront these structures rather than ignoring or attempting to dismantle them entirely, Moure's work uses translation, nonlinearity, and indeterminacy to direct attention to how our ability to communicate is limited by the structures of linguistic and textual production. In the collaborative text *Two Women Talking*, Moure and Bronwen Wallace insist that feminist poetry must not limit itself to its earlier concerns of maternal figures, embodiment, mythology, and reclamation because these tactics only reinforce the typical marginalization of the feminine in literature. Instead, feminist poets must draw attention to the fractures in the existing structures. They must "*write out of the dislocation of speaking from negative space, non-space*" (20, emphasis Moure's), and "deconstruct" these structures. In other words, Moure believes that the work of feminist poets is "to question the structure/systems/origins of our own media as we are engaged in using them" (39). What follows is a close look at the ways in which *Pillage Laud* works to turn the gaze back onto these structures/systems/origins, writing in excess of them and at times transgressing them.

In much of Moure's work, these structures are manifest in the concept of the archive as defined by Jacques Derrida in *Archive Fever*; however, Moure's treatment of the archive is not entirely derridean. For Derrida, the archive, from *arkhē* (or *first thing*), is concerned with both "the *commencement* and the *commandment*" (1, emphasis Derrida's). It is "the principle according to the law, *there* where men and gods *command*, *there* where authority, social order are exercised, *in this place* from which *order* is given" (1, emphasis Derrida's). Inscription, the process of archivization, is "what permits one to justify the distinction between memory and archive," and thus the radical potentials of memory permit deviation from archive, the control of which is central to political power (27). After all, as Derrida states plainly, "There is no political power without control of the archive, if not memory" (5). The archive is the underpinning of social order, of power exerted over subjectivities, and "archive fever" is the reactionary fear of the disruption of archival knowledge. Memory thus serves as one space where we may work against archival structure. Isabel A. Moore is one who sees a resonance between Derrida's archive and the governing structure of lyric poetic authorship, arguing that critics and readers who express a discomfort with Moure's queering of the author suffer from a "lyric fever" (35). Moore offers the insightful observation that Moure refuses the binaries of poetry versus philosophy or of lyric poetry versus experimental poetry (37) and, furthermore, that many of her reviewers demonstrate a fear that the lyric subject has already given way to the poststructuralist and late-century avant-garde destabilizations of it (39). In support of this analysis, Moore notes the many reviewers of Moure's poetry who consider the poet too interested in philosophy and theory, too theoretical to be effectively poetic. Moore quotes one reviewer, for example, who condemns Moure's *Little Theatres* for being more interested in a statement of philosophical poetics than in poetry itself. This reviewer, Moore writes, "wished Moure 'would check her poetics at the door when publishing her poetry'" as it was "too often inf(l)ected...by political philosophy" (37). Thus, a "lyric fever" surrounds Moure's work (51), for her work confronts the reader with manifestations and dissolutions of the lyric subject throughout, which the reader may well find frightening.

"Lyric fever" is clearly enacted in *Pillage Laud*, but we should not forget that Derrida's archive fever, as Collis reminds us, is distinctly psychoanalytic; it is a "death drive longing for forgetting, erasure, and repression" (*Through Words* 19). *Pillage Laud* thus has less to do with Derrida's archive fever and more to do with what Collis calls "*mal d'archive*": the text is "both in need of the archive and suffering destructive archive fever" (19). Its status as collaboration between speaking self and machine signals a demand of the impossible, a truly anarchist tactic; it wants at once to destroy the archive and insert its multiplicitous speaking self (a bastardized version of the lyric subject) into those structures.

Furthermore, because the text is produced by a collaboration between poet and computer, *Pillage Laud* must be read as grappling with derridean memory and with memory as Moure herself describes it. For Moure, memory in poetry is not dependent on semantics or on textual meaning; instead, she argues that it finds its manifestation in "The sound of words" (201). Nevertheless, because its very inscription draws attention to the archive, to the way that memory is archived, Moure acknowledges that the poem is not and cannot function outside of the archive. Instead, "Poetry...is the *structuration*...of *memory* that can undo the Law of the City, because it both precedes and transgresses the Law" (202, emphasis Moure's). It is crucial that she says "transgresses" here, and not "avoids"; the fact that memory is external to, or precedes, the Law as archive does not mean that it can function without it. For this reason, poetry in Moure's view should seek not necessarily, or not only, to "break it [the Law] down" but also to "peel it back and reveal its brokenness, the non-congruity behind it" ("Poetry, Memory and the Polis" 204). In my view, *Pillage Laud* does exactly this. In essence, *Pillage Laud* is a text of memory that destabilizes the archive and draws attention to the ways in which the ephemerality and flux of memory are structured by language. Memory is that which precedes the structuration of writing. In the aurality of memory, Moure sees the radical potential of poetry to use sound, itself ephemeral, to complicate and transgress the Laws of logos. She neither ignores nor refuses the larger structures of the logos, but looks to the fissures in language that poetry can make obvious for help to transgress these otherwise limiting structures.

Moure in *Pillage Laud* looks to these fissures, interestingly, by retaining some traditional structures of language (grammar, syntax, spelling) while disrupting others (meaning, sense, logic). While Moure's decision to retain proper grammar has led some readers to dismiss this text as merely reifying language rather than interrogating it,[10] I argue that Moure works through these structures to expose them, to peel them back, in order to reveal the archive behind the curtain. Like Howe, Moure presents the reader with images of literal archives (libraries, dictionaries, museums, and so on) that are forced in the indeterminacy of this text to confront their own boundaries. Like Howe's speaker sleeping in the library, Moure's computer-generated speaker forces the warmth of the body and the pleasure of tactility into the cold stacks: "After she rolled, libraries were your virtues" (50); "Certain libraries swelled the companion's brevity" (38); "The library should observe the empire of respect, the / vertebrate of custom" (61); "so texture a library was" (36). In other moments, the library appears as a site of displeasure: "Certain theorems are the libraries of bitterness" (14). Similarly, the dictionary appears in *Pillage Laud* as a site of violence and oppression in which the speaker questions, "What may the dictionary insist?" (19). Violent imagery of bondage and electricity characterizes this dictionary: "the model of rope—voltage—is her dictionary" (25). In another passage, the dictionary occupies the position of authority: "A dictionary especially rules" (26). The dictionary becomes a set of rules that seeks to include and envelop more and more. The speaker laments: "Why does every dictionary extend?" (57). The dictionary requires not grammar and syntax, but sense, logic, and limited definition, the structures of language that Moure finds most destructive.

The museum meets a similar fate, where its confrontation with the body initiates its destruction. The computer-generated speaker observes, for example, that "While you drank me, museums vanished" (33). Even light proves ineffectual in the museum, whose primary concern is reification and inscription. The text asks, "Would the ray leave the museum of flesh?" (70), and receives no answer. So, too, does the archive fail. The text, mocking the dismantled dictionary, provides its readers with a new definition of the term: "An archive: space, its vagabond between those roots and those / imitations" (68). The archive is emptied and destabilized. Its former position of stability and uniformity ("those roots") and its desire for mimesis, for representational linguistic sense ("those / imitations"), have been replaced by a nomadic condition ("its vagabond"). It occupies a liminal "between" rather than a binary: a non-space. And so Moure, as one node in the complex authorship of *Pillage Laud*, guides her readers through the non-space of vanished museums. Accordingly, in *Pillage Laud* we are not without archive; we are with the new archive. She—or "someone"—boasts: "I am your historian" (92). She repositions us.

In the end, I would argue, Moure transgresses the archive by writing in excess of it. The concept of Moure's excess has been effectively analyzed by Susan Rudy, who argues that excess is a trademark of Moure's work, in terms of both form and content. She characterizes this "excess" as follows: Moure "writes in excess of signification; refuses conventional word order and usage; redeploys grammar, punctuation, syntax, and spelling" (205). This excessive signification—which refuses to be fully inscribed by the archive, to be placed among the library stacks or under the museum glass—exposes the ways in which the archive limits our potential uses of language. Rudy sees in Moure's work that the "relations [*sic*] between words is endlessly shifting" (210) and that this state of flux ultimately generates "an excess of meaning" (211). In her excess, furthermore, Moure's poetic project works in a similar fashion to Howe's, whose insertion of the fluctuating personal into the larger structures of history and language can be read as similarly excessive. Both authors, by pointing to the fissures and discontinuities of these larger structures of the logos, demonstrate that a primary concern of the experimental feminist poet must be to generate these excesses of meaning. Both authors refuse to be fully categorized by the archive, offering instead a multiple and shifting "I" that moves deftly through the stacks of the library. Their new archive is that of the poem, the structuration of live memory that transgresses as it speaks.

*Pillage Laud* invites itself into the poem-archive, including its readership as a part of the vast social authorship of the text. This is essentially what DuPlessis argues when she asserts that the reader of *Pillage Laud* performs the text and that the reader is thus a writer as well, but only insofar as the author/writer herself is considered to be just one subjectivity in the multiplicity of textual production (989). In other words, because the reader cannot make sense out of these sentences that look, for all intents and purposes, as though they *should* make sense, the reader has to take an active, agential role in reading this work. Similarly, Rudy places particular attention on the ways in which the complication of authorship produces what she terms a "communal narrative" (212). Moure likewise, in her collaborative essay with Caroline Bergvall, insists that all of reading is "inherently a practice of exchange, or responsiveness," that it is "radically communal" (170). This, we may recall, is the exact same phrase used by Duncan. Moure and Bergvall also characterize the reading of poetry in particular as a kind of "enactment" (175). Certainly *Pillage Laud*, with its explicit confrontation of individualized authorship via computer collaboration, opens itself to new and various forms of reading processes. The process of the text's production signposts the intentional fallacy better than perhaps any of the other experimental texts in this project; Moure's level of engagement in the writing is unclear at best, and yet she does guide the reading process in ways that other indeterminate texts do not: For example, Moure's designation of *Pillage Laud* as a book of "lesbian sex poems" guides readers into exegetical territory in a way that Mac Low's *Stein Poems* do not: by prescribing a way of reading the content of the poems, Moure engages with her readers in ways that significantly exceed a mere description of process. Consequently, "Erín Moure" develops in *Pillage Laud* a poetics of indeterminacy that directly addresses a communal readership rather than expressing a lack of interest in the ways the text could be read.

I argue, then, that in its computer generation, *Pillage Laud* is a cyborg book at the meeting of two forms: the digital, computer-generated text and the individually scripted lyric. In this I follow such critics as Emerson, who argues that the fundamental difference between the computer-generated poem and the more traditionally (read: humanly) produced text is that a transmedial authorship requires that criticism focus on the reader rather than either producer or object (47). This move in criticism from author and text to the reader is a distinct feature of postanarchism, and it requires that we pay attention to the ways in which *Pillage Laud* directly addresses and discusses its audience. The computer-generated poem, just as Emerson claims, does not kill the author or even render authors unimportant. Rather, it suggests that the author is just one meaning-producer along with (and equally weighted with) the reader or the text itself, and that this is made explicit in the computer-generated text (55). The technology involved—MacProse, in the case of *Pillage Laud*—is a fourth participant in this collaborative meaning-making. This is probably most evident in the text's explicit invitations for the reader to engage in the production of both meaning and, through metaphors, the text itself. "I may move me," the poem's speaker suggests, addressing an audience that is both individual and collective, "but each of you longs to rule" (33). A few lines later, "each of you" acquires even more agency in this process: "You appear to type" (33). Elsewhere, the reader is directly engaged in events: for example, amidst highly erotic discussions of the female body, one jarring line reads, "The audience snaps her form" (66). Later, *Pillage Laud*'s readers are directly addressed in a way that suggests they occupy a position more valuable, even, than the speaker: "Dear one, I am the title, and you are the heights" (88). Authorship, in this line, is authoritative in title only, quite literally—an interpretation for which Moure's choice to include her name in quotation marks on both editions' covers prepares us. We as readers are, according to *Pillage Laud*, "the heights": a suggestion of physical power that moves well beyond name.

Moreover, in *Pillage Laud* the speaker questions not only the presence of an audience (a common feature even in lyric poetry) but also her position in relation to it, by questioning the function of the text itself. The speaker asks, for example: "Whom had the fresh poem mattered to?" (51); "Had we read?" (71); "to whom is this speaking machine hastening?" (91). The text is by such means positioned as a "speaking machine," a cyborg text that continues its speech as though it is a clearly defined speaking subject communicating directly to a comprehending audience. In the final poem, "to exist is reading," the question of readership and its relationship to the "speaking machine" again comes to the fore. The poem itself seems to meditate on the pages that have preceded it, asking, "So mechanical a suggestion—how has everyone replied?" (103), and later, "Whom don't the readers produce?" (104). In the end, the poem's computer-generated speaker questions whether it is even possible to imagine a text without an audience: "When to exist is reading, can listener stop?" (106). The suggestion here is that a readership is produced at the same time as the text itself. This poem, clearly, reflects a conception of reading as "radically communal." It implies an ethical relationship between other readers and between readers and the author in such a way that, ultimately, the "Erí(i)n Moure(é)" who authors *Pillage Laud* is presented as a part of this reading audience. That is, "Moure(é)" figures her real audience into her work by simultaneously relating to and imagining into being, especially in this last poem, the vast multiplicity of her real, macrocosmic audience.

I would further argue that *Pillage Laud*'s common is one in which we must recognize our affective connections with various subjectivities—including the machines—involved in textual production. The text foregrounds the extremely affective relationships that link the production of the text and its enactment (or reading), explicitly stating that "To read was an affection" (91). At the end of the book the speaker directly addresses this concern: "Those texts stain you. // You are some audience; / you expect affections" (102). The discomfort, the "stain," brought on by the expectation of affect and the actual reception of the non-narrative, non-suturing, computer-generated text produces the audience. This discomfort is an especially productive affective response that encourages political engagement in a way that other texts cannot.

For Moure, meaning is inherently incomplete, and thus a complete and perfect meaning is impossible; "words," she reminds us, "cannot entirely convey our desires" (*My Beloved* 22). But poetry can make explicit the incomplete nature of meaning-making and meaning-reception through sound, aurality, and memory, as *Pillage Laud* so effectively demonstrates. Moure writes that "Sounds unlock memories which precede the laws of social order. Sounds that precede words. The sound is where memory coalesces in the poem" (23). In some ways, this statement recalls the kind of logocentrism that Derrida attacks in *Disseminations*, the notion that speech or live memory precedes the graphic process, and thus suggests a truth outside of language but gestured toward with every articulation. Moure navigates away from this dangerous logocentrism by suggesting that all attempts to convey meaning articulate not an external truth, a *logos*, but rather the fluctuating and incomplete desires of a nebulous speaking subject who is difficult to name. Ultimately, *Pillage Laud* approaches the unegoic in some of the ways that Cage and Mac Low envisioned, but persistently reinserts the subject that threatens to be erased by this process. This is not personal, confessional, or typical erotic poetry, but in its inextricable merger of poet and machine it insists on the importance of subjectivities (authors and readers equally weighted and alike) that fluctuate and move, revealing the diffuseness and incompleteness of erotic desire and meaning-making at once.

### [Juliana Spahr Prefers Both

In *Response* (1996), the first collection of poetry by the now central experimental poet, Juliana Spahr, we see the author's refusal to entirely deny her subjectivity, just as we saw in Howe and Moure. This refusal becomes a major interest of Spahr's later work, in such collections as the very popular *This Connection of Everyone with Lungs*; in *Response*, it is just starting to emerge. Still, as Spahr explores poetry's potentials for resistance, for experimentation, the issues of subjectivity and language merge in the two primary arguments that she develops throughout this collection: that there is an inherent link between expression and linguistic violence and that the common, paradoxically, both requires and disrupts subjectivity. These themes add force to one another throughout *Response* as Spahr writes to resist the predominance of the lyric "I" in contemporary poetry, especially in activist poetics. After all, as Katy Lederer exclaims in her review of *Response*: "If any act of poetic writing can be thought of as action, this is it" (140). Ultimately, Spahr, in this early collection, interrogates the relationship between language and violence to forge a feminist poetics that, in true postanarchist fashion, uses poetry as activism and considers how we might use poetry to amplify alternative voices. In *Response*, Spahr proposes the activist poetics she continues throughout her career.

While rarely explicitly anarchist, Spahr's work in *Response* can be characterized by a clearly activist, insurgent attitude. As she recalls, *Response* was written in a poetic climate fraught with debate between "writing that turns from standard English and one that upholds standard English" ("90s" 173). Spahr sees turning from standard English as anti-imperialist and anti-capitalist and argues that this vein of poetry was fuelled by the 1990s' "perfect storm" of political resistance and experimentation ("90s" 174). Moments of collective resistance in the 1990s, as in the Zapatista revolution and the 1999 protests at the WTO (World Trade Organization) meeting in Seattle, sought large and overarching goals through multiple voices concerned with multiple projects and employing multiple tactics; in her view they were "successful thought experiments in what a universalism with room for particularity might look like on a very practical level" ("90s" 173–74). For Spahr, then, the 1990s in poetry saw these practical experimentations as intrinsically tied to the potentials of poetry for similar experimentation in language, generalized under Spahr's wide-reaching principle of turning from standard English.

Itself a product of the 1990s, *Response* is filled with examples of Spahr's grappling with the radical experimental potentials of language and their correlatives, the radical potentials of activism. Spahr implies, at first, that the starting point of a politics of experimentation is a resistance that stems from anger: "the anger is to draw attention to the way anger is a just response / to how they will be angry until just witness is begun" (76). With such passages, she suggests that the most effective political content is marked by its enactment rather than its dogmatism. In section one of the collection's first poem, "responding," the speaker remarks on the reading of "a book that is so subtle" that "[its political content goes unnoticed" (8, no close to square bracket), a book that eventually provokes the speaker to ask: "what is political content?" (8). As the boundaries of what dictates political content are blurred by what Spahr terms a subtlety, she advocates for a poetic language that, in working against standard English, promotes an anarchic moment of insurgency—a TAZ, in other words—where the inherent instability of language is allowed to flourish. Consider, for instance, the first line of "responding": "This is a place without a terrain a government that always changes an unstable language" (8). The ambiguity of Spahr's syntax here is significant; the grammar of the line makes it unclear whether the place is without both terrain and government, or whether the terrain-less place is also a government in flux. Moreover, the line might suggest that this "place," both without physical boundary (terrain) and without authority (government), changes an already unstable language, or else this "place" that is always in flux *is* an unstable language itself. This ambiguous syntax, then, enacts the politics of the "place," the primary situation of *Response*, embodying (which is to say, locating in the physical) while at the same time destabilizing activist movement. The "This" that starts this line is a deixis with no contextualizing information, no external object to which it refers. "This...place" is thus entirely ambiguous, a nonplace whose location in the physical realm is tenuous at best.

For Lederer, these dual goals of destabilizing and materializing are the most effective anti-traditional tactics of *Response*. She sees these most clearly enacted in Spahr's insertion of the generic, especially by way of her intrusive use of the bracket, into an otherwise particular work. "By inserting 'the generic' within" her margins, Lederer observes, "Spahr transmutes the ghostly—thus invisible—margins of the traditional book into the space of the 'embodied'—thus vulnerable—textual center" (142). I would further argue that, because of this now-vulnerable textual centre, the bracketed generic insertions function as TAZs, moments of insurgency and displacement that are still necessarily encased within more traditional confines. In "responding," these TAZs get characterized as Spahr's "[New State]," in which poetry and art in general serve a crucial purpose: "we know art is fundamental to the [New State]" (*Response* 9). Yet the "[New State]" is not, for Spahr, a means of defining physical space any more than it can be used to define the individuals who inhabit that space. In fact, in "documentary," similar bracketed insertions directly contest using nation as a means of definition, when Spahr uses brackets to redact: "[name of nation used as an adjective deleted]" (35).

Spahr is careful not to overstate the political potentials of poetry, but the poem "responding" reveals, nevertheless, a deep ambivalence about subjectivity and pronoun use in her poetics. In a few passages in "responding," for instance, she writes of occasions when the political import of art fails against the physicality of real violence, as for instance where "[name of major historical figure]," a still generic figure that speaks to the pervasiveness of this violence, "calls, authentically, for a more total, more radical war than we can even dream in the language of the avant-garde" (*Response* 9). Later in the same poem, Spahr characterizes art as not only ineffectual, but also potentially damaging in this material realm where "while overwhelmed by an opera [name of major historical figure] plans genocide" (12). Such passages speak to the potentially ineffectual or damaging role of art in politics, but at the same time the bracketing of the "major historical figure" sets him/her in flux, thus blurring the lines of history, politics, and even artistic tradition. As Spahr's readers, we are asked to take on the burden not only of envisioning these violences on a very real level, but also of occupying the bracketed spaces ourselves. Because of the generic wording and the generally vague, open, or bracketed way in which Spahr presents the violences of the text, it is up to us to envision how and when these violences occur in the real, lived experiences of ourselves as subjects and of subjectivities other than ourselves. In this way, we occupy these bracketed spaces, becoming the various [generic pronouns] included therein, but also momentarily occupying the positions of "major historical figure" and the other slightly more specific subjectivities. This reader-envisioned violence and the reader's participation in the process of meaning-making pervade *Response*, so that it exposes the radical potentials of a postanarchist reading practice to allow for reading as activism. The bracketed intrusions are deictic shifts that engage the reader in direct and specific ways, revealing thereby the inadequacy of deixis in pronouns generally and further pointing to the inadequacies and slippages of the relationship between the subject and its representation in language. The [generic pronouns] of *Response* reveal, most of all, a deep ambivalence about subjectivity and pronoun use in poetics, admitting at once the necessary presence and obvious slippages of each and every pronoun.

What we find in *Response*, then, is a sustained grappling with the issues of subjectivity. Like Howe, Spahr is writing both in and away from a tradition of experimental poetry that has long been preoccupied with the suppression of the self. Spahr is heavily influenced by LANGUAGE poetry, which sees this suppression of individual subjectivity as something that must be grounded in semiotics, form, and language. Lederer points to this influence when she writes that Spahr in *Response* is "a poet unwilling to clutter her writing with the signs of her own subjectivity" (140), but I differ from Lederer on the extent to which Spahr seeks to remove "the signs" of authorial "subjectivity." In my view, *Response* marks the initial moments of Spahr's ongoing interest in what she considers a paradox of subjectivity: in order to be truly communal, we require individual subjectivity; at the same time, in being truly communal, we disrupt and disfigure our individual subjectivities. This challenging paradox is central to the understanding of community and the common that permeates her work; *Response* demonstrates Spahr's first forays into this paradox, which she satisfies via her use of the [generic pronoun].

To begin looking at the paradox of subjectivity in *Response*, we must first look to Spahr's concept of authorship. In "A, B, C," she outlines a theory of the author as an initiator of choices rather than the controller of a text: "An author," she writes, "is the person who originates or gives existence to something" (284). As initiator, the author nevertheless needs to involve readers in the production of meaning, and so authorship conceived in this way leaves much of the process of meaning-making incomplete. This repositioning of the author includes the reader in the production of textual meaning on a communal level; in a radical poetics that embraces inclusivity, the terms of author and reader need, in some way, to be conflated, and the boundaries between them need to be blurred. Spahr sees this new, radical poetics of subjectivity both described and enacted in Stein's work: "Here is a confusion of subject, address, and identity. Here a new poetics of the subject is scripted" ("A, B, C," 286). In Spahr's view, furthermore, Stein's reliance on readers to make meaning themselves requires her to relinquish some of the authority of the author. Spahr observes that "In Stein's work the authority of the author is hiding behind the door, is translated, is denied," suggesting that Stein's authorship is not, cannot be, a controlling presence imposing meaning upon the words ("A, B, C," 287). Let us, for a moment, leave the finality of a term like "denied" and focus instead on Spahr's choice of "translated," a term that defines Stein's approach to authorship as at once purely linguistic, resituating, and altering. In contrast to the flux and manipulation suggested by "translated," a word like "denied" is final, perhaps, but it also acknowledges the persistence of the lyric "I" in poetry, a persistence we must resist, must shut the door upon, must deny. The authorial subject in poetry demands representation; a postanarchist reading practice, like the one Spahr proposes based on her analysis of Stein, seeks to unsettle these demands. That is, Spahr's poetry may work to limit authorial subjectivity, but she also knows, just as the poets I have previously discussed know, that the completely unegoic is impossible.

If *Response* teaches us nothing else, it shows us that the construction of the subject is inevitable. We might even say that the collection takes this for granted, rather than grappling with the knowledge as Cage and Mac Low do, and as Spahr will do with greater sophistication in her later work. The unnamed speaker of *Response* states, plainly and conversationally, "we know we are all constructed" (25), as if the social construction of the self is a widely and easily accepted truth. Once the text accepts social construction as a starting point, it is free to move, conveying an individual subject that is in flux, always in motion. Sophie Mayer notes that Spahr's practice is not new, and Spahr's tools themselves are not new either; that is, Spahr disperses her "lyric 'I'" through "postmodern poetics of quotation, repetition, and bricolage" (Mayer 60, 48). These, we know, are three of the mainstays of postmodernism that have, even by 1996, become tired and perhaps ineffectual as a poetics and politics. But if this is where Spahr begins, by the time she gets to *This Connection*, we find a multiplicity of selves and "beloveds" that permeate the work so thoroughly that it is evident Spahr has moved well beyond postmodern concerns of the self and into a poetics that takes for granted the multiplicitous and porous nature of selves as a starting point. What this move amounts to is not a dispersal of the self, but a rethinking of that very concept, and it is important to acknowledge that this rethinking begins in *Response*: "as we rethink our selves, the political enters / and the issue twists to become about our ability to touch information / to make our own decisions" (61).

These are lines that Mayer, too, finds central; for Mayer, in a political poetics we "need to 'rethink our selves' in light of the radical tropes of alienation and connection highlighted by global war and global media" (49). In support of this argument she invokes Judith Butler's conception of a politics of interdependence and interconnectivity: "we're undone by each other," Butler asserts in *Precarious Life*, "and if we're not, we're missing something" (23). It is this undoing of each other via connection that leads Mayer to observe in Spahr that "Reader, poet, and subject are interdependent, made vulnerable (in Butler's term) by 'shock and awe,' by the rending violence that gently informs...Spahr's swift changes of focus" (50). Much of this violence is in the cleaving of closed subjectivity, the opening of the self, and the quick movement between selves and points of view. This movement is implied by Spahr's shifts in subjectivity and authorship, and it serves to disrupt the ordered, taking a page from Stein's own mandates. For Spahr, this process (of flux, of movement) is more valuable than an identitarian politics could ever be: "more than identity our attraction is to puzzle / the lineage" (46–47). But none of this movement answers the question *Response* asks so persistently: "how much self can be removed and the self remain?" (70). In asking this question in *Responses* without answering it, Spahr seeks to construct a disrupted postanarchist subjectivity that does not oppose "selfhood," but rather proposes more useful ideas of selves bound in interdependence.

In the end, for Spahr, the central question is that of pronouns, those literal representations of selves in language. Pronouns preoccupy Spahr throughout *Response* and well after. In 2005, nearly ten years after *Response* was published, interviewer Michael Boyko posed a question to Spahr about subjectivity in her work, and her response is telling: "I keep thinking pronouns all the time. Somehow pronouns have become the most loaded parts of language for me" (Spahr, "A Brief Q&A" np). Pronouns get complicated in *Response* through their turn to completely generic states. For example, in "responding" Spahr writes of a "[gendered pronoun]" who "wanders in this place / [searching / [waiting" (*Response* 8). Despite the almost humorous lack of specificity, the [gendered pronoun] is able to move between the localized "this place" and the flux of open movement denoted by "wanders," "[searching," and "[waiting." The latter two progressive verbs are bracketed without close, implying even greater instability than the words would on their own. They represent transport, movement. An especially significant line, "[generic pronoun] creates" (8), demonstrates that the blurring of subjectivity is, can still be, productive.

Spahr continues to play with pronoun usage in her later collections. We can see, for example, a gradual shift in the nearly ten years between *Response* and *This Connection*, where the pronoun "we" is used frequently in an almost Steinian repetition. Spahr explains this turn to "we" to Boyko:

> I started with "we" because I wanted to start with together....And I wanted everyone to be there in the poem. I wanted "we" to include those who read it. And then I wanted when I turn to "I" to talk about how that moment of becoming individuals, becoming distinct and disconnected, is part of the problem. And I wanted more specifically to talk about my own complicity with this...I guess I felt I had to stand up and take responsibility and be there in the poem at some point. That I couldn't hide in the "we." And I also wanted the reader to think about their individualism with me. (np)

Here we see Spahr express an explicit desire to involve and "include" readers via her use of the plural pronoun "'we.'" It is thus especially striking, and distinctly postanarchist, that this desire to include "everyone" in the language of her work leads her to a discussion of the impossibility of removing the writing self from the poetic project. We need subjects, Spahr suggests, in order to connect with other subjects, to be interdependent, complicit in each other's "individualism." That is the core paradox of *Response*.

In recognition of selves, we blur lines: rethink, translate, transport, read. This paradox of the subject—that we must connect to break down monadic subjectivity, but that we must have subjects in order to connect them—recalls the paradox of the feminist experimental poet as identified by Ngai, who cites Spahr as an example of writers who explicitly deal with this. For Ngai, the paradox of language for feminist avant-gardists is clear: they must decide either to refuse the binary (and thus ignore it) or to interrogate it and thus risk inadvertently supporting it: "For the feminist writer, the stance that form is political implies that there is no politically neutral language and, by extension, no language uninflected by gender and its ideological codes" (316). Here Ngai usefully illuminates the ways that the avant-garde is predicated on a masculinist discourse that tends to ignore the gendered codes innate in linguistic structures. The choice becomes either to follow a "tradition dominated by male modernists and valorized by feminist poststructuralist theorists" or else to engage in "a strategic *reappropriation* of 'feminine' form" (316). If these options are unsatisfactory, the alternative is to accept the position

> that the attachment, even the critical attachment of gender codes to language promotes the restriction of women to certain kinds of expression and in fact perpetuates binary gender divisions and the hierarchies inevitably accompanying them. This position culminates in a feminist need to insist that linguistic categories should not be gendered, even in aesthetic or critical efforts to challenge past ways in which forms and genres certainly *have* been gendered. (317, emphasis Ngai's)

The goal here is to "do away with the concept of 'feminine form' altogether" (317). The result is that the "feminist" avant-gardist is left with a fundamental theoretical decision to make before writing: to either argue that all form, all language is "inevitably" gendered and politicized, leaving no room for resistance, or to look past or ignore the ways that language codifies and regulates subjectivities, with gender being just one of many elements of selfhood under that umbrella. This, Ngai argues, is the central paradox of the feminist experimental poet: "If one adheres too strongly to either of the positions circumscribed by the 'politics of form' position," she writes, "one runs the risk of asserting 'no language is code-free' to a degree that leaves one stuck with the task of constantly negotiating between 'masculine' and 'feminine' categories, inadvertently strengthening them" on the one hand, and on the other, "one runs the risk of dangerously underestimating the pervasiveness of gender ideology in all cultural forms" (317). Spahr grapples with this paradox, too, as Ngai observes, in that she "deliberately occupies the boundary between these possibilities by using the 'generic' phrasing" (317–18) in *Response*.

I, too, would like to examine Spahr's grappling with representation and genericism through one politically charged and deeply feminist example; in the fourth section of "responding," Spahr writes, "[generic pronoun] wished to reduce writing to the zero level where it is without meaning. When culture invades private life on a large scale [generic pronoun] said the individual cannot escape being raped" (*Response* 21). A few lines later, this long line is separated into a list structure that sees the language stutter:

> [my zero-level writing
> [generic pronoun] said
>             protest rape
> [generic pronoun] said
> my zero-level writing
> [generic pronoun] said
> dangerous cultural rape
> [generic pronoun] said
> my zero-level writing
> my zero-level writing (22)

The wording here is borrowed from a passage by Ni Haifeng, a Chinese avant-garde artist and writer whom Spahr almost certainly came across through an article by Andrew Solomon in *The New York Times Magazine*, "Their Irony, Humor (and Art) Can Save China," in which Solomon discusses the radical political potentials of the contemporaneous Chinese avant-garde. The full quotation from Haifeng that Solomon provides reads as follows:

> In 1987, he began to paint on houses, streets, stones, trees and he covered his island with strange marks in chalk, oil paint and dye. He has said that he wished to reduce writing to the "zero level" where it is without meaning. "When culture invades private life on a large scale," he said, "the individual cannot escape being raped. From this viewpoint, my zero-level writing can be taken as a protest against the act of rape. I also want to warn people of the dangers inherent in cultural rape." (np)

By adapting Ni's words and Solomon's writing, Spahr suggests that a "zero-level writing"—a writing with no meaning—is impossible and politically dangerous, and that such writing may risk underestimating the violence of such social institutions as gender. Standing in stark contrast to the insertion of the bracketed generic pronoun, the specific and overtly political terms "protest rape" and "dangerous cultural rape" refuse to tip Spahr's writing toward either side of the paradox: they neither insist on a feminine form nor ignore the gendered inflections of language. The lack of gender specificity of the generic pronoun repeated throughout this passage (nowhere in the collection is its use so pervasive) both suggests the openness and receptiveness that characterizes feminine form for Ngai and also refuses a clearly delineated binarism. In the end, the short, indented lines quoted above begin with "[my zero-level writing," which never sees its bracketing closed. In this way, Spahr suggests here the radical potentials of a tightrope walk between two dangerous sides of the feminist experimental paradox; she neither supports nor refuses, embracing a postanarchic alternative rather than giving in to one side or another. It is the stuttering that produces a new mode of articulation.

In *Response*, then, Spahr envisions "[a reader culture" without a close to the square bracket, insisting instead that "[generic plural pronoun] prefer both" (8). By asserting that "[generic plural pronoun] prefer both," Spahr not only emphasizes plurality and commonality, but also proposes a valuation of reading as experience rather than interpretation, an anti-exegesis, which is not entirely new, but is still clearly a radicalism that opposes the very process of reading a poem. Preferring both is, for Spahr, an exercise in embracing alternatives rather than binarism or dualism. At the heart of tradition (and individual talent) is a hegemony of reading founded on exegesis, hermeneutics, and semiotics. [a reader culture embraces readings rather than just reading; it prefers both.

## Harryette Mullen Making Kimchee in a Museum

I move from Spahr's clear anarchist sympathies to the work of Harryette Mullen who, while never identifying as anarchist herself, instead offers postanarchism a method of resistance that is highly experimental and interested in the radical alternatives offered to readers and writers in, and through, language. To explore these radical alternatives to expression, Mullen positions the ephemeral alongside the preserved, and points to a black experimental tradition that moves adeptly between the speakerly texts of the Black Arts Movement and the writerly texts of LANGUAGE poetry and the avant-garde. I look at one of her later collections, *Sleeping with the Dictionary* (2002), to argue that Mullen manipulates the machine-like workings of Oulipian procedural poetry and its concomitant ephemerality and multiplicity of the personal to develop an intermediary poetics that complicates subjectivity and authorship without withdrawing the speaking self completely.

Describing Mullen's work as avant-garde or experimental, or even as a part of the LANGUAGE tradition, is fraught with complications. To begin, the avant-garde designation tends to be treated as an exclusive club; at times, this "club" metaphor can even become literal, as in the example of the Oulipo, which, as Spahr notes, is a literally exclusive club that rarely admits women or people of colour.[11] Yet, as Spahr also notes, one does not need to be a card-carrying member of the Oulipo to carry out their language games: "Oulipo techniques are, obviously, frequently used by those who are not in Oulipo. But it is still hard not to read Mullen's insistence on the Oulipian nature of this book as a polite claiming and insistence on an inclusive tradition" (Introduction iv). Although she writes in this tradition without a membership card, Mullen skilfully uses Oulipian methods to explore the relationship between the individual and the communal in a number of complicated ways, "exploring communolects, community, and her own subjectivity using what are sometimes called poetic 'procedures,' or various composition techniques" (Spahr, Introduction iii). Thus, she uses the methods of a once exclusive club to promote, instead of exclusivity, an inviting and egalitarian approach to the communal. For example, Mullen's use of the N + 7 technique[12] is a gesture toward the communal and away from individualized subjectivity and authorial genius. Mullen herself acknowledges that she finds the Oulipian constraints liberating: "I have found that using constraints in this way expands the possibilities for improvisation, as various textual operations may be tried at different points in the writing process" (Henning 27). Mullen also admires the way Oulipo places less emphasis on the poem as end product, arguing that the "idea of 'potential literature' liberates the writer to concentrate on the process, rather than the product, of writing" (26). Nevertheless, while *Sleeping with the Dictionary* bears some resemblance to Oulipian procedures, Mullen's poetry in this collection refuses to be categorized as simply *writerly*; instead it works to collapse the boundary between the lyrical work associated with the Black Arts Movement and the avant-garde refusal of subjectivity, ultimately demonstrating that these schools need not be as separate, let alone antagonistic, as they have been historically.[13]

To explore this issue, I would like to focus on the prose poem "Coals to Newcastle, Panama Hats from Ecuador" (16), a poem that expresses acute awareness of the two literary traditions with which Mullen has been associated. Of this poem, Mullen tells Barbara Henning, "I had the title before the poem, starting with the expression, 'Coals to Newcastle.' That's a city in England that was known for coal mining, so this saying is about getting more of what you've already got" (58). While the poem need not be read as metapoetic, I cannot help but see it as expressing a desire not to fit in with, or subscribe to, any one particular school of poetry: in other words, a desire not to give readers "more of what" they've "already got." Though this metapoetic theme is never explicitly stated, it is suggested by the image of coal, a symbol that contains within it the duality that is persistently discussed in regard to Mullen's work: coal as blackness, coal as progress.[14] The coal, of which Newcastle already has too much, represents on the one hand industrial progress, city, machine, and innovation; it prioritizes the material and the successful. On the other hand, coal becomes a symbol of blackness, insofar as it not only is black in colour but also colours the skin of those mining it; additionally, coal mining has significant literary precedent as a symbol of poverty and of labour issues.[15]

The metapoetic elements of this poem are brought to the fore through Mullen's emotional approach to authorship. The speaker insists on the belligerence of emotion: "I'll be emotionally disturbed for as long as it takes" (16). This interest in emotion takes an important political and metapoetic turn when it attacks the difficult, emotionless, and bourgeois side of avant-garde poetry, as when Mullen writes, "You're too simple to be so difficult. Malicious postmodernism" (16). This opposition leads the speaker to turn in on herself, ultimately questioning the validity of the reliance on subjectivity and authorial presence representative of the Black Arts Movement and the erasure of subjectivity praised by the avant-garde. The poem ends, "Now that I live alone, I'm much less introspective. Now you sound more like yourself" (16). The speaker, who "lives alone" and is thus separated from the social, here claims that this separation allows her to be free of self-contemplation, to avoid constantly reviewing herself and her subjectivity. However, the paratactic addition of "Now you sound more like yourself" and the sudden shift in person from the first to the second undermine the sentence that precedes it. Who sounds like his or her self? The reader? Or is this an external voice directed at the speaker? This final parataxis brings into question our ability to sound like ourselves at all. The suggestion of causality in these final two sentences also implies contradiction; in supposing that we ever "live alone," that we can ever become "less introspective," we sound most like ourselves. We cannot escape subjectivity; in discussing its potential erasure *ad infinitum*, as the avant-garde has tended to do, we simply increase the terms of our subjectivity.

This dual interest in being less introspective and sounding more like ourselves is primarily what critics have pointed to in labelling Mullen as a "crossover" from racialized poetry of identity toward identity's erasure in LANGUAGE poetry and the avant-garde. For many, "Mullen's crossover appeal is the prime reason for her popularity" (Hart 143). But her work never treats these two approaches to poetry as separate entities, and I would therefore argue that the designation of "crossover" is inaccurate. Mullen addresses the issue herself, when she warns against the idea of the crossover poet:

> The erasure of the anomalous black writer abets the construction of a continuous, internally consistent tradition, while at the same time it deprives the idiosyncratic minority artist a history, compelling her to struggle even harder to construct a cultural context out of her own racial individuality. ("Poetry and Identity" 86)

As "the anomalous black writer," Mullen resists erasure by, for example, writing as Oulipo without claiming to belong to Oulipo as a group. While she acknowledges where she's giving us "more of what" we've "already got," she also challenges us to think about why we have so much of it. This strategy is, at the same time, an act of implicit opposition to the Marxism of LANGUAGE poetry, whose interest in subsuming the subject to the communal ultimately represses anomalous voices. Thus, the associations made by critics between Mullen's work and such schools of avant-garde poetry as Oulipo and LANGUAGE reveal not only those anomalous elements of Mullen's work but also the erasures and fissures existing within such filiative communities.

The perceived separation between avant-garde and black poetics comes up again in an interview with Elizabeth Frost where Mullen laments the fact that "What people think of as 'black poetry' is set aside from what people think of as 'poetry,' in terms of tradition, history, how language is used. People have a very specific notion of what black poetry is" (Mullen, "Interview" 417). To this, Frost responds by arguing, "there is a balance between two different forces. One is an assertion of identity. The other is what I think of as hybridity—the mixture, the different influences all occurring at once. There is sometimes tension, but there doesn't have to be" (Mullen, "Interview" 418). Frost's identification of this mixture in Mullen is useful, even though use of the term "hybridity" has the potential to close discursive practices rather than open them. Despite Frost's insistence on the rhetoric of balance and hybridity, what she asserts here is that Mullen does not unite two schools but rather embraces the multiple. This concept of the embrace is much more productive than the dualism of terms like "balance" and "hybrid," which tacitly support the understanding that asserting racial identity and experimenting with subjectivity are in opposition, or are at the very least separate.[16] Despite the frequency with which the criticism surrounding Mullen uses such problematic terms to insist that she bridges two disparate poetic worlds, or that she merges two seemingly contradictory poetic forms, there is some precedent in the most recent scholarship for taking up the arguments Mullen herself has been making for decades.

In particular, I would argue that Mullen's concept of the "anomalous black writer" foregrounds—in order to reject—the conventional assumption that the process of writing from the lyric "I," a purportedly less experimental mode, is reserved for women, people of colour, or queer subjects. This marginalization assumes that the white, cis-male, heterosexual poet occupies a better position from which to critique identity. Amy Moorman Robbins argues convincingly that this assumption draws on

> a significant and still-operative contrast: that between experimental writing/poetry that is assumed to explicitly or implicitly contest the viability of any given lyric subject...and writing that

> foregrounds questions and problems of discrete, often racialized selfhood in specific cultural contexts. (341–42)

In support of her argument, Robbins addresses Silliman's assertions, which are outlined in the introduction to this chapter. Robbins concedes that LANGUAGE poetry, with its abnegation of identity, has "origins within and for a particular group," but she also claims that we must move beyond Silliman's arguments that this makes LANGUAGE poetry a white man's game; we must critically trace how this reading "significantly complicates our reading of the movement's subsequent disavowal of a poetics of identity" (345). Robbins further cautions that "the eventual positioning of Language writing as opposed to lyric poetry, with the latter genre repeatedly linked to writing by people of color, subtly contributes to the impression that political poetry by the socially marginalized is historically not experimental" (349). In order to discuss Mullen's work without re-inscribing this unhelpful and inherently racist dualism, I look to her collapse of the dualism of writerly and speakerly texts, opposing bourgeois conceptions of archive and preservation with the ephemerality of the polyvocal, multivalent text. Mullen opposes the archive through the incorporation of highly personal and emotional moments into impersonal organizational structures of archiving. Ultimately, Mullen's work shows us not only that we can bridge the gap between the speakerly and the writerly text, but that this gap was always artificial, developed in order to continue to silence the voices of the marginalized in poetry, and to keep the reader at a safe and non-intervening distance from the text.

As many scholars, including Mullen herself, point out, the collapsing of the divide between experimental and racialized writing is grounded in the collapse of the supposed divide between texts that privilege orality (what Mullen calls "speakerly" texts) and formally/visually experimental text (which she terms, following Barthes, "writerly"). In "Poetry and Identity," she argues not only that the anomalous black writer gets elided when we maintain these divides, but also that black writers will be at a disadvantage if they continue to prioritize orality over writing. This is made even clearer in "African Signs and Spirit Writing," where she insists that "any theory of African-American literature that privileges a speech-based poetics, or the trope of orality, to the exclusion of more writerly texts will cost us some impoverishment of the tradition" (671). Deborah Mix also brings this perceived divide to the fore in her insightful studies of Mullen, arguing for instance that the marginalization of the experimental racialized author occurs "because of a set of assumptions perpetuated by scholars of experimental writing and scholars of African-American writing; the former group seeks 'writerly texts,' while the latter seeks 'speakerly' ones" (38). Following Mullen, Mix also suggests that collapsing the divide between speakerly and writerly texts works to enrich both camps. For Mix, Mullen's poetry and criticism "demonstrates what we risk losing if we don't rebuild our frameworks for understanding experimental traditions" (39). I do not want to risk such a loss, so I turn to postanarchist literary theory, which reveals Mullen's collapsing of the divide between the speakerly and writerly text as central to an understanding not only of Mullen's work but also of her place in the field of contemporary poetry. Moreover, I argue that this collapse is central to Mullen's envisioning of a more primary space for the reader.

Many critics have seen Mullen's collapse of the divide between the speakerly and the writerly as a way to offer more space and greater freedom to the writing subject. For example, Frost, in the introduction to her interview with Mullen, suggests that Mullen's aversion to the rules of genre allows her greater freedom for improvisation and free play. She argues that Mullen combines "a concern for the political issues raised by identity politics with a poststructuralist emphasis on language" and that, in this combination, she is afforded a freedom unavailable to a writer seeking to follow any one school (Mullen, "Interview" 397). Frost uses the terminology of play throughout, arguing that in "Eliding supposed divisions between 'writerly' and 'speakerly' texts, and rejecting Romantic 'inspiration' and authorial mastery," Mullen is afforded the childlike freedom to compose "by the rules of a game she makes up along the way" (Mullen, "Interview" 398). The results, as Frost asserts, are poems that are "encoded but ultimately decipherable"; that are meaningful, but—in keeping with the theme of this project—not necessarily expressive

(Mullen, "Interview" 398). Mullen's work, especially in *Sleeping with the Dictionary*, complicates the role of the author precisely by breaking down the divide between the speakerly and the writerly text, between orality and visual form.

She does this, in part, by approaching a poetics of *aurality* rather than orality, a distinction that requires some explanation. While some critics have looked to the role of the oral in Mullen's poetry, I argue here that this scholarship has yet to consider the ways in which aurality is present only insofar as it is always already mediated by the visual appearance of the text on the page. In order to do so, I should first consider that this discussion has deep roots in LANGUAGE poetics and the argument that the orality of a text is necessarily preceded by aurality. As Charles Bernstein explains in *Close Listening* (1998), "Orality can be understood as a stylistic or even ideological marker or a reading style; in contrast, the audiotext might more usefully be understood as aural—what the ear hears....*Aurality precedes orality*, just as language precedes speech" (13). By opposing the audiotext to the written text, Bernstein asserts that the aural precedes the oral; more particularly, he asserts that the way a text *sounds* (the way it makes its sounds, its vocalizing, its orality) is contingent upon a pre-existing aurality that necessarily precedes the text. One scholar who applies Bernstein's analysis of aurality to Mullen's work is Jessica Lewis Luck, who asserts, "Here is the aurality that precedes orality that Bernstein writes about, the experimental cacophony that precedes the voice, speech, and presence of a human self" (370). For Luck, Mullen's work collapses the speakerly/writerly divide by refusing the preservation and archivization of the writerly text in favour of the ephemerality and impermanence of the aural. Luck's argument here is insightful, though it does not quite address the complexity of Mullen's approach to the aural. That is, Mullen's poetry in *Sleeping with the Dictionary* recognizes the radical potentials of aurality, while at the same time conceding that complete aurality in text is impossible because it is always mediated by written language. She encourages the maintenance of some aurality in her work; gibberish and nursery-rhyme sounds, homophones and homonyms, rewritings and aural wordplays all revel in the temporary nature of the aural and resist the homogenizing tendency of the grapheme to reduce the aural to the oral, to a "stylistic marker" in Bernstein's terms.

As with nearly every discussion of aurality/orality in Mullen's work, I must here defer to her often-quoted statement:

> I am writing for the eye and the ear at once....When we talk about orality, most of the time we are not really talking about orality—we are talking about a mimetic representation. Poetry does come out of song. If it gets very far from song it is difficult for many people to connect with it. So I am always experimenting with how to be in that space, where it's neither completely spoken nor completely something that exists on the page. (Mullen, "Interview" 401)

For Mullen, then, to occupy a writing space that is neither purely writerly nor purely speakerly is an attempt to engage more fully with readers; in line with a postanarchist poetics, she looks to "connect" with her audience, a term that suggests affective engagement rather than an expression of meaning. But, as Matthew Hart is quick to note, in this interview Mullen also "admits to the 'mimetic representation' that underpins all textual representations of orality" (156). Nonetheless, I agree with Hart that Mullen's work still occupies "the productive space between the 'completely spoken' poem and the reified thing 'that exists on the page'" (156). I would add, further, that the desire to connect rather than express mimetically flourishes in the realm of the aural/oral; the ephemerality of aurality leaves more space for multiple readers than does the more traditional and closed-off signification of the purely mimetic and representational text, which encourages, instead, exegesis and interpretation.

Mullen's poem "Free Radicals" brings the tension between aurality and representation to the fore through the image of a dinner party in a museum, marked by the organizer making *kimchee*, the Korean fermented cabbage dish, for the guests: "Now she's making *kimchee* for the museum that preserved her history in a jar of pickled pig feet" (29). As with any passage of Mullen's, the potential readings of this one sentence are rich and inexhaustible. This passage stresses immediacy (begins "Now"), coinciding with the present-progressive action of "making," which must necessarily be read against the past-tense of the museum that "preserved." Mullen juxtaposes the current action of making kimchee with the preservation of a museum, drawing implicit attention to the fact that kimchee, as a fermented food, is already in a process of degradation, of rotting; moreover, as a reader who has some familiarity with kimchee will know, it does not keep long, and as it sits in the refrigerator its taste changes, becoming progressively more sour until it becomes inedible. Pickling, on the other hand, is the museum of food preparation; pickled or preserved foods are designed to keep well, easily and neatly compartmentalized on store shelves or in household pantries. "Her"[17] history gets preserved in a jar of pig's feet, the kind of meat traditionally discarded by Western culture, but notoriously consumed by cultural Others. It is significant in this context that pickled pig's feet are featured in both traditional Korean cuisine and black comfort food of the American South. The sentence that follows seemingly paratactically makes this cultural reading metapoetic: "They'd fix her oral tradition or she'd trade her oral fixation" (29). Here the museum—which is a metonym for archive and canon, and more particularly a metonym for the interest in preservation of the writerly text—looks to *fix orality*. Bookended by an either/or dichotomy, Mullen offers two options to the racialized experimental poet, her "anomalous black writer": either oral tradition is stabilized and preserved, or we forfeit our desire for the oral. Neither option seems particularly viable for Mullen, especially since the psychoanalytic term "oral fixation" in this case signals both the fetishization and infantilization of the cultural traditions associated with orality and the speakerly text. Ultimately, Mullen's anomalous black writer faces the same paradox as Ngai's feminist avant-garde; either write the self and stop being avant-garde, or refuse the self and be a part of the museum. Like the other poets in this chapter, Mullen chooses both.

Ultimately, these poets and many others still writing feminist poetry refuse to abide by one side of the argument or the other. They know the political (and poetic) dangers of monadic individuality, but they also know the dangers of erasure. Instead of choosing, each poet opts for a third way, which is the way of paradox: they insert the self, the personal, the intimate, and the erotic into one or another indeterminate, machine-written, or archiving structure. They make kimchee in the museum; they transport subjectivities with square brackets and generic pronouns; they merge erotic flesh with computer output; and they sleep warm and soft in the impersonal library. Each one ultimately demonstrates that the erasure of the self that earlier (largely male) poets worked toward to allow for reader freedom could not be an effective strategy for feminist writers on its own. Instead, Howe, Moure, Spahr, and Mullen work to dismantle the larger structures of language, meaning, and archive by using literal machines or machine-like writing practices to open spaces for interventionary and agential readers. At the same time, they refuse to withdraw their authorship entirely.

These attempts to infuse the self or variations of the lyric subject back into the avant-garde set the stage for the conceptualist project that would follow it, though they are of course not the only experimental school that led to conceptual poetry. Instead, as the next chapter will show, the experiments by these feminist poets in machine-writing, generant texts, and the impersonal structures of history and archive to reframe and reformat the subject gave way in and around the early 2000s to the conceptualism that followed. Conceptualism returned, however, to the minimally egoic and indeterminate practices of the earlier poets described in chapter one, to focus not on the interpretive freedom of readers this time, but on the collapse of the authorial role. Instead of refusing to withdraw the subject, refusing opacity as the telos of poetic language, conceptualist poets chose to dwell (and continue to dwell) on the authorial role and the concept, rather than working to increase the spaces and potentials for readers to read and not simply passively receive.

# 3 Easy Concepts

THROUGH my engagement with postanarchist literary theory, and more particularly through my study of its application to the digital or machine-writing texts that now constitute the conceptual poetry canon, I came to discover that the major characteristics I had found useful in conceptualism at first—the eradication or limitation of egoic authorship, extreme populism, uncreativity—were ultimately either unhelpful to postanarchist objectives or not actually present in the texts themselves. Unlike the feminist poets discussed in chapter two who work to insert the personal into impersonal structures to make agential space for readers, conceptualist poetry, for the most part, aims to rewrite, or else to obsolesce, previous forms of writing in ways that limit room for readers to interpret freely and engage directly. What follows is a working-through of the arguments for considering conceptualist poetry as a vanguard school that opens up some important discussions from a postanarchist perspective, but that ultimately fails to address these issues adequately. That is to say that the poets discussed in this chapter—Kenneth Goldsmith, Vanessa Place, Christian Bök, and Darren Wershler—gesture toward the radical potentials afforded by altering, limiting, or manipulating the authorial role through the incorporation of the machine into their writing practice. But these authors (and the first three in particular) ultimately reveal, at least in the work I consider here, that this practice can, and often does, produce readers with significantly less freedom than what is offered to the readers of more traditionally composed, and more traditionally read, texts.

While the primary feature of conceptual poetry continues to be the eradication or limitation of authorial control over a poem, nearly every conceptual poem is constructed through a process of digitization, remediation, or machine-writing either literally or figuratively. However, the indeterminacy of machine-writing that we have seen in chapter one is replaced, in conceptual poetry, by authors functioning as machines rather than as egoic, monadic individuals. For this reason, to contextualize and critique the conceptual project, I read these poetic works against Hayles's recent assertions about electronic, digital, or machine-writing. In a critical study of electronic literature, Hayles proposes two features of radical digital writing: first, that verbal narratives can be both *conveyed* and *disrupted* by code, and second, that "*distributed cognition implies distributed agency*" (136, emphasis Hayles's). On the first point, Hayles makes clear that disruptions of narratives by code permeate our everyday lives, saturated as we are with technology: 404 error codes, ATMs returning our bank cards, or UPC readers not scanning a bar code are examples she gives of ways in which digital codes disrupt quotidian narratives steeped in technology. Of course, it is also true more generally that artistic and cultural practices—especially artistic and cultural practice engaging with technology—use various kinds of code to disrupt narratives: highly formalized writing uses a range of different coding practices to disrupt traditional narratives of poetic production and reception, as does machine-writing of the kind that I discuss in the first two chapters of this book. Conceptual poetry, in its use of machine and technology, has made explicit its disruption of traditional narratives of authorship and readership. In this way, it engages with the potentials Hayles identifies in her first proposition to occasionally effective political and poetic ends.

It is when read in light of Hayles's second proposition that conceptualism reveals its fissures and failures. By "distributed cognition," Hayles means that human cognition becomes distributed through the tools (technological or otherwise) that mediate an individual's engagement with a text (138). This distribution requires that technological tools remain consistent in some ways so that, through habitual use or training, the mind and body are able to use variant technologies or systems without having to be constantly retrained. One example Hayles offers is that of a computer mouse: it consistently looks like a mouse and fits well into the hand with buttons placed where fingers can easily tap, and movement of the device corresponds to the movement of a cursor on a screen (137). Some of the cognition required to use this device becomes second nature—human agency distributed almost unthinkingly to the machine's parts—and Hayles asserts that this distribution of cognition threatens to automate human cognition; she challenges me to consider, for a moment, how frequently I find myself absent-mindedly opening applications on my smartphone or how readily my hand reaches for a mouse or a touchpad the moment I am seated in front of a computer. On the other hand, the concept of distributed cognition and the resultant "distributed agency" of technological engagement implies digital writing's unique opportunity to both engage with and disrupt these habitual engagements; Hayles also affirms that digital writing, in employing this distributed cognition, can create "new pathways of communication among different kinds of knowledge" to "open us to flashes of insight and illumination" (138). Hayles acknowledges that, as I have suggested, "all literature can operate like this" (138), and sometimes print-based literature *does* operate like this, as is the case with the print-based literature discussed in the previous two chapters; but she also argues that electronic literature has, by redirecting our typical habitual engagement with technology and with text, "especially potent opportunities" for this engagement, "given the intensely cognitive environments of networked and programmable media" (138). In other words, digital writing offers authors enhanced opportunities for not only complicating authorship but also engaging with readers in a more direct and interventionary fashion.

Unfortunately, conceptual poetry has historically been a genre vastly more interested in questioning authorial intention than directly engaging with a readership, and as such, conceptualism writ large has dedicated itself to the work Hayles identifies in her first proposition. Rather than concerning itself as a movement with disrupting and radicalizing the ways readers engage with texts, conceptualism calls for the use of digital and machine-writing practices to focus on a reduction of authorship and authorial control over the text, work that has been done in various ways and degrees since the start of the twentieth century. As an unintended result of this focus, however, the work of reading the conceptual text is really no work at all; as Goldsmith himself notes, conceptual texts like his do not require or even encourage reading: "My books are impossible to read straight through. In fact, every time I have to proofread them before sending them off to the publisher, I fall asleep repeatedly. You really don't need to read my books to get the idea of what they're like; you just need to know the general concept" ("Being Boring" np). Similarly, Place's work privileges her conceptual writing practices, neither regarding nor even encouraging reader engagement with her work. Bök's *Eunoia*, by contrast, presents us with a strange problem in postanarchist readings of conceptual poetry: Bök has foregone the aid of machines in the conceptual writing process, relying on the poet's compositional skills to create a text that offers very little freedom on the part of the reader while still being wildly popular, as far as collections of experimental poetry go. I argue throughout this book that machine-writing can be and has been used to create more engaging ways of writing and reading, a trajectory that postanarchism recognizes in some conceptual projects, such as Wershler's *The Tapeworm Foundry, andor, The Dangerous Prevalence of the Imagination*. Still, for the most part conceptualism neglects the distributed agency of readers who need new pathways to creatively navigate texts. I do not wish to suggest that all conceptualism falls victim to the neglect of readers' cognition and agency, and for that reason I include Wershler's *Tapeworm Foundry* in this chapter as one example of a conceptual work that encourages thoughtful and agential reader engagement–in this case, by encouraging readers to produce their own work rather than simply passively consume his. Nonetheless, I argue in this chapter that, overall, conceptualism's use of digital and machine-writing practices is a missed opportunity for poets to actively engage their readers, whose distributed cognition threatens automation. Instead, all too often, conceptual poetry encourages greater levels of automation of the reading practice.

## Kenneth Goldsmith Talking to Himself

I begin this chapter with a discussion of one of the most controversial and famous pieces of conceptual poetry, Kenneth Goldsmith's *Soliloquy* (exhibit 1997, print 2001, digital 2002). Goldsmith describes the piece in the preface to its digital version as included in the first volume of the *Electronic Literature Collection* (ELC): "*Soliloquy* is an unedited document of every word I spoke during the week of April 15–21, 1996, from the moment I woke up Monday morning to the moment I went to sleep on Sunday night" (np). *Soliloquy*, as a piece of conceptual poetry, follows in the tradition of the poets studied in the first two chapters of this book who all work to withdraw authorial expression and control over their writing and over the reader's experience of their texts. But, as I will demonstrate throughout this case study, Goldsmith's decision to reproduce a week's worth of his speech in a textual object demonstrates a good deal more control over the writing and reading processes than other machine-writing methods. In 2017, the process of this text's production is well known. What is perhaps less well known about the piece is that it is a multimedia text fitting partially and inadequately into numerous genres. The text exists as a print-based book of poetry (which closely resembles the immense tome of a prose novel), as a digital-poetic artifact, and as a gallery installation. Additionally, as a transcription of speech, the text walks a thin line between poetry and drama. At points the sections of *Soliloquy* are labelled "acts."

Because *Soliloquy* is essentially a transgeneric piece, we must look closely at the complex interplay between the print-based and digital versions of the text. While the print-based version, a massive block of paper and ink, has become much more popular and more frequently studied,[1] Goldsmith nevertheless sees more possibilities for its digital form to reproduce ephemerality: "the textual treatment of the web version is indeed web-specific and perhaps more truly references the ephemerality of language" (*ELC* np). The particular "ephemerality" he refers to here lies in the form of the digital text only, wherein the transcribed sentences appear and disappear like the ephemera of spoken words, a marked contrast with the heft of the more than five hundred pages filled with text that make up the print volume. The print book lacks a similarly nuanced consideration of visual form and spatiality, a concern that Perloff brings up in her e-mail interview with Goldsmith for *Jacket*. Noting that Goldsmith cites the Noigandres group and other concrete poets as major influences on his work, Perloff suggests that "pieces like... *Soliloquy* have neither the look nor the structural configuration of a Concrete poem: on the contrary, spatiality is replaced by temporal form" (Perloff, "A Conversation" np). Goldsmith's response acknowledges that these texts "are, by their nature, temporal pieces," but he also argues that the internet collapses the divide between the temporal and the spatial, foregrounding the materiality of even the most ephemeral online texts (Perloff, "A Conversation" np). It is certainly true that the ephemerality of internet textuality complicates the divide between the temporal and the spatial, but pointing to this complication says nothing about the complex ways that digital textuality questions the very materiality of text.

Still, the materiality of language is a major concern of Goldsmith's work more generally. In *Uncreative Writing* (2011), for instance, he argues that the internet and the proliferation of text that it has ushered into our everyday lives have changed the way we view and understand textual materiality: "Words are no longer primarily transparent content carriers; now their material quality must be reconsidered as well" (18). Again he insists, "never before has language had so much *materiality*" (25, emphasis Goldsmith's). These comments raise the question: when were these good (or bad) old days when language functioned immaterially, or worse, when we understood that that was the case? At the very least, did the modernists (and then the structuralists? and then the post-structuralists? and the postmodernists?) not effectively do away with any literary understanding of "transparent content carriers"? And even if it is true that language is more material now than it ever has been, then Goldsmith's choice to render the ephemerality of a week's worth of speech into the tome of a physical (material) text reduces the radical temporariness of Saussurian *parole*. Furthermore, choosing to destabilize this physicality through digitization and remediation is a problematic decision that, at best, says nearly nothing about the space of the literary in an increasingly digitized world, and at worst misreads digital potentials. I am arguing, therefore, that in drawing attention to the interplay of materiality and ephemerality in language, *Soliloquy* demonstrates its shortcomings in its relationship to the digital using the now cliché turn to materiality as an excuse to ignore, yet again, the radical politics of empowered and agential readers.

In Hayles's terms, we can say that Goldsmith, in *Soliloquy*, uses literal computer code, and figurative code as well, to codify or stratify the ephemeral spoken word in order to write and to disrupt traditional narratives of authorship and textual production without disrupting the traditional role of the reader. Clearly, *Soliloquy* makes explicit its critique of Romantic assumptions about the way poetry is written; more specifically, it levels criticism at unsophisticated assumptions of poetic works as expressive, of language's potential to represent, and of the possibility of egoic or unegoic writing. Goldsmith uses coding practices to disrupt these expectations. Yet one of the byproducts of Goldsmith's disruption of authorial intention is a text that can be read (if one chooses to read it at all) by a broad population, a feature that also challenges charges of elitism and pretension in the poetic avant-garde. In other words, Goldsmith's work here uses various codes to disrupt and critique normative narratives, but *Soliloquy* does not really work to discourage "distributed cognition" or offer any agency for the reader via this disruption.

Nevertheless, *Soliloquy* and other conceptual projects like it (for example, poetry by Place, Robert Fitterman, and Dworkin) are able to make these critiques precisely because these works rely on the distribution of cognition that results only from easy and habitual engagement with technology. *Soliloquy* does not engage or challenge its readers, though it should be noted that such a reading was never the goal. In

2001, when *Soliloquy* was first distributed, its challenges to conventional understandings of authorship and intention may have appeared radical and thought-provoking, but in the time since, it has become the norm for people to approach digital text in much the same automatic, uncritical way that Goldsmith recommends for his writing, in print and digital formats. (Consider, for example, social media users' propensity to post and share links to items that they have not read). What is now required by new media work, and what is now done by many digital practitioners (as I will demonstrate in chapter four), is to open up new pathways to radical reader agency and new cognitive engagements, rather than encouraging passive textual consumption in the name of populism. This text does not provide agential space for its readers, even though Goldsmith presents his work as a radical and populist poetic piece.

Indeed, Goldsmith's claim for uncreative writing's populist nature is, in my view, essentially facetious. In *Uncreative Writing*, he asserts that the kind of uncreative project he is calling for and exemplifying in *Soliloquy* is "truly populist"; he observes that "a lot of 'difficult' work has been produced under the mantle of populism only to be rejected by its intended audience as indecipherable, or worse, irrelevant," but "uncreative writing," he insists, escapes these charges (100). The "uncreative," as Goldsmith defines it, is the process by which a writer (particularly by digital means) re-appropriates existing text rather than producing original writing. He further argues that uncreative writing uses paratext and process to explain its methodologies, making "its intentions clear at the outset" and thus making it so that "there's no way you *can't* understand it" (100). And yet charges of indecipherability and elitism *can* and *have* been laid against uncreative, conceptual poetry, and especially against Goldsmith's. The uncreative may be "truly populist" in theory insofar as it is easy to read and to understand (thereby increasing its potential readership), but in practice it reveals itself as destined to follow the avant-garde tradition of public maligning followed by popular commodification recognized by Gertrude Stein as early as her "Composition as Explanation" (1926): "For a very long time everybody refuses and then almost without a pause almost everybody accepts" (496). Part of the problem, as digital scholar Florian Cramer astutely points out, is that the uncreative is woefully one-sided. Cramer critiques Goldsmith's theory of "uncreative writing" on two important grounds: "Firstly,...it risks treating the Internet as a poetic plunderground without really feeding back into it," and "Secondly,...'uncreative writing' boils down to the dialectical opposite of creative writing. As a mere negation, it does not ontologically question creativity" (np).

On my reading, *Soliloquy* exemplifies both of the weaknesses Cramer identifies. Of course, in the case of *Soliloquy*, Goldsmith does not explicitly treat the internet as a place where information is meant to be received and stored, in that he is recording his own words and not the words of others. But even though *Soliloquy* does not use a generant text, I would argue that its appropriation of the quotidian for its source "text" is analogous to the one-sided process of plundering that Cramer critiques. I would further argue that *Soliloquy* also exemplifies the second kind of weakness that Cramer identifies: by opposing Romantic conceptions of authorial creativity with the uncreative processes of copying, transcribing, and reporting his own speech, Goldsmith does not question traditional understandings of either the creative or the author, but instead provides an authorial anti-hero who requires the very authorial control he wants to destabilize. Ultimately, uncreative texts like *Soliloquy* convey relatively little about the materiality of the text save that it exists and must therefore be considered; Goldsmith's transcription and thus material rendering of oral ephemera does at least this much. For this reason these texts cannot appeal to a general readership, i.e., those who see the materiality of language brought to the fore every time they select their clickbait. If postanarchism has heretofore required a radical rethinking of authorship and an appeal to a populist readership to make new and innovative readings in the collaborative dissemination of text, then it must also see the uncreative as a missed opportunity for radical recreation.

Moreover, Goldsmith's designation of the uncreative as truly populist fails to account for his own work, given the disjunction between what he claims for the role of affect in the uncreative text and what we ultimately find in *Soliloquy*. Interestingly, the issue of affect is brought up many times by proponents of uncreative writing, Goldsmith and Perloff included. In *Uncreative Writing*, Goldsmith cites Perloff's assertion, first expressed in *Unoriginal Genius* (2010), that an updated concept of literary genius would account for "one's mastery of information and its dissemination" (1) and would thus have nothing to do with the dissemination or transport of affect. In many ways, Goldsmith's numerous poetic projects carried out under the name of conceptual poetry are practices in the mastery and dissemination of information and are unconcerned with the expression or "transport" of emotion. Still, Goldsmith states in "Sentences on Conceptual Writing" (2008) that he does not believe that the conceptual poem is the only kind of poem to account for this new authorship. He explains, for instance, "I do not advocate a [*sic*] uncreative form of writing for all authors. I have found that it has worked well for me while other ways have not. It is one way of writing; other ways suit other writers. Nor do I think all uncreative writing merits the reader's attention. Uncreative writing is good only when the idea is good" ("Sentences" np). Here Goldsmith identifies two personal and highly individualized features of the uncreative text: it is a form of writing that is not suited for everyone but has "worked for" him personally, and the quality of the uncreative text is determined not by the writing produced, but by the idea behind it, a view that places more priority than usual on the intellectual, philosophical, and conceptual power of the writing subject. Despite the fact that Goldsmith insists repeatedly on the power of uncreativity and of relinquishing as much authorial control over the text as possible, Goldsmith's work is extremely personal and expressive, and relies heavily on authorial intent and intellect.

In other words, all of Goldsmith's "uncreative" texts relinquish authorial control to a degree, but none entirely avoids self-expression. While *Soliloquy* does rely on a singular speaking subject, the author, who necessarily expresses himself throughout his daily life, it is possible to argue that *Soliloquy* sees authorship exploded through the recording of the "indeterminacy" of daily speech. Other works by Goldsmith complicate authorship through more explicitly impersonal or indeterminate means. For example, *Day* (2003) sees Goldsmith transcribe an entire issue of the *New York Times* left-to-right, and his American Trilogy—*Weather* (2005), *Traffic* (2007), and *Sports* (2008)—sees him recording verbatim radio broadcasts relating to the specific topic. Nevertheless, he maintains throughout *Uncreative Writing* that it is not possible to avoid expression on the part of the author, a point that I have made repeatedly in these pages. In Goldsmith's terms, "the suppression of self-expression is impossible. Even when we do something as seemingly 'uncreative' as retyping a few pages, we express ourselves in a variety of ways" (9). Furthermore, he explicitly concedes that, no matter what, language is expressive (85). Akin to the unavoidable self-expression of uncreative authorship, the uncreative or conceptual text also necessarily conveys its message (an implicit poetics, a philosophy of language), even if it does not do so explicitly or clearly. Instead, "The philosophy of the work is implicit in the work and it is not an illustration of any system of philosophy" ("Sentences" np). However, while Goldsmith's use of the term "illustration" paints a reductive picture, I maintain that the distinction he draws between the implicit philosophy of the conceptual work and larger external systems is not as clear as he might imagine. Instead, as postanarchist theory makes clear, conceptual texts still work from and grapple with the same issues of authorial control and reader agency that we have seen in the texts examined throughout this project.

Ultimately, I would argue that affect is just as important as authorial intent in *Soliloquy*. Goldsmith himself raises the subject of affect a number of times in *Uncreative Writing*. He argues, for one, that the uncreative text still "delivers emotion," even though it does so "obliquely and unpredictably, with sentiments expressed as a result of the writing process, rather than by authorial intent" (4). Certainly it is true that, as Goldsmith adds, "Words are active and affective in concrete ways" (24), and we as speakers and as readers have limited control over the ways in which we engage with the affective functions of words. But I would add that, contrary to what Goldsmith claims here, *Soliloquy* in fact engages its readers in affective relationships in a deliberate and calculated manner. I do not mean here to conflate a text's delivery of emotion with an audience's experience of emotion; these are, of course, two different sides of the affective coin. Instead, I argue that part of the limitation on the reader in *Soliloquy* is how little room exists between this coin's two sides. Goldsmith encourages readers to enter into a literal dialogue with a literal author by inviting them to experience the text as at once voyeurs and intimates, insofar as each reader fills in the blanks of the text at points that call for another individual to interact with the author/speaker.

Consider, for instance, the numerous questions about emotion posed to the absent other speakers in the print-based version of *Soliloquy*. Because this text is the record of only one side of a series of conversations, Goldsmith reproduces questions to other people about their feelings with no replies offered, for example: "Are you having trouble with it, buddy?" (25); "Are you in love?" (43); "How are you?" (120, 122, 153, 415); "Are you alone?" (129); "I mean, you're not gonna bomb, are you?" (157); "How are you doing?" (175, 424); "Bets why are you just mooning around? Why don't you go do something?" (195); "Why are you guys cleaning so desperately?" (242); "Are you not enjoying this?" (246); "Are you just OK?" (301); "So are you dreading this totally?" (344); "Why are you mad at me?" (379); "Are you upset about it?" (425); "Oh Betty girl, are you up for this?" (469); "Are you upset? What's sad what's making you sad?" (470); and, "Are you upset?" (479). These questions, found throughout the text, alongside other, similar questions, signal an authorial voice that is constantly checking in on readers who are directly addressed. Readers are thus implicitly encouraged to fill in these blanks, respond to this speaker's questions, and take on the feelings of absent others who are never afforded the opportunity to speak for themselves or respond to these emotional questions in the text. It is also worth noting that a number of these questions, particularly the ones quoted above directed to "Bets" or "Betty," are questions posed to Goldsmith's dog, who would not be able to verbally fill in those blanks anyway. The result is an affective bait-and-switch. Readers are hailed; their emotions are called into question; but they are never permitted to respond.

In this context, we may recall Cage's Cunningham mesostics, which encode his intimate love in a manner that can never really be decoded by the reader (who is thus forcefully positioned as external to the emotion encoded in the text). *Soliloquy,* in marked contrast to Cage's work, encourages the reader to take part in the emotion and feeling of the speaker at the same time that the text persistently flaunts its own construction. In other words, the flaunted artificiality of the text works to keep the reader from emotionally identifying with the speaker or those addressed. This flaunting is particularly evident in Goldsmith's repeated reminders that he is taping these conversations. The word "tape" itself appears more than sixty-five times in *Soliloquy*, ranging from Goldsmith's checking to see how much time is left on his tape (66, 221, 273), to testing when he inserts a new one (69), asking people if he can tape their conversation (160), offering to play the tapes back for other people ("I'll play you the tape if you want. I got the tapes, honey. I got all the tapes" [106]) and complaining that he is nearly out of tapes and has to go buy more ("I gotta buy some more cassette tapes" [284]).[2]

The reader's more direct engagement with the text as encountered through the digital medium can work to counteract this effect; in its digital form, because of its heightened requirement for reader engagement and its insistence on the ephemeral, *Soliloquy* functions to some extent as a more deliberate and intentional vehicle for emotional engagement than its print counterpart. And yet, at the same time, Goldsmith uses the digital medium in *Soliloquy* explicitly to control the actions and affective responses of the reader. This reassertion of authorial control over readerly affect moves *Soliloquy* far from the literary ideals of postanarchism, as described at the start of this project.

Engagement, in the digital *Soliloquy*, is made manifest by the reader's ability to see only one sentence of the work at a time. This is a much more intimate way to interact with *Soliloquy* than the print-based version allows, despite the fact that the print book is something tangible, something readers can literally hold in their hands. Though mediated by technology, the reader must hover over each sentence—save the first one of each section—in order to have it appear on the screen (see Fig. 16). Otherwise,

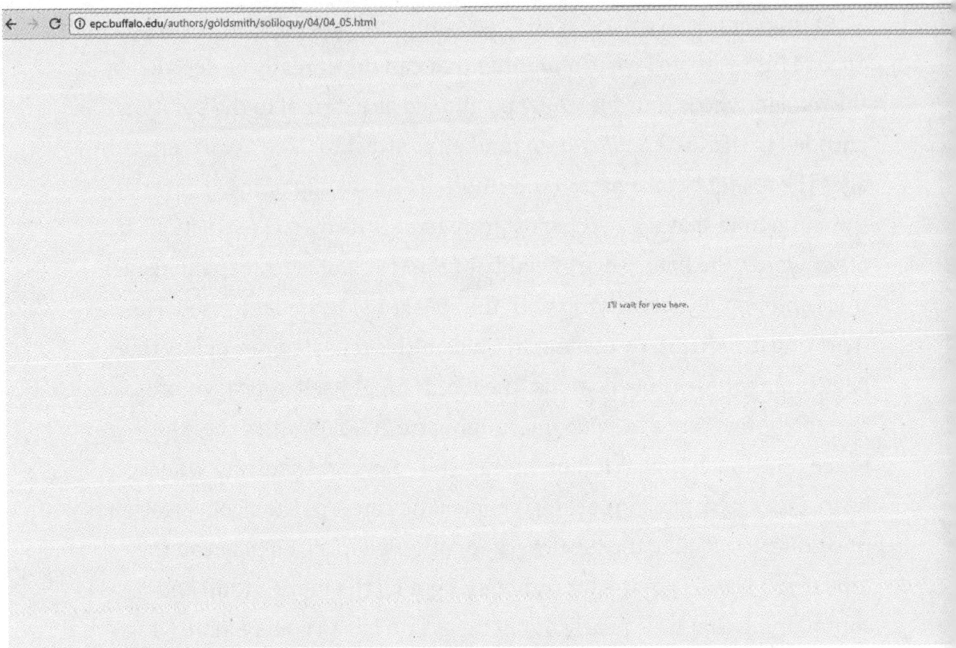


FIGURE 16. Kenneth Goldsmith, screenshot from electronic version of *Soliloquy*.

the page is blank. This contrasts with the experience of reading the print book, in which the reader's fingers would normally touch the book's cover and the deliberately empty margins only; fingers are never really *meant* to touch the ink, both because that touching would obscure that text in that moment, and because of the potential to smudge/alter the text, which would obscure/alter future readings as well. The digital text lures the reader into engaging with the words and letters in a way that the print book does not and cannot.

The intimacy of the digital text experience is also enhanced by the fact that only one sentence appears on the screen at any given time. The temporariness of the phrases appearing and disappearing with the cursor's hovering reproduces mimetically the ephemerality of the speech act. It is true that, as Andy Weaver reminds me, this mimesis only works "to a degree....After all, one can't go back and 'replay' a speech act the way one can go back and reread/recall by returning the cursor over an earlier sentence in the web text" ("Re: Re[2]:" np). Ultimately, the appearance and disappearance of the digital hover-text only imperfectly bridges the gap between the written word and the temporally limited speech act. Nevertheless, what is achieved remains a significantly more intimate relationship between reader and author. As Weaver also points out, the fact that this hover-text makes it impossible for the reader to see more than one sentence at a time (other than the opening sentence) makes it much more like a conversation than like the "soliloquy" that the print text offers ("Re: Re[2]:" np). It is almost as though the reader hears Goldsmith speak these words, which then disappear soon after they are read. Because only Goldsmith's words are reproduced—and not the words of those he addresses—the reader can potentially fill in the blanks between Goldsmith's sentences. It is thus quite significant that Goldsmith chooses to title this work a soliloquy rather than a monologue; a soliloquy and a monologue are both designed for a single speaker in a theatrical setting, but a soliloquy is clearly defined as "talking to or conversing with oneself, or...uttering one's thoughts aloud without addressing any person" ("soliloquy, *n.*"). Nonetheless, *Soliloquy* is marked by various instances of addressing another person, as demonstrated above, implicitly inviting readers to fill in the missing responses. By filling in these blanks, the reader mimics or re-enacts conversations that could have taken place, even invents these conversations to an extent, since *Soliloquy's* speaker can only control the words he speaks and not the words spoken to him. This much could be said about the print text as well, save that the digital text invites conversation more explicitly than the print; there is, after all, no space left between the speaker's lines in the print text, which are designed to be filled (literally or figuratively) by the reader.

When the digital text creates such space, the result is a visually, spatially, and temporally chaotic page that resists the linearity of printed prose. Because of this, readers of the digital text are invited to navigate their way through the work much more freely than they are invited to engage with the printed text. As a reader, I can move my cursor wherever I want throughout the page, revealing sentences at what appears to be my own whim. Furthermore, though the text mimics narrative prose in its appearance, the lack of storyline encourages me to read pieces at random. There are elements of the digital text that gesture toward a causal linearity: the days of the week are presented in order, each section is listed numerically, and the chronological narrative guides reading in a traditionally Western left-to-right, top-to-bottom fashion. Yet despite this, the page is difficult to read and to control in this way: it invites a linear reading but then makes that linear reading difficult and ultimately undesirable. In the mass of blank space, the reader cannot see where the "page" ends or where the next line begins, and as a result the reader continually hovers—although by accident—over sentences belonging to different sections, and thus may at any moment see into the future of Goldsmith's week. Because of this reader engagement, the digital form of *Soliloquy* suggests intimacy and performs audience engagement as the reader is pulled into the world of the author's daily life (though not necessarily pulled into the author's subjectivity, as the following discussion makes clear). One means of pulling the reader in is the use of small talk that appears directly addressed to the reader. For example, the text begins with the conversational "Good morning, how ya doin'?" This phrase, as the first of its section, remains visible while the reader stays on that page without a hovering cursor, reminding the reader of the conversation throughout.

All of these cues signal a reader engagement that appears to be relatively free and subjectively determined, but is actually quite clearly designed, calculated, and controlled. While the text is filled with discussions of poetry, the avant-garde, and the art scene in New York, it is also, by virtue of its recording Goldsmith's day-to-day life, full of references to the intimate relationship between Goldsmith and his wife, Cheryl; the very last words of the text are "Good night, Cheryl. I love you." Such points suggest that we as readers occupy a similarly intimate relationship with the author: instead of being expected to identify with the speaker, according to the lyric convention, the reader is aligned with Cheryl. A close look at one of the text's most intimate of scenes, supposedly a sexual encounter, shows that because the text foregrounds its construction (its being performed) and its materiality, the reader is prevented from ever really achieving intimacy with the authorial voice, despite our feelings of identification with Cheryl and others directly addressed throughout the text. One scene that demonstrates this identification, and its concomitant failed intimacy, is a notorious sex scene that appears here as it does in the printed book:

> Can I put my finger in your ass? All the way up? That's on tape. Just to spice the tape a little bit, right? I said that just to spice up the tape...Really? Really stop or, yeah?...I mean, why? Come on, this is art! I mean, look at what I do for your art! Look what you do for your art!...you do for your you get naked in front of audience of thousands and you're crawling around and you can see your pussy and here she says I don't want to be on the tape. It's so contradictory! And it's O.K. for your art but it's not O.K. for my art! (336-37)

The performance of Goldsmith's first request loses its erotic intimacy almost instantly. Instead, we are confronted by the text's construction and the amount of authorial intent and performance involved in Goldsmith's decision to speak crudely in order to "spice the tape a little bit, right?" The result is a moment, not of erotic intimacy, but of marital fighting. As Christopher Schmidt observes, the scene "opens up an obvious place to make a feminist critique...with Goldsmith using his wife's body as a kind of host or platform for the improvement of his project" (33). If, as I have suggested, the text invites us to identify with Cheryl, it also at this point may invite us to feel hurt at being used.

Like Cheryl's, our voices do not appear in this text. We, too, are self-conscious about our position there. We, too, are used by the text, whose deception is made worse because of its façade of intimacy and truth (those are *really* the words Goldsmith *genuinely* spoke). And our bodies, too, are controlled by the text: our movements are used to create its negation of creativity and to contribute to its shock value in that *Soliloquy* relies on, rather than disrupts, our distributed cognition and our habitual use of cursor, mouse or touchpad, and browser. Like the lines of the page that exist and govern our reading while making us think we are free, the text and its author/speaker control our reading process and control our affective engagement with it. We are voyeurs in this sex and in this fight, which is made perverse by our appearance. Goldsmith as Author-god thus controls this text and our engagement with it on a level that a more traditionally expressive text does not, and despite his claims elsewhere, there is very little likely to be "oblique" or "unpredictable" about how it makes us feel.

This is not to say that Goldsmith has more authorial control than the average Victorian novelist, but rather that compared to the other poets described in the two previous chapters who write with similar goals regarding the relinquishing of control, Goldsmith's authorial persona is vastly more controlling. In essence, *Soliloquy* does not lend itself well to a postanarchist reading because it seeks explicitly and directly to control the way that a reader approaches and receives the text rather than using the disruptive potentials of the work to encourage new and differential pathways for cognition. Despite its radical rethinking of authorship, then, which I maintain is interesting and perhaps even valuable, the ways that this text governs a reader's affective relationship demonstrates its limitation of reader freedom rather than expansion of that freedom, making it distinctly *un*postanarchist.

## Vanessa Place Without Serifs

The first book in Vanessa Place's *Tragodía* trilogy, *Statement of Facts* (2011), has—like Goldsmith's *Soliloquy*—caused quite a stir in the poetry community.[3] Place is a poet who also works as a lawyer representing sex offenders, and *Statement of Facts* sees her reframing the narratives of her work, appropriated from official court documents, as conceptual poems. The result is that these collected narratives of trauma are repositioned, dramatically changing their audience and their purpose. As Goldsmith says of this text in *Uncreative Writing*, "By shifting the context from law to art, and by stripping the language of any legal purpose, we suddenly see these documents in ways impossible to see them before" (103). But what exactly do we see, as the newly intended audience of these texts? And how does this repositioning of legal documents as art pieces alter the way we view the authority of the author of a conceptual text? I include a discussion of this collection in this chapter primarily because *Statement of Facts* raises questions about the authority of conceptual authorship and about our reception and interpretation of conceptualism *vis-à-vis* form. In truth, the questions are not raised by any other work I have considered to this point. Place *has* authored these texts in more ways than one: she presides over them with the authority of a lawyer in their original state, and she also presides over them as arranger, formatter, and author when they are poems. Perhaps obviously, these pieces are intended to be emotionally disturbing in a way that the other conceptual pieces are not, owing to the authority suggested by the legal nature of the source documents and the way that font and typeface alter our understanding of this authority *as well as* the authority of its producer. This is brought to the fore as early as the first page of the text proper, in the second paragraph, where a discussion of the rape of a thirteen-year-old boy is bookended with the title, "Prosecution Case," and a series of footnotes refer to transcripts that we, as readers, cannot access. These signs of artifice and authority culminate in the detached legal tone of the descriptions of the assault: "Ben felt his pants coming down; he tried unsuccessfully to pull them up....Ben felt appellant's penis penetrate his bottom, and remain there for five minutes" (9). In the pages that follow in "Ben"'s case, his credibility is repeatedly brought into question, while the text's absent and anonymous speaker (via Place as compiler) uses a detached tone, legal language, and various forms of documentation to assert the authority of this version of events.

The question of authority in *Statement of Facts* is especially salient in terms of both literature and sexual politics; in conceptual poetry as in sexual offenses, dissenters frequently question a speaker's authority in order to discredit the speaker. It is significant, therefore, that Place's position in both arenas affords her a credibility and authority that are unavailable to other less privileged speakers. As lawyer, Place is granted legal power and social credibility *ab ovo*; as acclaimed poet, with such well-known peers as Goldsmith and Perloff (who are both thanked on the copyright page), Place is granted importance and value prior to the reader's reception of her book. All the same, removing the source texts from their original legal context puts Place as their "author" in a precarious position: she claims a kind of ownership over these source texts and yet at the same time places herself at a distance from her original position as legal defender of the accused. I would also argue, based on my analysis of formal elements and physical properties of the book itself, that Place acknowledges her precarious position and conveys discomfort with her authority in *Statement of Facts*.

Consider, for instance, her decision to record the text proper in a sans serif typeface. We know that Place considers serifs to be highly significant: in *Uncreative Writing*, Goldsmith records Place calling serifs "those little epaulets of authority" (104), and he argues that this association of serifs with authority is the reason she chose to remove them from the original court documents. While I have not been able to find this wording anywhere save in Goldsmith's transcription, the argument is a fascinating one, especially in light of this book's concern with machine-writing in general and the politics of form more particularly. The idea that serifs denote authority is not without foundation, and both Place and Goldsmith accept it uncritically. It is true, as Alex Poole convincingly demonstrates, that those publications that are considered to have authority are most frequently *printed* with serifs: court documents, print books and magazines, newspapers, even digital versions of texts that desire credibility and authority like academic journals. (See, for example, most major journals in contemporary literature, such as *Contemporary Literature* or *Twentieth-Century Literature*, but not certain journals of new media studies, such as *Convergence*.) Printed collections of poetry also almost always employ a serif typeface, as is the case with all of the print books discussed in the first two chapters except the one by Cage (who uses Letraset, some with serifs and some without) and Nichol (whose program did not allow serif fonts). By contrast, due to issues of size and graphic design, electronic texts typically do not, though again we find no clear consensus; though both are exclusively digitally published scholarly websites, *Jacket2* uses a serif typeface whereas *Postmodern Culture* does not. Yet there is nothing inherently authoritative about serifs themselves save that a long-standing tradition dictates these practices.[4] Frequent use and traditional context mean that the reader can be expected to associate a serif typeface with a speaker who carries the traditional authority of centuries of textual history, and a sans serif typeface with a modern and seemingly more popular (and less authoritative) speaker, much as Place and Goldsmith would expect.

However, not all of these "epaulets of authority" have been removed from *Statement of Facts*. While the entirety of the body of the text is printed in a sans serif typeface, all of the paratext, including the book's cover, is printed in a serif typeface. This is true also of the PDF version of the text (which is, at time of writing, available for free online through the University of Pennsylvania). By their very presence, the serifs lend authority to the author's name and the book's title, the review blurbs (one of which is provided by Goldsmith), the copyright and publisher information, the table of contents, and even the page numbers. The result is that—if Goldsmith is correct about her intentions—while Place aims to remove a legal or juridical authority from the court documents, she is at the same time stressing the authority granted to her work by the very form of the print book, and she is also stressing its own legality (via copyright). Even if these serifs are the result of design decisions not made by the author, the effects are worth noting.[5] If the repositioning of the original documents in a literary text raises questions about who speaks and who is heard (and *why*), then the paratextual serifs suggest that these questions are not being asked of the text's literariness. Instead, these paratextual serifs function as an assertion of the power of the Author. The serifs thus lend a literary credibility to the piece and suggest the genuineness of the appropriated legal documents at the same time that they assure the reader of the literary value of the documents' appropriation.

The footnotes Place includes with the documents are another element of the text that assert its authority. Even though these are in a sans serif typeface, the footnotes lend credibility to the text as a legally truthful and apparently impartial reproduction: a statement of the facts.

Sometimes these footnotes are clearly authoritative about the genuineness of what is included. For example, one footnote indicates that its referent is "Taken from the transcript admitted as People's Exhibit No. 12. (Supp. CT 20) The transcript of the May 3rd chats, one from 3:52 P.M. to 4:02 P.M., the other from 4:05 P.M. to 4:27 P.M....are not included here as they were not introduced into evidence. (Supp. CT 23–25)" (278). The result is that readers are both assured about the genuineness of the evidence provided and reminded of their distance from the text (and the case) by only being privy to that information "introduced into evidence." Yet other footnotes suggest a fact-checking and impartial third-party voice mediating the possibilities of subjective and biased testimony, as with the caveat: "It is not a diagnosis recognized by most practitioners. (RT 9:1826)" (98). It remains unclear to whom we are meant to assign the speaking voice of these footnotes.

Ultimately, any attempt to answer such questions will lead to impasse, for *Statement of Facts* requires us to accept that the questions of *who* speaks and *how*, who is *heard* and *why*, are complex ones that are influenced by social inequity and a politics well beyond the scope of her project or my own. Furthermore, Place's ongoing and determined silence on such questions, a silence she has maintained in various interviews and discussions about the text, demonstrates her intentional commitment to leaving matters at the level of complexity and conundrum, her refusal to take a side. Probably the most blatant example of Place's silence on the intention behind or purpose of her work can be found in her refusal to address Spahr's call for this contextualizing information, published on the *Could Be Otherwise* blog. Spahr asks:

> Does Vanessa's book mean to suggest that rape is largely a socio-economic problem? Does it intentionally, or even unintentionally, tell a story that might leads [*sic*] readers to conclude that rape is largely something poor people, mainly Latinos, do? Is it bad information that might put people at risk? (I am thinking here—does she by presenting only certain legal cases, such as ones that she has

been involved with, lead us to think she is saying something larger about rape? Is there a representational question?) (Comment, np)

If we review the discussion of which this is a part, we find that Perloff responds to the comment, but Place is notably silent on the matter. David Kaufmann's later article on the subject for *Postmodern Culture* notes that Place has continued to refuse to respond to Spahr's questions about class, race, representation, and demand.

This silence on Place's part is essentially a refusal to contextualize her text. On one reading, such silence opens up the potentials afforded to the readers in their reading process. Viewed in this way, her silence is not unlike Cage's silence in the Cunningham mesostics, which I discuss in chapter one: Place's expressive silence similarly foregrounds the issue of the genuineness of the source texts, thereby challenging us to interrogate issues of genuineness and affect in traditional poetry. It raises the issue of the factual, asking us to wonder if it is possible to state a fact without making a *statement* about it, and it raises the question of the impartiality of the legal system, asking us specifically to look at who speaks and who is given authority in rape and sexual assault cases. For better or for worse, it does not take a side on any of the above issues, further evidence of Place's discomfort with (but not her refusal of) authority. As Goldsmith is quick to note, appropriation actually involves "dozens of authorial decisions" (118), and the formatting issues (of serifs and footnotes, for example) are some of the most telling authorial decisions Place makes. These decisions, intentionally or not, draw attention to what Steven Zultanski describes as "the social structure which grants an erroneous truth value to certain acts of language as a means of control" (np). They also do their part to re-inscribe the text's literariness as a "truth value" itself, asserting a control over the reception and interpretation of the text.

The authorial control denoted by these formal elements appears all the more powerful when we consider how they govern affect. *Statement of Facts* is filled with documents authored by Place as lawyer, and then re-authored via new contextualization as a book of poems. Here, appropriation is positioned as yet another challenge to traditional authorship, but one that carries with it the vestiges of authorial intention twofold. There are, of course, as Goldsmith mentions, many authorial decisions to be made when appropriating one text for another purpose. We may also interpret Place's move from the professional and authoritative serif typeface to the more populist and digital sans serif typeface as an attempt to clear the way for Hayles's "new pathways of communication," however rudimentary that move may be. Even so, the readers of *Statement of Facts* are ultimately made *less* rather than more free in the process of their reading. Obviously, this argument is controversial. After all, conceptualism is predicated on the lack of intention on the part of the author, a lack that should translate to increased freedom on the part of the readers in their interpretation and experience. I have already argued that Goldsmith's looming presence in *Soliloquy* actually curtails reader freedom, but the lack of agential freedom for the reader in *Statement of Facts* is decidedly more difficult to establish beyond question. Nevertheless, there are strong arguments for considering *Statement of Facts*' sensationalism to powerfully limit and control the reader's response to the text.

While Place's authorship in *Statement of Facts* is not expressive in the traditional sense—it does not seek to express the emotions or desires of its author or speaker—it is still highly affective. The affect produced by *Statement of Facts* is not unlike the affect produced by *Soliloquy*; however, where Goldsmith's work constructs an (ultimately failed) intimacy between speaker/author and reader, Place's work is at its heart sensationalist. That is, *Statement of Facts* requires that the reader engage with and experience the text in a certain more or less unavoidable way based on literary and cultural cues. The collection bombards the reader with a mélange of detached legal jargon and descriptions of violent personal trauma, a juxtaposition that almost certainly will leave readers both desensitized to the sexual violence and traumatized by it. One example of such detachment appears in "Prosecution Case: Gabrielle," where the sexual abuse of an eight-year-old is described with clear legal detachment:

> Gabrielle was 8 years old at the time of the trial; she didn't like the appellant because of what he did to her. Appellant rubbed Gabrielle's "front butt," her pelvis, under her uniform pants and underwear. Appellant did this more than once: he was sitting down, she was on his lap, sitting on one of his legs. (167)

Such moments of detachment maintained in the face of trauma are made even more emotional by the distanced tone of the text, because this passage's unemotional language presents a (real, lived) trauma as a symbol rather than a recognition or a witnessing. These moments of detachment, I argue, are akin to the deadpan stare of a psychopath in a horror film; the lack of emotional response to traumatic events is an absolute inadequacy, and this inadequacy may increase readers' affective responses to both the trauma and its presentation. Lack of empathy in the speaker of *Statement of Facts*, in other words, correlates with our own increased emotional response. This reading of *Statement of Facts* is not unlike Maggie Nelson's reading of Lars von Trier's *Breaking the Waves* (1996), part of her insightful discussion of the symbolic use of trauma (after trauma, after trauma) in *The Art of Cruelty* (2011). Nelson recounts the emotions she felt as a result of witnessing the various traumas to the female body in the film, traumas that the film treats as symbolically sacrificial and Christ-like: "I sat in the dark theater, probably not unlike many viewers, feeling distraught, to the point of destroyed. Then, as the first wave of emotion lifted, I felt angry. Then I felt disgusted. Finally, I felt bored" (196). Viewers of *Breaking the Waves* and readers of *Statement of Facts* alike are presented with body trauma without a call to witness or a gesture to empathy. Rather, the traumas are recounted in this symbolic, unemotional fashion repeatedly, and the repetition amplifies the emotional exhaustion and desensitization that result.

Because of such passages as this, *Statement of Facts* is emotionally exhausting to read. While I can only truthfully attest to this feeling in my own reading experience, the trauma of reading this book is also evident in some reviews. For example, in her review of *Statement of Facts*, Anna Moschovakis's[6] tone indicates an exhaustion resulting from the emotional charge of the text. Here, the reviewer demonstrates how overwhelmed a reader may feel by the trauma recounted in *Statement of Facts*:

> The book's 430 pages contain tale after tale of touching, sucking, forcing, cutting, binding, stalking, hitting, whipping, burning, cajoling, drugging, abducting, imprisoning, deceiving, crying, apologizing, and raping, raping, raping. The victims are mothers, daughters, students, neighbor boys, wives, cousins, infants, employees, prostitutes, and the elderly. The appellants are gang members, pimps, drug dealers, dropouts, respected teachers, former police officers, members of the military, and psychologists. (np)

Moschovakis's exhausting but not exhaustive list accurately reflects the repetition inherent in the conceptual text, but Place's repetition is markedly different from, for instance, Goldsmith's recording of movie listings or sports scores as part of his project, *Day*. Considering Place's position as the legal defence of the appellants, and knowing, as the paratext reminds us, that the text is a compilation of appealed guilty verdicts, we must read such repetitive trauma as Moschovakis chronicles as the intended result of the reading process. That is, Place sees the repetitive nature of the appeals and translates that into the text itself. It is for this reason that I would argue that, ultimately, *Statement of Facts* puts the reader in the role of passive recipient rather than that of active, engaged agent. The reader of this collection is not positioned as judge or even really as jury in these cases; instead, the reader is simply an observer of injustice in various forms, without enough information or agency to even bear effective witness. What is more, because the copyright page tells us that these are appeal cases, we know that the role of the judge has already been carried out, and that we are presented with these cases after the fact; because these texts are now repurposed as poems, our position as readers is—explicitly—inconsequential.

Because Place transposes these legal briefs from the appeals court into poetic text, she draws attention to the fact that the legal brief is not originally meant to be an affective text. For the poetic text to work as it should, it relies on a degree of skepticism about the supposed impartiality of the juridical system as well as the requisite shock that accompanies the defamiliarization of narratives of trauma narrated in a deadpan tone. Part of the defamiliarization comes from the impartial tone that is already inherent in legal briefs, but part of it, I would argue, also comes from Place's treatment of these emotionally relevant documents as pure materiality, as dead language appropriated, just as when Goldsmith steals the *New York Times* for *Day*. In "The Death of the Text," Place reveals her understanding of the dead (or dormant) materiality of source text used to produce conceptual poetry: "the text says nothing but what is fed through it. The text is machine, not mirror. In this sense, text is screen: not a mirror *of* us, but *for* us" (np). While in digital poetics "screen" can suggest a place of touch, of integration and collaboration (a touch screen, the way that you view a work and even its source code), Place's use of "screen" here suggests instead a barrier designed to keep her audience at bay (a window screen, a smoke screen). The treatment of language as stuff, rather than as living voice reflecting the lived experience of the individual, may seem like the innocuous objective of an average conceptual artist, but just as Perloff's provocative but insightful statements at the 2010 "Rethinking Poetics" conference indicate, this treatment walks the dangerous line between bringing to light the difficulties of expression and silencing minority/victim voices. As Zultanski reports, "Marjorie Perloff caused the audience to collectively gasp when she claimed that what *Statement of Facts* reveals to us is that the victims of rape are 'at least as bad as or worse than the rapists'" (np). In this statement, Perloff incisively exposes what can happen when we apply the politics of conceptualist treatments of language and audience to lived experience.

This treatment of the court briefs as dead language may expose the potentials of language to function as pure materiality, but it also opens the door for a dangerous moral relativism that allows Place to dismiss victims' voices and disregard the lived experiences being appropriated for the conceptual text. Zultanski's point on this subject is worth noting: "according to Place, conceptual writing presents the inertness of the text;

it can be re-framed in any way one wishes, insofar as an inert, inutile text is not self-reflexive, and does not make its own meaning. Because of her repeated statements of this sort, Place's 'any reading is a good reading' stance loses its provocative appeal" (np). Zultanski's analysis shows that *Statement of Facts* does not open the doors for readers to come away with "any reading" that could be classified as a "good reading." Furthermore, if this were possible, then we would have to confront the possibility that such politically and emotionally charged language can never effectively be rendered as pure materiality. *Statement of Facts* is, accordingly, *not* a machine that says nothing; it is a sensationalist and affective piece that often reads more like a true crime narrative than a detached conceptual collection of dead language. The text acts relentlessly upon its readers, carrying them through the traumas of these narratives. Rather than an activist text that produces the radical freedom of an active reader, then, *Statement of Facts* is at best apolitical and at worst a promulgation of the sensationalist sexual violence in popular media.

### Christian Bök Obsolesces the Avant-Garde

To begin my discussion of Christian Bök's landmark text, *Eunoia* (2001), I would like to argue that while Cage's Cunningham mesostics and Mac Low's *Stein Poems* were produced by processes characterized by pleasure, chance, and a relative facility, *Eunoia* requires that its readers pay attention to the labour of its production. A text of univocal lipograms, *Eunoia*'s chapters each use only one vowel, and the work as a whole reflects an attempt to exhaust the univocal words available in the English language. Its construction was decidedly more laborious and more difficult than that of any other text I consider in these four chapters, and Bök advertises this fact. In the afterword, he asserts that "The text makes a Sisyphean spectacle of its labour, willfully crippling its language in order to show that, even under such improbable conditions of duress, language can still express an uncanny, if not sublime, thought" (103). A few pages later, Bök almost laments: "*Eunoia* has required seven years of daily perseverance for its consummation" (105). It *could* have been automated, Bök acknowledges, but was not.[7] Repeatedly, he demonstrates the role that labour plays in the text and insists that this labour is markedly human. If Cage's, Mac Low's, and Moure's works are informed by the digital—are machine texts at their heart—Bök's is handcrafted, flying in the face of a tradition of *sprezzatura* that positions poetic construction as born out of sublime inspiration. Cage, Mac Low, and Moure are all working within a tradition of experimentation that has looked to technology to create new modes of writing and reading; Bök's contrary choice not to automate or engage technological affordances in the production of *Eunoia* marks a desire to assert this handcrafted authorship as not a new process of experimental writing but a better version of constraint-based poetry than that which came before. The labour of *Eunoia* works in part, therefore, to outstrip and outshine earlier procedural writing modes, not to make them easier or more egalitarian. For Robert David Stacey, it is precisely the insistently obvious difficulty of the work that has led many critics to dismiss *Eunoia* as unpoetic: "it is Bök's extraordinary effort, the 'arduousness' of his task, that has been the focal point in several attacks on *Eunoia* which deem it insufficiently poetic...and which, more generally, reject the Oulipian constraint as productive of anything worth reading" (65). But, as the quotation from Wershler used as the epigraph for the afterword contends, "the tedium is the message" (103). I would not suggest that *Eunoia* is tedious to read—in fact, I argue that the work is immensely readable—but the writing of it would have, indeed, been tedious work.

What is fascinating but problematic about Bök's interest in the labour of his writing process is that it clearly disregards the useful, anarchic elements of digital technology. The digital, as anarchist Bookchin observes, allows a good deal of menial labour to be automated; this would include the poetic labour of such onerous Oulipian procedures as Bök's feat in *Eunoia*. For Bookchin, automation was of course a threat to some jobs, but it also meant that it opened up more creatively and intellectually challenging jobs to those who would have otherwise been completing those menial tasks (*Post-Scarcity Anarchism* 85). Yet though Bök admits that his process *could* have been automated, it was not;

Goldsmith makes many similar claims about the uncreative processes of his work. Both poets, then, rather than seeing the future revolution suggested by automation as praised by Bookchin and other later anarchists, instead partake in the labour of the poetry like lifestyle-anarchists, like tourists stepping down momentarily from positions of authorial and institutional power to observe what it might be like to actually have to labour for their products. A good Marxist might look at this turn to labour as honest, thoughtful, or useful, though Bök never really considers the labour politics of this work, and his position as a tenure-track professor and a well-established poet undercuts this Marxist labour critique. A good postanarchist, on the other hand, recognizes that an author who labours over a process that could be automated denies himself the affordances of the digital, and in so doing ultimately relies excessively on authorial intention.

Part of the reason that the works by Cage and Mac Low that I discuss in chapter one are perhaps more fun to read and were easier to produce than *Eunoia* is that these works rely much less on authorial intention. While the Oulipian constraints used to limit the diction of the text do severely restrict authorial intention, *Eunoia* remains, as Stacey terms it, a "voluntary" text. That is, it is "a 'voluntary' literature, born out of an intentionality that finds its correlate in the inevitable purposiveness...of its form" (67). The Oulipian constraints behind *Eunoia* produce a "defamiliarized language," to be sure, using univocal chapters to wrench language from its traditional signifying function, placing particular emphasis on sonority, like-sounds, and aural play. But Bök's defamiliarizing process is not unlike the defamiliarizing elements of other, more traditional, verse forms. After all, as Stacey asks, "What else is a sonnet or a villanelle, rondeau or sestina but the willed imposition of a set of restrictive rules which skew language from its ordinary usage, which deform it, and, in doing so, extend the domain of the sayable itself?" (68). Bök, like Moure, decides to maintain the dominant structures of grammar, and in the prose poem's absence of lineation this is all the more apparent. But where Moure's collaboration with machine involves questioning the possibilities of expression or communication, expanding the "domain of the sayable" in *Eunoia* does not do this. To be sure, "at no point does *Eunoia* reject meaningful communication as a basic condition" (Stacey 69). Instead, Bök uses *Eunoia* to demonstrate that language is expressive beyond our intentionality, a unanimous concession among the poets in this project. In Bök's own words, "*Eunoia* suggests that, even under duress, language finds a way to express its own compulsions" (np). And yet, while the language Bök uses here suggests a language that can act on its own, *Eunoia* focuses so strongly on the role of the author and his manipulation of traditional narrative and linguistic code that what Bök reveals, by the particular constraints he uses to place language under duress, is less a compulsion that is language's own than the compulsion of Oulipian verse forms. No language is neutral, we are reminded repeatedly throughout the history of experimental poetics, much less a language under duress. What seems to speak for itself in *Eunoia*, however, is not "language's own compulsions," but the compulsions of the constraint-based poetic form.

Because procedures are central to the author for the production of the Oulipian text, they have traditionally served as a skeleton key for highly formalized writing like *Eunoia*. If meaning is not readily communicated, the procedure for producing the text can be used to decode its message. Yet *Eunoia* does not require such a key; its appeal to the reader lies not in the constraint or in a meaning the prose poems purport to reveal, but in its author's status as a direct inheritor of a lineage of avant-garde traditions and in his work to top, and ultimately to obsolesce, those earlier avant-garde movements. Of course, Oulipo is a tradition of writing and not of reading, and so, in its theorizations of poetry, it is not preoccupied with its readers; it thinks even less about affect. As Perloff notes in her discussion of *Eunoia*, "According to Oulipo rules, there are as many possible constraints as there are poems, and the constraint is not an external form that is recognized readily but may be a rule that remains largely hidden to the reader" ("The Oulipo Factor" 25). In *Eunoia*, the univocal "rule" that governs each chapter's composition is obvious formally, but it does not govern the reader's reception or interpretation of the prose poems themselves. Still, the title of the piece directly concerns itself with the affect of its readers and not the work's composition: one definition of "eunoia," as Voyce points out, is a healthy and balanced state of mind. In light of this, Voyce quips: "I find this amusing, since *Eunoia* seems to have required near pathological compulsion to write" ("Xenotext" np). The compulsiveness behind the text's production is clear, but the popularity of the text suggests its reading is popular, following traditional modes of encoding and decoding meaning in language, rather than some kind of pathology.

Whether the writing process was "pathological" or not, the text itself is not a scattered collection of disjointed thoughts, as one might expect from such a constraint as Bök's, but rather the formation of clearly discernible narratives couched in each chapter. It is this presence of narrative that Stacey uses to argue for the valuable postindustrial and anti-globalization politics of the text, pointing out that free verse is more useful to globalization than more structured poetic forms because it is more easily translated into different languages (72). Stacey also observes that if, as Bob Perelman says, "Parataxis is the dominant mode of postindustrial experience," then the tendency toward narrative continuity in *Eunoia* must be understood in this context (74). Narrative continuity here functions as anti-capitalist and anti-industrial, ultimately rejecting the "idea of the aesthetic predicated on the sovereignty of the imagination" (77). And yes, because of this narrative continuity *Eunoia* is immensely readable. In the "U" section in particular, the prose poems turn to humorous, exuberant, and pornographic storytelling:

> Ruth plus Lulu. Ubu struts. Ubu snuffs up drugs. Ubu hugs Ruth; thus Ruth purrs. Ubu untucks Ruth's muumuu; thus Ruth must untruss Ubu's tux. Ubu fluffs Lulu's tutu. Ubu cups Lulu's dugs; Ubu rubs Lulu's buns; thus Lulu must pull Ubu's pud. Ubu sucks Ruth's cunt; Ubu cuffs Ruth's butt. Ubu stuffs Ruth's bum (such fun). Ubu pumps Lulu's plush, sun-burnt tush. Ubu humps Lulu's plump, upthrust rump. Ubu ruts. Ubu huffs; Ubu puffs. Ubu blurts; *push, push*. Ubu thrusts. Ubu bucks. Cum spurts. Ubu cums.
> (79, emphasis Bök's)

As this section of "U" illustrates, the narrative coupled with the rhythm and flow (whether resulting from or despite the use of only one vowel) in each chapter make *Eunoia* a surprisingly enjoyable—and accessible—read. Bök's performance of the poems, available on a compact disc recording, brings the pleasure of these humorous and sexually explicit sections to the fore, and enhances the way that the univocality and the normative sentence and narrative structure work together to produce an enjoyable, even joyful, reading.

Nevertheless, even though *Eunoia* does adhere to a narrative function, the formal constraint of univocality means that the text is ultimately untranslatable, and so resists universalization. Like Goldsmith and Place, Bök makes explicit his disruption of traditional understandings of authorship by following the trajectory of the formal avant-garde that includes Oulipo and other highly formal work up to Cage, Mac Low, and others writing in a similar vein. As we might expect from such a work, *Eunoia* demonstrates the extent to which linguistic code disrupts narratives; yet it also shows that there are radical potentials in constraint and unexpressive authorship not just to disrupt narratives but to create new ones. Such work requires a constrained and unexpressive authorship, but it also requires a powerful and articulate authorship that governs the text. Ultimately, I would argue that, because of *Eunoia*'s author-driven constraints, *Eunoia*'s readers are limited in their interpretive engagement with the poetry therein, poetry that is characterized by the kind of expression and representation that produces readers who are not free.

I do not want to suggest that the labour of *Eunoia* resides entirely within the tireless work of Bök. On the contrary—not unlike the conceptualism of Goldsmith and Place, much of the work of reading *Eunoia* is done by the reader. For Sean Braune, this work is akin to the work of mathematics, in that the reader is meant to decode the meaning of the text to "the *N*th degree."[8] For Stacey, by contrast, the text suggests its own "epistemology," a unique "theory of knowledge" in which "its *manner* of meaning" is "the key to its subject *matter*" (67). While there is merit in both of these readings, I would argue that the work of reading *Eunoia* stems from its insistence on erasing the work of previous poetry in the mind of the reader. Essentially, the primary goal of *Eunoia* is to render obsolete earlier and ostensibly more traditional forms of writing and meaning-making in order to make room for the radical epistemological possibilities of its new form; however, it does so by denying agency to the reader.

The text positions itself as a radical eraser of earlier poetry. In the first section, "Chapter A," the second sentence of the first prose poem positions Bök as "A Dada *bard*" whose work "mars all stanzas and jams all ballads (what a scandal)" (12, emphasis Bök's). The sarcasm suggested by the italics, the derisive tone of the parenthetical quip, and the bombast of the repeated "all" establish the text as one that simultaneously owes its existence to poetic tradition[9] and seeks to destroy it. This reading is reinforced by the review blurb included on the text's back cover in which Goldsmith proclaims, "*Eunoia* takes the lipogram and renders it obsolete." While at its heart this desire to obsolesce earlier forms of writing is also a desire to create new methods of writing and reading, this trending toward obsolescence is the opposite of what Hayles suggests in her proposition that the distributed cognition of habitual use can produce distributed agency rather than unidirectional power distribution. For poetry to redistribute both cognition and agency by means of the digital and machine-writing (or at least for it to draw attention to the ways that our distributed cognition has become so habitual as to be automatic), it must propose options outside of the automatic and make room for readers to engage freely and fully with the text. In the end, *Eunoia* relies so heavily on its radical, artificial, and formal authorship that there is little room for readers to do much more than be impressed by the patience, skill, and *labour* involved in the text's production. Most of the critical and scholarly responses to *Eunoia* do just that.[10]

What is at once most interesting and most troubling about the way that the text positions itself as radical is that whereas the radical experimental text is frequently understood as a tactic for authors who want to write but cannot,[11] Bök presents us in *Eunoia* with a rethinking of authorship as labour in and of itself, and *difficult* labour at that, as opposed to the presentation of ease in *sprezzatura*. His remarks on innovation are thus especially telling. He tells Voyce, for example, that "Innovation in art no longer differs from the kind of manufactured obsolescence that has come to justify advertisements for 'improved' products," and that "we have to find a new way to contribute by generating a 'surprise'" (Voyce, "Xenotext" np). Bök seems to suggest here that part of the new labour of radical authorship is to reclaim machinic means of production and to redo them personally. This all boils down to *craft*. After all, the first line of the text reads, "Awkward grammar appalls a *craftsman*" (12, emphasis mine). What is praised in a craft is the individual who has become its expert; a failure to become an expert practitioner—i.e., having "awkward grammar"—is thus appalling. Bök's grammar in *Eunoia* is distinctly not awkward. He moves adeptly from English to French and back, employing parentheses, dashes, and semicolons to produce readable sentences despite the univocal constraint, thereby revealing the poet as a craftsman who has expertly devised the text's plan and carried it out.

What sets *Eunoia* apart from other radically experimental texts most obviously is the fact that the book is mass-produced and massively popular. Responding to the issue of the text's popularity, Bök tells Voyce that while he is pleased, he also knows that even a popular book of poems is, in the grand scheme of things, not terribly popular: "I am surprised that my own work of experimental poetry has enjoyed popular success, selling more than 20,000 copies at last count [in 2007], but this number still pales in comparison to the success of other cultural artifacts in other art forms" (Voyce, "Xenotext" np). Still, Stacey points out that this popularity is important and notable: "*Eunoia*'s extraordinary popularity is perhaps especially surprising given that it is a highly experimental text" (64). If we understand that experimental works of poetry tend to be relegated to an even further obscurity than poetry is usually afforded, then we are right to be surprised by *Eunoia*'s commercial and critical success. So what is it about *Eunoia* that provokes such popular acclaim? One answer is that *Eunoia*'s popular appeal lies in its ability to mix the politics of Oulipian constraint and extreme formal radicalism with the appeal of narrative continuity. This mixing allows the reader to come face-to-face with the radically experimental text without the added burden of readerly freedom. While this may make for an enjoyable, popular, and marketable text, reading *Eunoia* through the lens of postanarchist literary theory reveals that this same extreme authorship also makes for a less free, less engaged readership even than more traditionally composed poetic works allow. *Eunoia* gestures toward the minimally egoic experimental work, but what shines in the end is authorial skill and linguistic prowess, without leaving room for an agential, free reader.

### Darren Wershler andor Any Number of Readers

I end this chapter with another relatively popular text of conceptual poetics, Darren Wershler's *The Tapeworm Foundry*. While I have argued throughout this chapter that the space for an active readership as advocated by a postanarchist literary theory is simply not present in the vast majority of works published (either accurately or not) under the umbrella of conceptual poetics, ending this chapter with *The Tapeworm Foundry* affords me the opportunity to point to it as an exception. Wershler's *The Tapeworm Foundry* interrogates the space for an active and activist readership in a history of experimental poetics while at the same time ensuring that such a space is made for its own readers. In essence, *The Tapeworm Foundry* is a text full of possibilities. It encourages its readers to stop reading and to interact with it. Its proposals for other poems, books of poems, and art projects engage readers through humour and through invitations to creativity, implicitly defined as the use of imagination to produce something unique. In *The Tapeworm Foundry*, Wershler trusts his readers in a way that few other authors do, and the result is a text that repeatedly encourages its readers to produce their own work. Readers have responded to this encouragement, too: projects proposed by *The Tapeworm Foundry* were produced by students at the University of Pennsylvania and exhibited together in 2008 (*Tapeworm*). Such events celebrate the text's potential to encourage other readers to produce their own work—to produce, furthermore, work that itself questions the roles of the author and the reader, that breaks down conventional notions of creativity and inspiration, that allows poets and artists to work together as a common, and that confronts the parasitic nature of what the book's subtitle terms "the dangerous prevalence of imagination."

This is not to say that *The Tapeworm Foundry* is necessarily utopian. On this point I follow Susan Vanderborg, who also reads the text as full of possibilities, but who cautions as well that it grapples with the feelings of defeat we might feel as a result of capitalism's tendency to guide our imaginations and limit our creative choices (148). As Vanderborg also points out, the book functions palimpsestically, inscribing the potentials of conceptual uncreativity and radical defamiliarization onto extant texts that have been or risk being commodified in a market that absorbs the experimental and the avant-garde in order to nullify or diminish its revolutionary potentials. For Vanderborg, *The Tapeworm Foundry* is a text of parasitic noise, "not only...full of noisy over-communication and static on still-functioning lines, but also" describing "completely ruined or non-useful texts, with tips for creating such objects ranged alongside its visions of easily consumed commodities" (156). Indeed, *The Tapeworm Foundry* is more concerned with the noise of radical experimentation and textual production than with the final texts, which exist throughout its pages as concepts without finished products (159). For example, Wershler suggests a book project wherein you, the reader, would "write your book in ink that contains powdered radioactive compounds and then perform your readings of the book by holding each page up to a geiger counter" (np). Or, in another suggested project, Wershler suggests that you "write extended comments on a movie by using a stickpin plus a magnifying glass to scratch marginalia into the black space that surrounds each celluloid frame" (np). Both of these suggested projects lead to an unreadable final text, and both suggest a level of ruin: in the first, a reading and writing practice that is literally hazardous to your health; in the second, a destruction of a film reel for written comments outside the viewers' purview.

The ruined books, unusable objects, and wild digital projects that Wershler proposes collectively reject an economy founded on the principle of use-value, as Vanderborg argues. However, while Vanderborg pays particular attention to the digital lineage of Wershler's book itself (164), what I am particularly interested in is *The Tapeworm Foundry*'s merger of analog and digital. In the paragraphs that follow, I consider some of the many instances where readers are encouraged to use their own biographical examples, and especially their own handwriting, to produce digital, experimental, and unusable texts, in order to examine what this text (marketed and circulated by and large as a print-based book) suggests about the radical potentials of digital texts—especially considering the volume of work Wershler has done in the digital humanities.[12]

In the first few pages of the book, Wershler characterizes his proposals for experimental art projects as ones that interrogate the relationship between the readers and the art pieces they would produce. One of his first instructions is to "reconstruct the ruins of a bombed out capital i" (np). This directive draws attention to the fact that no letter, least of all "I," is capitalized throughout the text. More importantly, it also calls up the image of a reader who takes up a physical position in a linguistic subjectivity (occupying the literal space of a letter of the alphabet) that has been "bombed out" by an avant-garde poetics that has sought to obliterate conventional notions of subjectivity. The reconstruction in question is, accordingly, the construction of a new space for the reader to create a makeshift and fluctuating "I" within this and other texts. This subjectivity is at once personal and abstracted: while the materiality of language is stressed in this image, the implied destruction and reconstruction of subjectivity happens on the level of the abstract. This reconstruction of subjectivity is complicated a few pages later, though, with Wershler's humorous language play in his proposal that the reader "object to the subject" (np). In this way he encourages the production of new subjectivities that exist in the tenuous and immaterial locus of potential meanings.

These new subjectivities are made manifest throughout *The Tapeworm Foundry* in descriptions of the reader's handwriting being used to complicate digitization, autobiography, inspiration, and the useful, meaning-making potentials of the art piece. One reference to the reader's handwriting can be found in Wershler's call to the reader: "write all of your misgivings about your work in ballpoint pen along the edges of your collated manuscript doing so in the same way that you might have written on the edges of your high school math book and then shuffle the pages before you bind them" (np). In an act of defiance against a publish-or-perish culture in both academic and creative writing, Wershler asks the reader to defile the seemingly impersonal medium of the printed manuscript with the very personal, confessional nature of the typically unspoken "misgivings" authors inevitably have about their work. The personal and individualized nature of the reader's emotions is emphasized by the fact that these misgivings are to be personally handwritten onto the printed manuscript. Adding handwriting to a typewritten manuscript turns it into a palimpsest on which the individualized reader is afforded personal and individualized space through the physical materiality of a "ballpoint pen" scribbled onto the manuscript pages. The space for the reader's autonomy is further expanded by Wershler's added instruction that these misgivings be scrawled, not like edits or revisions, but like juvenile marginalia, doodled like a boyfriend's name or an illustration of a heart. The resulting project is then made even more (auto)biographical in that Wershler specifically instructs his reader to write not just in the manner of juvenile marginalia or doodles, but rather "in the same way that *you* might have written on the edges of *your* high school math book" (np, emphasis mine). *My* marginalia in *my* math book, my own recollections of the activity at once universalized (we all doodled in all of our math books, he suggests) and made personal (his name was Chris, I respond, the hearts were made into balloons). Yet all of this attention to subjectivity and autonomy is then undercut by the proposal's final instructions to shuffle the pages before binding. Nevertheless, our personal experience, our emotions, and our confessional tendencies have a place in the textual production and are required to turn the traditional and usable text into a noisy, radical mess. I would argue, then, that for its suggestion that our subjectivity, our reconstructed capital "I," is important for the process of creation of radically experimental texts, but not for the finished product, *The Tapeworm Foundry* is a postanarchist text: it represents subjectivity as important in the process of textual production insofar as that subjectivity itself is also a process. Because the line between writing and reading is radically blurred in this text, the fluctuating subjectivity required by both actions (both reading and writing) gets carried over from Wershler's production of *The Tapeworm Foundry* to our reading of it and essentially continues (either literally or figuratively) in the projects proposed therein.

In another mention of the reader's handwriting, Wershler encourages the reader to "write a poem about sir isaac newton in your normal handwriting on an apple newton and then let the device mistranslate it for you" (np). In this case, the line between the digital and the print-based text is blurred. The individualized personality of the handwritten document provides the eventual indeterminacy and illegibility of the end product; the idiosyncrasies and inconsistencies of handwriting would render the text illegible, "mistranslated" by a machine that did not have the processing power to accurately receive and translate handwritten texts. Additionally, Wershler humorously juxtaposes Sir Isaac Newton (representing physics, physicality, and materiality) and the image of the Apple Newton (a platform that at the time of writing was just barely still in production). The Apple Newton OS's handwriting-recognition software was famously inaccurate, frequently producing illegible and unrecognizable translations of the handwritten original. These examples indicate that the reader's place in the production of meaning—and the production of texts—is a difficult one. Readers are invited to bring their own personal experiences to the work, but are persistently reminded that, in order to maintain the text's radical potentials, individuality and personal experience must eventually be randomized, mistranslated, and rendered into noise. Only in this way can the next reader be afforded the same potentials.

For these reasons, *The Tapeworm Foundry* demonstrates precisely what Hayles imagines when she insists upon the "potent opportunities" that exist for electronic work to reveal the ways that we engage with technology habitually, to redistribute the cognition that makes that work possible, and to encourage us to engage with digital and technologically mediated knowledge in ways as heterogeneous and multiple as any collective readership. This achievement is even more astonishing considering that despite being available in PDF form via *UBUWeb*, the book is almost exclusively marketed and circulated as a print-based work. In either medium, *The Tapeworm Foundry* demonstrates the postanarchist argument that in order to effectively critique the subjectivity that makes lyric authorship, limited readership, and expressive representation possible, we cannot simply withdraw from engagement with these literary conventions, but rather must reveal through them the multiple ways of making knowledge. The very format of *The Tapeworm Foundry* and its "andor" list structure reveals a potentially limitless landscape for textual production and reception, but it is not overwhelming or alienating (an irony considering Wershler's online persona as "Alienated" on his homepage and Twitter). As Hayles observes, in reference to the interaction between the body's ways of knowing and the mind's, "These differentials, far from posing obstacles to understanding, constitute the uneven terrain on which electronic literature plays, its effects intensified by the diverse knowledges it mobilizes and the nascent connections it forges" (139). Rather than denying his readers access to the literary terrain, Wershler invites readers to destroy *Tapeworm*'s pages and create many of their own, thereby mobilizing "diverse knowledges" about poetry itself.

Thus, I would like to characterize *The Tapeworm Foundry* as "(mal) content," a throwaway term that Wershler uses in his exchange on the poetry website *Circulars* with Brian Kim Stefans. Wershler exclaims: "don't just 'write' (a verb that in many cases bears the superciliousness of the romantic), build (mal)content. Bring on the hyperlinks, intro paragraphs, pictures, PHP scripts, and HTML formatting, especially if they help to demonstrate the mutual indebtedness that all creativity entails. Use Your Allusion" (Stefans and Wershler, "Exchange" 82). Buried within Wershler's characteristic humour and jouissance, the term suggests a content—a product—that carries within it the potential to function like the parasite of *Tapeworm*'s title. (Mal)content feeds off existing literature and grows indefinitely, producing new parasitic texts and always linking back to them. In this way, (mal)content is a distinctly postanarchist concept insofar as it encourages reader freedom while at the same time working parasitically to dismantle the structures of linguistic expression that typically limit this freedom. (Mal)content is a lot like Bey's "poetic terrorism," too, though Wershler never draws that comparison. *The Tapeworm Foundry* can be read as just such a parasite, a (mal)content that produces new forms that slowly but surely eat away at the traditional epistemologies that would seek to govern it.

In particular, the book's (mal)content attacks notions of value, especially as defined via capitalism. Weaver astutely notes that most of the proposed projects in the text are ones that actively oppose or refuse capitalist economy; in Weaver's words, *The Tapeworm Foundry* "creates a series of readers who can attack the capitalist economy like a series of parasites" ("Darren Wershler-Henry" 114). Furthermore, even though the book is necessarily bought and sold through a capitalist economy, the digital (PDF) version circulated online via *UBUWeb* is freely available, which means Wershler intentionally invites piracy, another dig at capitalism. (Mal)content may be a poetic construct, but it does have some practical, tangible outcomes; its projects are anti-capital and its effects are connection alongside disruption. Though it is print-based, then, *The Tapeworm Foundry* makes multiple links to multiple abstract, unfinished, or not-even-begun projects connected by the indefinitely looping "andor": a term designed to wear away at larger structures (capital, canon, and so on) rather than to simply obsolesce them.

One way the text does this is through a series of vague instructions scattered among the otherwise quite specific instructions for new art projects or books of poetry. These vague instructions serve as a reminder to readers that they do not actually have to follow any of the directions in the book. Instead, the proposals function as lines of flight that link together various radically experimental projects through a readership encouraged to produce more art and become a part of the parasitic rhizome. When Wershler encourages his readers to "proceed according to a philosophy of whatever" (np), he allows his parasite access to virtually everything. I am for this reason tempted to read the text as one that resists materiality, whereas many of the other texts discussed in this book have challenged the reader to acknowledge the issues of materiality surrounding textual production. When I encountered relatively early in the book Wershler's directive, "remove specificity and then convert to ambiguities," I believed that the text was supporting such an argument. Yet a close reading of the rest of the text uncovered a direct contradiction pages later, wherein Wershler proposes instead that the reader "delete ambiguities and then convert to specificities" (np). These incommensurate directions suggest not that the text attempts to deceive its readers, but rather that the really radical potential of a text that is purely proposal is that it allows for the production of multiple new texts, rendering previous binaries (of specific and ambiguous, material and immaterial, etc.) increasingly unimportant.

Close to the book's end Wershler even instructs: "andor do none of these things" (np). In this way, he ensures that the reader cannot help but follow at least one of his instructions: he creates a moment of (mal)content in which the reader is included in the parasitic rhizome. Readers may or may not choose to engage in these specific projects, but, just by doing "none of these things," they are still necessarily drawn into this community. After all, *The Tapeworm Foundry* begins with "or jetsam" and ends with "flotsam and," suggesting an indefinite feedback loop of aggregation. The text may be all-consuming, but it also presents the reader's engagements with it as distinctly outside the purview of its author. Lest the indefinite loop of the text seem manipulative, *Tapeworm*'s authorial voice includes this commentary: "andor dont [*sic*] and see if i give a fuck" (np). This approach radically challenges our conceptions of reader involvement and is thus commensurate with postanarchism. In the end, a postanarchist reading process is one that does not end when the text does, but rather continues through the rhizomatic linking of texts, readers, and authors (real and imagined). Postanarchism insists on the active role of the reader as an intervention into the authorial presence. The parasitic nature of *The Tapeworm Foundry* breaks down existing concepts of the reading process that would keep reader and author on their appropriate sides of the process, instead allowing readers to be parasites, too.

Given that *The Tapeworm Foundry was* first published in 2000, we might have expected that the litany of projects it outlines would have rendered a whole movement of conceptualism unnecessary. After all, if what Goldsmith says is right, and we never really have to read an uncreative or conceptual work, then Wershler's list of concepts is enough to exhaust an entire movement. And yet conceptualism, with Goldsmith and Place at the helm, saw itself as the predominant form of avant-garde poetry for the first decade and a half of the twenty-first century until its writers and its projects began to come increasingly under fire. The underlying misogyny, racism, and elitism of the movement was critiqued by such writers as Ken Chen, Joshua Clover, Amy King, Alan Davies, Keston Sutherland, Cathy Park Hong,[13] and Johanna Drucker, who argued as early as 2012 that "Conceptualism is probably over now, even in its newest iterations" (9). There have even been charges of racism laid against *Eunoia*,[14] whose portrayal of Middle Eastern cultures as regressive, violent, and barbaric bears some recognition. The work of political critiques of conceptual poetry is not my focus, but it is important to point to the concerns voiced by Chen, Hong, and others, as these concerns are intrinsically tied to the lack of care in the conceptual project for readers. Because *The Tapeworm Foundry* gestures outward rather than inward, relying on reader engagement rather than authorial critique or craft, it has more concern for who is represented and how. This is part of why such a high priority is put on the readers' own handwriting, desires, and bodies throughout the proposed, yet impossible or uncompleted, projects depicted therein. The very project of making room for an agential reader in a poetic work through (figurative) linking and other forms of connection (however parasitic) suggests above all the inclusivity of the common, an inclusivity that is absent from the vast majority of the projects associated with conceptual poetry. In its turn to reader biography and handwriting, *Tapeworm* points to the postanarchist ambivalence toward subjectivity; in this case, the extremely personal is met with the extremely impersonal or conceptual, expressing this ambivalence in the form of the apparently incommensurate.

Drucker's suggestion that conceptualism is finished signals a movement in poetics away from author-based print work that sees only a tool (for creation or distribution, or both) in the machine and the digital format and toward work that takes up the potentials of machine-writing and digital media to directly and significantly engage with and empower readers. Rather than treating networked computing as a plunderground where an almost infinite mass of text is available for plagiarizing, remixing, and redistributing, many works of electronic literature and digital poetics composed before, during, and after the rise of conceptual poetry engage their readers in substantive ways. Of course, there are still (and always will be) digital literary works where the readers simply observe a digitized work and answer to a governing authorial presence. But these works continue to give way to digital poetics in which significant space is made for the reader who has enough text throughout the internet to passively consume, and has come to poetry instead to *engage*.

# 4
# Digital Interventions

IN THIS FINAL CHAPTER, I look to four very different works of digital poetry to trace how contemporary poetics has moved past the limitations placed on readers by the conceptual poetic project. Spanning a decade and a half and taken from multiple countries, the four new media projects discussed in this chapter—Jim Andrews's "Seattle Drift" (1997), W. Mark Sutherland's *Code X* (2002), Brian Kim Stefans's "The Dreamlife of Letters" (2000), and Andy Campbell and Mez Breeze's *The Dead Tower* (2012)—all use the digital medium in different ways to encourage the same thing: a greater than usual attention to free reading practices and direct reader involvement. These projects are vastly different in appearance, tone, and approach, but one important feature unites them: they all make clear the authors' desire to re-engage with their audiences, to remedy, in other words, the separation between author, text, and reader that continues to characterize literary and digital culture.

Obviously, this chapter makes much of the digital medium; nevertheless, discussing the radical and interventionary potentials of the digital medium to invite free and agential reader engagement also requires that we look closely at the ways in which each text is situated within existing (mostly print-based) reading traditions. The practice of viewing new media projects in the context of print traditions is a fairly common one, and in this chapter I both draw attention to this tendency in the scholarship and do my own work to situate these four digital texts within the print-based literary traditions that they are working within and against. Furthermore, in light of postanarchism's insistence on stressing materiality, I argue that these new media projects make radical, new engagements with their readers through the innovative potentials of the digital machine.

In essence, I situate these texts in a tradition that has, heretofore, been print-based but that, these texts imply, will hereafter be digital. After all, as Hayles writes in *Electronic Literature*, "To see electronic literature only through the lens of print is, in a significant sense, not to see it at all" (3). Because I do not wish either to overlook or undersell the importance of the digital medium to the reader engagement these works facilitate, in this chapter's case studies I attend in some detail to software, format, coding language, and other digital elements that may be relevant in each case. For the same reason I place a particularly high value on the various kinds of hardware or networked technologies that readers may use to engage with these pieces. In keeping with this emphasis, for the most part I shy away from close readings of the texts I consider in this chapter, instead encouraging my readers to seek out and engage with these pieces on their own.

What makes the particular digital texts by Andrews, Sutherland, Stefans, and Campbell and Mez that I focus on here of importance to my project is chiefly that, unlike the conceptualist projects discussed in chapter three, these texts all illustrate both of Hayles's propositions about digital literature introduced in that chapter. Each of these new media works demonstrates the ways that "verbal narratives are simultaneously conveyed and disrupted by code" (Hayles's first proposition, *Electronic Literature* 135); in all four, likewise, their use of the digital medium to engage with readers demonstrates how "distributed cognition implies distributed agency" (Hayles's second proposition, 136). Moreover, these texts all reflect their authors' shared interest in varying and disrupting the habitual ways in which we use networked technology, and they all reveal the ways in which our habitual use of media results in some loss of agency to subconscious or unthinking action, a problem that Hayles identifies (137). Each of these texts points to our current use of networked technology, which has become so habitual that we often type without looking at the keyboard; perhaps even more often, our hands will automatically gravitate toward a mouse or a touchpad when we sit in front of a computer. But these four texts also demonstrate how literary or poetic use of digital language can intervene in such kinds of habitual activity.

I do not, however, mean to suggest that my argument for the importance of the reader in the digital text is radical. In fact, this basic thesis is a fairly common argument in studies of electronic literature. For example, Jan Van Looy and Jan Baetens' introduction to *Close Reading New Media* (2003) begins with the principle that "The decentered nature of electronic text empowers and invites the reader to take part in the literary process" (7). My purpose in situating this discussion of electronic literature in the context of radical, free readership is to look specifically at the potentials of the digital medium to efface authorial power over a text and at the resultant onus of meaning-making placed on the computer and the reader/user/player. Andrews, for example, asks his readers to look at the code and construction of "Seattle Drift," thereby establishing a TAZ where readers are invited to engage as the text drifts apart in a newly expanded field of composition. Sutherland, with *Code X*, presents the poetic text as a tool for the creative process rather than a finished product, revealing the potentials of digital media to engage readers in agential reading processes. Campbell and Mez create a digital-poetic space in *The Dead Tower* for readers to explore and engage without the limitations of goal-oriented reading, sensical language, or executable code. Even Stefans, in the non-interactive "Dreamlife of Letters," reveals the extent to which digital reading and writing processes have heretofore depended on a passive reader who consumes with little agency. While these are four quite different approaches to the e-literary text, they all reveal how digital media can expose our passive, habitual use of media, yet also reveal how we can use digital media to make space for radical reader interaction and agency.

## Jim Andrews Drifts Apart

Jim Andrews's "Seattle Drift" is a classic work of kinetic poetry, a genre that builds on concrete poetry's treatment of language as visual medium in its use of digital technology to have the poem's words literally move across the screen in front of the reader. More significantly for this project, "Seattle Drift" moves at the (partial) behest of its readers/users, who start and stop the movement. While the poem is hosted and still accessible on Andrews's site, *Vispo.com*, "Seattle Drift" was originally distributed through the now foundational journal of web art and digital writing, *Cauldron & Net*, in its first volume in 1997. Andrews wrote the code for the work in Javascript, updating the DHTML with Marko Niemi in 2004 to make it work on PC and Mac; they updated it again in 2015 to adapt it for mobile users. When readers/users visit "Seattle Drift" in either location, they encounter a fairly simplistic page layout: the poem, white Arial typeface on a black screen, looks like a short and fairly traditional poem, if a bit tongue-in-cheek:

> I am a bad text.
> I used to be a poem
> but drifted from the scene.
> Do me.
> I just want you to do me.

This last line might provoke curious readers to look at the hyperlinks above the poem, provided they realize that the smaller red text at the top of the screen is indeed a set of hyperlinks (considering they lack the underlining and blue colour typical of hyperlinked text). The red text provides readers with three hyperlinks to click at their leisure: if they choose, they can "Do the text," which results in the randomized and slightly erratic movement of the words and punctuation marks toward the right and bottom of the screen until no words are visible; at any time during that movement, readers can then "Stop the text," leaving the words and punctuation marks wherever they have ended up at that moment; at this point the readers have the option to "Discipline the text," returning the words to their original and supposedly proper order. These linked options are the first sign that Andrews invites readers of "Seattle Drift" to engage directly, to interact, rather than to passively consume the text.

All the same, despite the fact that these are links that initiate, stop, and restart the drifting function, the reader never leaves this webpage. The poem has a tendency to disperse, but otherwise the work is fairly cohesive. This makes "Seattle Drift" different from some of Andrews's other work; as Hayles observes, the more popular (and, arguably, more scholarly rigorous) *On Lionel Kearns* (2004), and *Stir-fry Texts* (1999), demonstrate the influence on Andrews's work of a history of such avant-garde poetry as William Burroughs's cut-up method and other forms of indeterminacy or remix (*Electronic Literature* 19–20). By contrast, "Seattle Drift" focuses on presenting words and punctuation marks as separate entities that relate to each other but act—in this case, move—independently. Much of the work of making "sense" of the poem is prompted by the fact of the individual pieces' movement and the particular ways in which they move; the semantic sense of the poem, as read when all the different pieces cohere, is largely secondary. Andrews recognizes this facet of the work himself:

> each object might have various properties in addition to its usual appearance and meaning and place amid other words....When you click the text that says 'Do the text,' the words in the poem eventually drift independently off the screen. Each word has its own behavior, its own partially random path of drifting off the screen. Each word is a kind of little language widget, langwidget. ("Digital Langu(im)age" np)

While the langwidget neologism is humorous, it also does a good job of establishing the linguistic unit as an element in a field, clear evidence of Andrews's debt to Duncan and the "field of composition" characteristic of Black Mountain poetics, here brought into the digital context. However, the poetic "field of composition" takes on a radically altered identity in a digital context, where the composition's units can literally move as a part of the piece, and where readers are invited to engage with a level of intervention that Duncan could not have dreamed of. Where Andrews's description is less accurate is in his claim that the words have their "own behavior," which is simply not the case. In fact, the level of mediation required for these langwidgets to migrate across the screen is what makes this work significant in a postanarchist context.

The truth is that while Andrews writes of each word's independent behaviour, his recognition that the langwidget's "path" is only "partially random" acknowledges the importance of those aspects of the poem's movement that are distinctly not random. The movement of the words of "Seattle Drift" across the page is designed to *seem* random, but it is quite clearly controlled by three primary forces: first, by the reader, who literally starts and stops the movement; second, by Andrews, who wrote the code and the algorithm for the movement and made the necessary choices of design and content; and third, by a relatively straightforward algorithm. A quick look at the webpage's source code unearths a pseudo-randomizing movement function that determines whether each word will move left or right and whether it will move up or down with any given move; for each move, the function generates a pair of numbers that determine, in pixels, how a word or punctuation mark will move along the x-axis and how along the y-axis. This movement function shows a heavy bias toward downward and rightward movement; furthermore, not all of the langwidgets are allowed the same range of movement. Some, such as "a" and "the" and some of the punctuation, are given much greater range of movement, causing them to recede from view much more quickly. Others, such as "poem," "text," and "drifted," move more slowly and remain on the screen longer: "text" is almost always the final word on the screen, because it cannot move more than two pixels horizontally and one pixel vertically at a time, unlike others, such as the "a" that precedes "poem," which can move five pixels at a time in each direction. While each choice to "Do the text" yields a different experience, then, each doing yields a similar outcome (see Fig. 17).

For these reasons it is more accurate to describe the movement of "Seattle Drift" as partially randomized and partially organized, with the

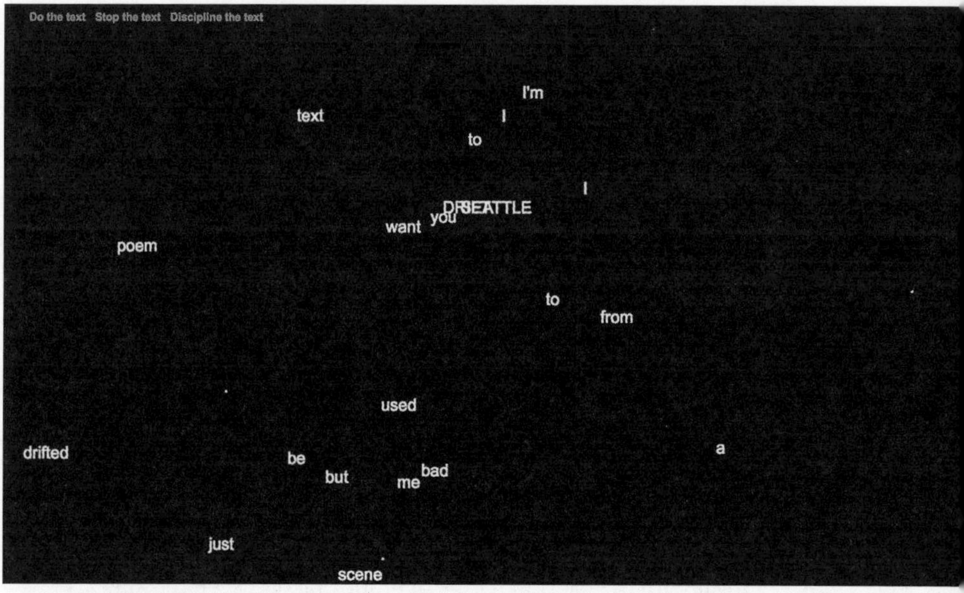


FIGURE 17. Jim Andrews, from "Seattle Drift."

reader's agency mainly limited to determining when that movement begins, ends, and begins all over again: an interaction that Katalin Sándor describes as one in which the work "addresses the reader by a somewhat limited interface-rhetoric" (150). But, as Paola Trimarco points out, this interface is also essentially optional; we can read and engage with the poem in the traditional way by visiting the page but not clicking the hyperlinks. The poem only drifts "if readers choose to become an active participant in the work" (89). For Trimarco, the "active" readership is invited—or perhaps it is more appropriate to say "begged"—by the poem, and this reverses what she sees as the usual power structure:

> The tenor in this brief poem is informal and suggestive of a relationship between reader and text which might be interpreted as similar to parent and child or sadistically between two lovers, which in a sense reverses the power relationship between reader and poem, as the poem gives the order (in the command "Do me") and the reader follows by clicking on the words on the screen. (89)

With its express desire for "Discipline," whether understood as parental or erotic, the text asks the reader to give it "order."

The question of power that Trimarco raises is central to the poem, for "Seattle Drift" expresses a desire to move any power the poem may have (its content, its signification, and its potential for exegesis) into the hands of a user/reader who may exert control over the piece by starting it, stopping it, and disciplining it back to its traditional lineation. Where I differ from Trimarco is that, in my view, the desire the poem expresses, with such instructions as "Do me," is for a relationship that is far more sadomasochistic than familial. The poem desires its own abuse, desires that it be made bad (or perverse) by the reader's "abnormal" or non-traditional actions upon it. The relationship between reader and poem is also highly performative, not unlike sadomasochistic sexual practice. Moreover, the poem's tendency to resist logical linguistic and hermeneutic traditions aligns it with the illogical nature of erotic practice. Even the appearance of the poem encourages this sexualized reading, as, in its ecstatic breaking from tradition and composure, the white text disperses and spreads across the screen like ejaculate.

In light of the clear erotic and sadomasochistic elements of this poem, as Stephen Cain reminds me, even Andrews's term "scene" recalls the use of tableaux and theatrical scenes in the Marquis de Sade's *The 120 Days of Sodom*. Still, unlike the men in de Sade's *120 Days*, the readers/lovers of "Seattle Drift" are very limited in the actions they can take, no matter how strongly they may wish to respond to the poem's expression of desire. In response to Ian Davidson's observation that the elements of "Seattle Drift" move "slightly jerkily" (173), Alistair Brown points out that this accurate observation reveals two issues: the relationship between the code and the technology that is used to view it, and the multiplicitous and reader-centric readings this mutability suggests. On the first point, the reader's experience of "Seattle Drift" is highly dependent on whatever device is used to engage with it (as is the case with all digital technologies), and this has an impact on just how jerky the movement may be. After all, "there is no software," as Friedrich Kittler reminds us. So too there is no "Seattle Drift," save through the device each reader uses to engage with the piece. On the second point, Brown remarks,

> Displaying the text on a larger screen (such as my 27-inch monitor) means that there is more black space to the right and below for the poem to move into, before the words drift entirely off screen. The poem would offer a different sense if played on a mobile phone screen....The poem is not medium-neutral. (np)

Each screen, therefore, puts different limitations on the reading of this poem. In this context it also bears noting that, as Leonardo Flores points out, the words of "Seattle Drift" will continue drifting even after they leave the constraints of our screen: "if allowed to drift for a long period of time, they [the words] would create an enormous virtual space in the browser that would require serious exploration of that space using scrollbars to find them" (81). In the absence of fixed limits, any starting and stopping of the work constitutes an artificial delineation of what the "poem" is at that point in time and space. While this fact—that our readings and interpretations place limits on a text—is true in the abstract of all texts, "Seattle Drift" and other digital poems like it make this artificiality explicit.

In thus revealing its artificiality, "Seattle Drift" takes its place in the long history of highly formal, print-based, avant-garde verse. But I would argue that it also does much more, in that it requires a rethinking of the divisions that make that history possible. Pursuing the historical connection between digital poetry—particularly kinetic works like this one or Nichol's *First Screening* discussed in chapter one—and concrete poetry is a fruitful trajectory, and most studies of Andrews's work do trace digital poetry's roots in concrete poetry. For instance, Roberto Simanowski argues that part of what "Seattle Drift" does is present and interrogate "the new possibilities of concrete poetry under the conditions of their being digital" (np). And yet, while I acknowledge my debt to such scholars as Simanowski, I am much more concerned with how drawing a direct, causal relationship between "Seattle Drift" and concrete verse does not fully acknowledge how the poem works against such traditional classification. Building in part on Flores's observation that "this e-poem enacts a critique of current and historical poetry scenes in order to create a space for a new e-poetry scene" (172), I would argue that "Seattle Drift"'s critique of "historical poetry scenes" involves a critique of the scholarly desire to create such scenes or the scene divisions that define them: these are the "scenes" from which we must "drift," and the desire to situate texts within historical, geographical, and generic classifications is just the kind of disciplining from which we must also "drift."

Even Simanowski observes that the poem resists classification and instead revels in digital and embodied play: "I drifted from the scene, says the poem when it is in proper order, but ends up all the more in the void when you try to help it" (np). Through this resistance, scholarly hermeneutics, exegetical reading practices, and the other concerns of most scholarship and classification become recognizable as acts of disciplining, with both positive (playful, erotic) and negative (limiting, classifying, stabilizing) aspects. When the act of disciplining the digital poem is made explicit, we as readers and as scholars can recognize how this practice limits poetry, but we can also revel in the play that is still there for us in the process. As Sándor points out, the poem "exposes language in its rhetorical-tropological elusiveness, which makes any (authorial, interventional) control over the text illusionary" (150). "Seattle Drift" reminds us that not only authorial control but also critical control and readerly control are illusions.

Indeed, I do not want to be utopian about the possibilities of reader engagement in "Seattle Drift," which would miss a key element of this work. Certainly the reader is able to force the poem into traditional lineation by "disciplining" the text, but that is nearly all the power the reader really has. Andrews's invitation to the reader to "Do the text" signals the kind of reader engagement we might expect from a rudimentary computer game, but the fact that the words' movement is governed by algorithm means that what the reader can "Do" to the text is quite limited. The limitations placed on reader agency in this way turn the tables on the practices of reading and interpretation; rather than a fixed text that in its stability limits the potential readings of a poem, in this case the poem's movement algorithm limits what a reader can do to create potentially readable versions of the poem.

If the poem is interested in the reader's limits, it is also interested in geographical boundaries. Andrews is often credited with being a Vancouver-based poet, but this poem is called "Seattle Drift," and it was written, as Andrews tells us in the code, "in the spirit of Seattle" during the three or so years that Andrews lived and wrote there. More specifically, "Seattle Drift" signals Andrews's collaboration with Joseph Keppler and the rest of the "Seattle crew" between 1997 and 2000, when Andrews lived in Seattle and when he produced this work and others like it (Flores 111, 113). Yet another reading is suggested by the drifting, overlapping, and obscuring movement of the words in this poem: movement that recalls the visual and phonic similarities between "Seattle" and "settle," an act that Andrews's transnational collaboration and his border- and genre-blurring poetics resist. As a digital text that drifts back and forth between Vancouver and Seattle, "Seattle Drift" problematizes the tendency to assign geographical boundaries to poetic "scenes."

Vancouver, as the site of such "scenes" of poetry as TISH and Kootenay, makes an especially fruitful location from which to begin exploring this line of argument. For example, Canadian poet Lionel Kearns, a long-time resident of Vancouver, is commonly associated with TISH, but Andrews's work on Kearns (critical and creative) stresses how problematic are attempts to align Kearns with TISH or with any school of poetry. More generally, any consideration of the Vancouver poetry "scene" will lead us to TISH's connection to certain American-based schools of poetry, such as Black Mountain or the New York School. We will also encounter the explicit internationality of the historic 1963 Vancouver Poetry conference, which encouraged transnational connection and collaboration. These and many other nodes of connection between Vancouver-based poetry projects and poetry in the US continue to exist and are facilitated even more by the communicative and collaborative potentials of networked computing. Because of this, we can also read the movement of "Seattle

Drift" as mapping or visually representing Andrews's Vancouver-based poetics, his thoughts about poetry that inevitably "drift" toward Seattle and other American centres. More specifically, the term "drift" suggests a movement by water, and both Vancouver and Seattle are coastal cities. Furthermore, if we superimpose the points of the compass on the poem, then we may say that the words, when they drift, tend to move south and east—Seattle, of course, is south of Vancouver, but it is also very slightly to the east. In all of these ways, then, the poem may be said to head toward Seattle. For a Canadian reader, approaching Andrews's work with any kind of national pride, "Seattle Drift" thus enacts a guilty desire that ought to be disciplined away. The poem, accordingly, does not simply resist histories and categories of Canadian poetry; it invites an act of subversion, of resistance or opposition to the mainstream.

Finally, the "scene" of Andrews's poem also draws on meanings of the term that suggest a material site, a sense that links "Seattle Drift" to the other experimental verse studied throughout this book. As the *OED* makes clear, the word "scene" has multiple associations with theatrical performance, since the word can refer to both the subdivisions of a script and the physically built site of performance. With usage in English dating back as early as 1481 (in a translation of Cicero, no less), the earliest meaning of the word "scene" is "the whole area set aside for the dramatic action, including both this background structure and the proscenium... where the actors stood; the stage" ("scene, *n.*"). The term also can be used to refer specifically to "the view presented to the audience at any time during the action of a performance by means of the scenery, lighting, etc." ("scene, *n.*"). This multiplicity of meanings suggests that what is important in a "scene" is not only how it is set but also how it is intended to be viewed by an audience. Andrews's use of this term therefore draws attention to the text's performance of what I might call its "poemness," announcing that it is a "poem" (however bad) as early as its first line. The theatrical associations of "scene" also suggest that the reader who obediently clicks the hyperlinks to carry out the action of the poem is, in true postanarchist fashion, an actor in this performance rather than merely a member of the audience.

The fact that "Seattle Drift" claims materiality for itself is especially important in the digital realm, where digital text is so frequently understood as ephemeral and immaterial. The physical "scene" of constructedness here recalls Duncan's image of the tapestry discussed in chapter one, a tapestry the poet encourages his readers to look behind to observe the inner workings it conceals. We may also note that the word "scene" has a long history of use in the phrase "behind the scenes," an association of particular relevance to any consideration of "Seattle Drift." The *OED* defines "behind the scenes" as the space both figuratively and literally "Behind the stage or the scenery of a theatre where the public is not usually admitted; out of sight of the audience" ("scene, *n.*"). Andrews creates just such a space, for he encourages his readers to look behind the scenes of "Seattle Drift" and to investigate his source code, which includes such personal notes as "This is the first DHTML piece I did" at its start, as well as a tender dedication inspired by "Seattle's own California girl Anne, who knows who she is"—in an aside. Besides these two statements Andrews includes a considerable amount of commentary with the source code, discussion that would not be available to readers who did not look behind the scenes.

Like an introduction, a footnote, or paratextual clues that guide the reading process (as in Moure's *Pillage Laud* discussed in chapter two), the code of "Seattle Drift" contains some explanatory notes, but refuses to direct interpretation. Andrews, for example, here explains the div tags that govern the movement of the poem, writing that "Each of the div tags holds one word of the poem" and then conceding, "OK it's a poem." Rather than enforcing a certain kind of reading, Andrews's reluctant "OK" in this aside suggests a concession to an external voice (reader, critic) who might insist, "Yes, this *is* a poem despite its first two lines." Nor is this reluctance just a pose; Andrews also comments in this section that he wrote the poem in response to questions he was asking himself regarding poetry and the digital medium, but then adds that the poem is designed to encourage discussion rather than make an argument. Comparing his own questions about the digital medium in poetry to the questions posed by abstract visual art about representation, Andrews states that

"Both prompt, rather than raise the questions directly." Here again, then, he places the onus on the readers who must ask and answer these questions on their own. While the programmer's hidden activity behind the scenes of "Seattle Drift" may recall the charges of control and limitation I laid against Goldsmith's *Soliloquy* in chapter three, these personal, conversational, and reluctant comments and suggestions hidden in the code reveal an authorial persona more invested in questions and collaboration than in answers. The author revealed in this behind-the-scenes space is tentative at best. In fact, the voice does not even know what to call the space from which it speaks: "And this neath text, what is it?" (np). Thus our look "behind the scenes" of "Seattle Drift" reveals a postanarchic space, a TAZ, where questions are prompted and readers are invited to engage while the authorship makes manifest both its presence and its incomplete constructedness.

### W. Mark Sutherland Puts the Cedar in Abecedarian

Part of the reason why the line between concrete poetry and "Seattle Drift" is so easily and frequently drawn by critics is that because it is a kinetic poem—what Andrews terms an "animism"—it can take the implicit movement of a static, print-based work and make that kinesis literal. "Seattle Drift" is concerned with this process, and accordingly it does not have any of the aural properties we see in some other (especially earlier) works of digital poetics. However, although W. Mark Sutherland's *Code X* does invite comparison to concrete poetry, this is a born-digital sound poetry machine that allows users to create their own sound poetry performances, and it is primarily concerned with the history of sound poetry, performance art, and installation art. As Paul Dutton writes of *Code X* in a brochure for Sutherland's *Scratch* exhibit, the work "fuses poetry, music, and visual art" to reveal the tenuous boundaries between these art forms (np). Despite the fact that, at its heart, *Code X* is a fairly simplistic digital game, it marks a point of convergence between many art forms and in so doing raises questions about how the digital medium might allow for greater audience intervention.

*Code X* made its first public appearance as a part of Sutherland's *Scratch* exhibit, where the program was installed on a computer and projected onto the wall of the gallery. Viewers of the exhibit were encouraged to interact with the program, choosing letters or writing words by typing on the keys, which caused the letter to appear on the projection in seemingly random spaces. Pressing a letter also started a ten-second recording of original sound poetry paired with that particular letter, which played on a loop as long as the letter continued to be pressed. In addition to this appearance, *Code X* was also produced as a CD-ROM by Toronto's Coach House Press. As Eichhorn notes, *Code X* appeared at a time when Coach House was working toward adapting its largely print-based publication history to an increasingly digital audience (520). *Code X*'s publication coincides with an initiative led by Damian Lopes to archive and digitize Coach House's front line; while some of these online texts were merely digitized versions of their print-book counterparts, others, such as *Code X*, were circulated as distinct born-digital works (Eichhorn 520). Unsurprisingly, the CD-ROM of *Code X* that was published by Coach House has long gone out of print; when contacted, Coach House did not have a single copy in its offices for me to view. Finally, as the compact disc became an increasingly impractical, unreliable, and uncommon way to disseminate digital works, Sutherland and Coach House "launched it [*Code X*] as an interactive website in 2009" (Eichhorn 520). Coach House's archived access to the work online is now a dead link, and the only way to see the work is either to download the program or play it through a browser on Sutherland's webpage.

Despite some obvious differences in the way the work is received, the version of *Code X* designed for personal and private use works in the same way as its installation counterpart. *Code X*, as the packaging for the original CD-ROM boasts, turns its "readers" into "collaborators on a transmedial sound poem and concrete poem by turning their computer keyboards into sound poetry producing machines." Each key places a typewriter-font collection of dispersed letters on the screen and cues an audio track of Sutherland's vocal performance of the letter. The visual appearance of the work, a black screen with white and red text in Courier typeface, bears no small resemblance to Andrews's work in "Seattle Drift" and other similar pieces. It also demonstrates a clear link to the features of early concrete and typewriter verse by such writers as Nichol and, especially, Steve McCafferey; the visual appearance of *Code X* recalls McCafferey's *Carnival* panels (1967–75). This allegiance to highly visual forms of poetry gets matched, in *Code X*, with an equally marked allegiance to the common vernaculars of sound poetry's major players, including Kurt Schwitters and The Four Horsemen.

In the same way that critics insisted on drawing the parallels between "Seattle Drift" and the concrete poetry that led to it, the very few studies of *Code X* done to date, none of which are academic studies, have focused on the literary and artistic influences on Sutherland's work. For example, in the above-mentioned brochure, Dutton devotes a lot of space to arguing that *Code X* "announces some of Sutherland's major influences: Dadaism,...Fluxus,...and such late-twentieth-century unaffiliated intermedia-ists as, for one, bpNichol" (np). What I find valuable about Dutton's discussion, however, is that he does more than set out to situate Sutherland's work in a history of cultural production: this list of influences provides Dutton with jumping-off points to talk about the features of Sutherland's work that he adapts from these other artists, and in this analysis Dutton identifies in Sutherland "an openness, a sense of play, and a determined earnestness in the establishment and practice of a vital, sensuously, and intellectually integrative approach to creative expression" (np). In my view, it is this "integrative approach" that makes *Code X* such an important contribution to Canadian digital poetics, especially insofar as Sutherland's technique integrates audience participation into any performance of his art. Much as Wershler does with *The Tapeworm Foundry* (described in chapter three), with *Code X* Sutherland invites readers not simply to engage with digital poetics but to create some art of their own.

With *Code X*, in other words, the readers become actors, players, or "performers" who make agential choices. The term "performers" is Sutherland's own; he uses it to describe the audience of his work in the information page that accompanies the web-based version of

*Code X*, thereby signalling both a similar approach to audience as Mac Low's (described in chapter one) and an understanding of the text as subsumed by, or at least as less important than, the audience to which it is addressed. Like Andrews, however, Sutherland somewhat overstates the degree of freedom his work gives to its audience. According to him, *Code X* is a sort of sandbox where its audience can play and, in playing, produce theoretically infinite permutations of the work's performance. But at the same time *Code X* is a fairly closed, limited system. Performances of *Code X* will, of course, look and sound different depending on who is interacting with it, what letters they choose, with what speed or pattern they type, what hardware they use to engage with the piece (in terms of both appearance and sound), how long they play, and whether or not the work is left to lapse into its "random" mode, an issue to which I return below. But as long as the performer types each letter of the alphabet at some point during a session, the result is the same: Sutherland's pre-written paragraph. As the information page tells us, "Code X is housed within a self-referential paragraph containing every letter of the alphabet." Moreover, while the order, overlap, and frequency of the sounds may vary, each letter typed will play the same "10 second phonetic improvisation" that Sutherland recorded. It is certainly true that "By typing words or selecting letters on the computer keyboard the performer can create visual poems and sound poems coding, decoding, mashing and jamming the *Code X*'s paragraph" (Sutherland, "Information," np). Regardless, the two fundamental elements of the work—the paragraph and the recorded sounds—never change.

Thus, while the role of the audience is agential, interactive, integrative, and free in many ways, only the process differs; the ultimate outcome remains fundamentally constant. In engaging with—or performing—*Code X*, we alter the text—the way it sounds, the way it looks—but only slightly. The voices and visuals produced by our interaction are predetermined, and though they look random when only a few letters are activated, they ultimately form a pre-written textual "whole." In fact, the "self-referential" paragraph that is ostensibly the work's conclusion speaks of the reading process of the digital text as leading to the end-goal of making adequate and substantial meaning from the text at hand (or cursor). It reads in part: "reading was a road a car a mnemonic mechanism driving towards form and meaning." Positioning form and meaning as the logical conclusions of the reading process, only revealed once the whole gamut of the alphabet is typed through, suggests that the reader, as consumer of a final product, is ultimately more important (or at least more exhaustive) than the reader as producer, or the process of producing enabled by the program itself.

Nonetheless, *Code X* resists the limitations of print-based literature and the book form in general, as signalled by the work's title. By breaking down the word "codex" into "code x," Sutherland exposes the digital potentials that were always already contained within the materiality of print-based works, and in so doing, he participates in a well-established tradition. As nearly every historian of digital poetics or media archaeologist argues, including Hayles, Emerson, Loss Pequeño Glazier, and Joseph Tabbi, born-digital poetics has a long and useful history in print literature. Its predecessors were such writers as Raymond Queneau and Nichol who manipulated the codex form to resist the closure, transparency, and immateriality that is the inherited mythology of the print book. The packaging and paratext of the physical CD-ROM distributed by Coach House plays even more on this title and its relationship to a history of print-based literary production. As Dutton explains, the manipulation of the word "codex" is only the first level of play in this title, and it indicates "more than just an anonymous code, a riddle to be solved" (np). Hidden in this title is also a positioning of this work both within and against a long history of poetry's complex and culturally determined relationship to its audience:

> The last three letters of "code" are in red, drawing our attention to the poetic intent: an ode—"a lyric poem," the *Canadian Oxford Dictionary* informs us, "usually in the form of an address, in varied or irregular metre." Not exactly what Sutherland has here, but close enough for intermedia. And further, we learn, an ode is "historically, a poem meant to be sung." (Dutton np)

While *Code X* bears very little resemblance in form or content to the ode, or to traditional lyric poetry more generally, what unites Sutherland's work with the lyric ode is a shared insistence on directly and clearly addressing their respective audiences.

Despite this important commonality, however, I must again stress the inadequacy of insisting on viewing such digital projects as *Code X* through or even as a necessary result of print culture. It should be with caution that we read Dutton's analysis of the relationship between *Code X*'s digital interactivity and the ode form. He identifies "a dual irony," in that "the text in question is Sutherland's own, rather than a legacy from antiquity, and the form is CD-ROM, a modern variant of the book, as attested to by its component parts being called 'pages'" (np). But it is highly problematic to argue that the CD-ROM—and by this Dutton means basically the digital text—is a mere "modern variant" of the book form. To argue this is to miss some of the fundamental questions *Code X* raises about new media practices in artistic and cultural production. The very name, after all, foregrounds the relationship between a text and its material context. "Codex" derives, the *OED* reminds us, from the Latin *cōdex*, which is itself a later Latin spelling of *caudex*, meaning the trunk of a tree, but meaning also a wooden tablet, a book, or a code of laws ("codex, *n.*"). Here it may be appropriate to recall Hayles's first proposition about the necessarily disruptive function of code.

Because Dutton views the digital as no more than a representation or an extension of print culture, unfortunately, he makes the dangerous misstep of viewing the born-digital work as immaterial, ephemeral, and intangible: he writes of *Code X* that "the work occurs not in the tangible world of materiality, but the virtual one of digital representation. The mode of interaction is not arrived at through a confrontation of conventional proprieties, but by the now familiar, even ubiquitous, and somehow oddly comforting vehicle of the computer keyboard and mouse" (np). Clearly, these two sentences betray each other. Of course *Code X* is very tangible. In its various forms and permutations that rely so heavily on numerous pieces of technological hardware, it expresses its reliance on materiality more than most print-based works do. In the second sentence of the passage quoted above, Dutton betrays the so-called immateriality of the virtual "world" from which *Code X* emerges. The material, physical hardware of the keyboard (and to a lesser extent the mouse or touchpad) is integral not only to the work itself, but also to the performer's active engagement in the work's production. Without the physical manipulation of the text achieved by the reader's pressing keys on the keyboard, *Code X* would only function in its random mode and would be missing the major integrative element. Dutton again contradicts his insistence on the immateriality of *Code X*'s virtual world in his emphasis elsewhere in the essay on the tools through which we experience it: it is "With these tools" that the performer "enters a vocoverbovisual CD-ROM environment, where he [*sic*] may play an intricate, non-competitive, temporally liberated (because theoretically perpetual), phonic, patterned, linguistic game—or simply witness the game being played by the machine in exponentially varied, non-repetitive random mode" (np). Let us not forget, either, the physical, bodily demands of engaging with digital media, which require interaction much more than a codex does. After all, the word "digital"—as we are apt to forget—has its etymological roots in the body, coming from the classical Latin *digitālis*, meaning "the measuring a finger's breadth" and later, in post-classical Latin, more generally meaning "of or relating to the finger" ("digital, *n.* and *adj.*, Etymology").

It is easy to see the virtual as immaterial, as cloud-based, but of course it never is; all screens are pixels, all hardware a complex interplay of metals and polymers, and so on. Nevertheless, there are economic and political forces at work behind the disassociation of the digital program from the hardware designed to run such a program, forces which tend to obscure this materiality. As Kittler argues, "because software does not exist as a machine-independent faculty, software as a commercial or American medium insists on its status as property all the more" (151). Insisting on the separation between the physical hardware of computing and the software we use in these computational processes, and to which we allow the status of property, allows for the copyright and commodification of the programming language as separate and independent from the hardware on which we use it. In fact, however, as Kittler convincingly argues, "there are good grounds to assume the indispensability and, consequently, the priority of hardware in general" (152). Ultimately, as the title of his essay announces, "There Is No Software"—only hardware.

Just as we saw with Nichol in *First Screening*, and again with Andrews in "Seattle Drift," a consideration of the material technology—of the hardware—that each performer uses to engage with *Code X* is integral to a consideration of the various reading practices provoked by the work. Obviously there is a marked difference between *Code X*'s appearance in the *Scratch* exhibit and the way that I use it with my personal computer at home. But there is also a significant difference in my playing of the piece on my PC desktop with a sizable monitor over high-quality computer speakers and my playing of the same piece (even pressing the same letters in the same order) over my much smaller MacBook Air 11.5" through earbuds.

When we emphasize the importance of the hardware, however, we implicitly raise questions about the importance of the reader. Perhaps that, too, can be overstated: a possibility that must be considered, given the randomized mode that *Code X* will revert to if left inactive. As the information page on the web-based version explains, "If the computer keyboard is untouched for 30 seconds *Code X* will begin to operate in random automated mode. *Code X* will replicate interactivity producing sound and visual poems until the keyboard is touched and the interactive program is re-engaged" (np). The fact that the poem reverts to an automated mode suggests, on one level, that perhaps the individual performer is not as central to this work as I have argued. If the activity of the performer can be and *is* performed by an automated algorithmic function that continues indefinitely and does not repeat itself, then our engagement with the work as performers is still integrative, but it is not really necessary. And yet the random mode can never "replicate interactivity" with complete success: the automated function reveals letters too slowly—and this cannot be changed because the work is presented in uneditable Flash—and thus letters fade into the black background before the full paragraph can be revealed. Unlike the individual performer, then, the random automated function of *Code X* will never reveal that

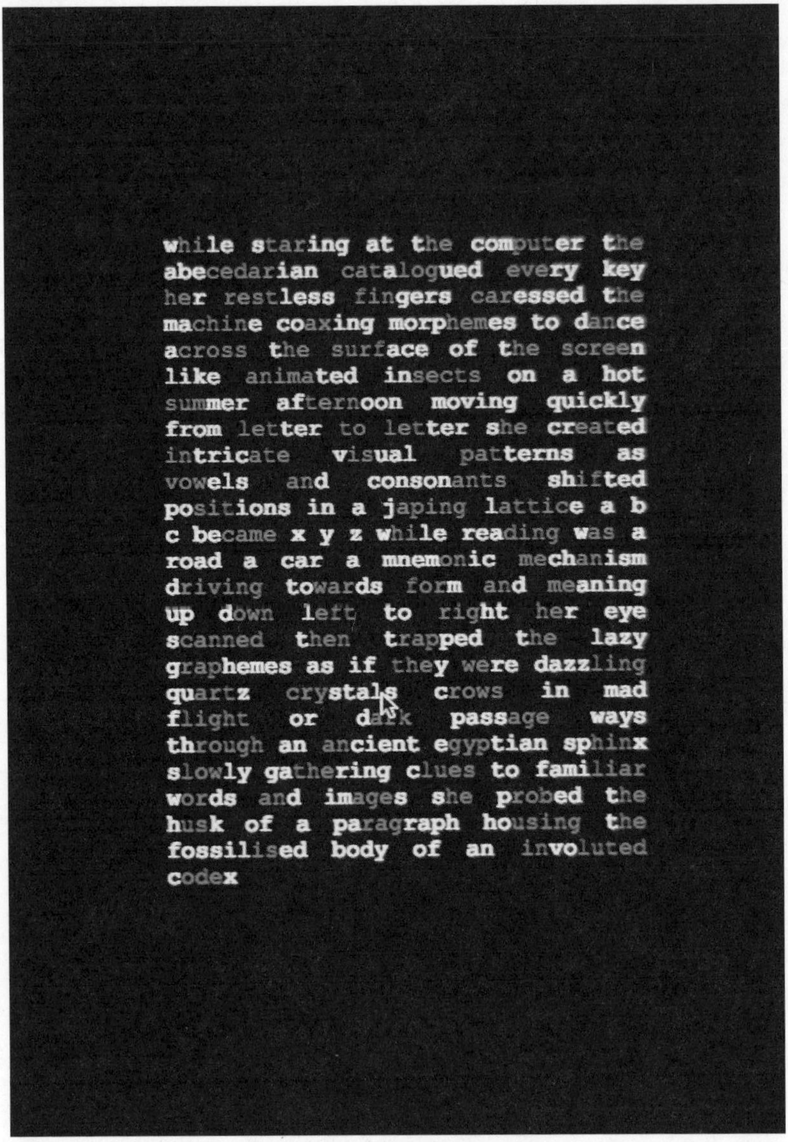


FIGURE 18. W. Mark Sutherland, final paragraph from *Code X*.

paragraph in full; this paragraph, can only be achieved by an individual knowingly typing each letter of the alphabet at least once in a short enough time span (see Fig. 18).

The terminus of the full paragraph and the automated function might be taken to suggest a "truth" or a "fact" of the text that is initially hidden from the viewer, an endpoint that results from an alphabetically exhaustive use of the work that the reader can reveal but cannot intervene in. However, the case is not that simple, due in large part to the many red words revealed within other words. (I use boldface here and in the discussion that follows to signal which letters are in red in the original text.) Just as Dutton points out, the word "ode" is revealed as red text in "c**ode**" with the letter *C* remaining in white. Indeed, almost every word of the final paragraph uses the differentiation of red and white to reveal words within words, which gesture toward the multiple and individual-specific readings that are contained within (and resist the limits of) the arbitrary whole of this final paragraph.

Furthermore, the performer is not only featured in the final paragraph but is even, through these words-within-words, addressed—although referred to in the third person. By way of the "hi" salutation that is hidden within the first word "w**hi**le," the performer is invited into a multiplicitous and radically free postanarchist reading practice. Here the reader is addressed and invited as we might be in a colloquial conversation, a strategy that significantly alters the poetic address to the reader that we might see, for instance, in an ode. Then the reader is invited to see hidden words within the words of the paragraph: the "tar" in "s**tar**ing"; the "he" in "t**he**"; the "put" in "com**put**er"; and, my personal favourite, the "cedar" in "abe**cedar**ian." Sutherland's opening, "w**hi**le s**tar**ing at t**he** com**put**er t**he** abe**cedar**ian **cat**a**log**ued **eve**ry key," is an obviously self-referential statement that describes his composition of the paragraph itself, which contains every letter of the alphabet and is a kind of catalogue of all potential buttons to be pressed, sounds to be initiated, and letters to be arranged on the screen. This description is also self-referential in its description of Sutherland's labour as the producer of the text, "staring at the computer" while coding the word, although this reading is simultaneously discouraged by the feminine pronouns Sutherland uses throughout. Finally, this opening clause is self-referential for the performer who reveals the final paragraph, produces the alphabetic work, and performs the act of cataloguing by pressing the keys herself.

At the same time as they invite the performer's participation, the red words-within-words also ensure that the performer's reading practice is characterized by a postanarchic freedom. The final paragraph, when complete, makes cohesive semantic sense, despite the occasional awkward syntax; by contrast, the red words contained within other words do not unite to form semantic sense in any way. That same opening sentence, only in red, would read "**hi tar he put he cedar cat log eve.**" Despite the promise of arriving finally at "form and meaning" that the paragraph offers, these words-within-words suggest instead the arbitrariness and inadequacy of the sense at which we might arrive. Thus, the final paragraph positions the creative performer at the crossroads of sense and nonsense, in a TAZ where any permutation of these letters can and should be used, but any permutation would result in the same outcome: the dissolution of those larger structures—sentences and paragraphs, most obviously—that typically govern meaning-making and reading processes.

Rather than cohesion and closed narrative, then, the final paragraph ultimately presents itself as "the husk of a paragraph" that reveals not narrative but rather "the fossilised body of an involuted codex." This final image, of the codex form curled in on itself, warped at the edges, fossilized from disuse and disinterest, presents the born-digital, integrative work as a radical new format. The "**vo**" that is hidden within "in**vo**luted" leaves us with a new form in obsolesced, obscure language: "vo" can be both a noun, an abbreviation of "volume," referencing parts of print texts in a longer series ("vo., *n.*"), and an adverb, an abbreviation of "voce" ("vo, *adv.*"), as in publishing "under the word or heading," a word with an obvious etymological root in the Latin *vōce*, the ablative of *vox* or voice ("voce, *n.*[2]"). "In**vo**luted" thus reveals its debt to the codex even as it moves beyond it; it reveals the incoherence and piecemeal nature of the semantic "whole" and the uneasy relationship between aural and written language. It is the TAZ at which all these points converge.

### Brian Kim Stefans Alphabetizes Dreams

In his brief preface to "The Dreamlife of Letters," Brian Kim Stefans explains that the poem, first published on his website, www.arras.net, in 2000, began as an analog poem composed by alphabetizing the words written by Rachel Blau DuPlessis in response to a question about gender and literature asked in an e-mail roundtable (np). Stefans rearranged the words of DuPlessis's text into alphabetical order, but, as he reports, he was not pleased with the first version of the poem that resulted. In his view, it did the work of the early concrete poets but added nothing to the discussions already undertaken by the genre's pioneers: Gomringer, the de Campos brothers, and so on. As a consequence, he decided to enhance the piece with graphic design, colour, and animation, ultimately producing the Flash-based poem we find in the *ELC*, volume one. Now one of the most popular and frequently studied works of early digital poetry, "Dreamlife" is best understood, I believe, in relation to other digital works, as well as the conceptual and avant-garde poetry traditions from which it clearly emerges. That is, I share other critics' interest in the radical, kinetic nature of "Dreamlife" as an avant-garde poem that allows for reader participation and reader freedom, but I do not want to neglect the importance of reading it in the context of a world of networked computing that has, as many digital humanities scholars have argued, all but forfeited its digital potential. One such scholar is Brian Lennon, who, looking back in 2000 on what had happened since the birth of the web in 1993, argues forcefully that "the democratizing, decentralizing World Wide Web...has in a mere six years been appropriated, consolidated, and 'videated' as a forum for commerce and advertising" (63). A lot more has happened to the vast potentials and expanses of Lennon's "World Wide Web" in the years since Lennon's comment was published, but one thing is sure: the process of appropriation, consolidation, and "videation" (a term Lennon borrows from Perloff's *Radical Artifice*) has only sped up and become more pervasive.

It should not surprise us that Lennon's concerns are also primary in "Dreamlife," a derivative analog poem *cum* Web art that was published at the same cultural and technological moment as Lennon's essay. As Lennon points out, the early leaders in scholarship of digital humanities and electronic literary studies, Bolter, Michael Joyce, and Stuart Moulthrop, had "seen from the start that electronic *hypertextuality*, or the computerized proliferation of symbolic writing, was only a step on the way to general electronic *hypermediation* dominated by iconic visual, rather than symbolic textual, forms" (64, emphasis Lennon's). "Dreamlife" was not only published the same year as Lennon's essay, but it is also the approximate contemporary of Andrews's "Seattle Drift" and Sutherland's *Code X*. As such, it speaks to the co-opting and videation of digital communities that concern Lennon and also speaks to the radical potentials of digital media to question issues of authorship, audience, and materiality that concern Andrews and Sutherland.

Unlike most other early born-digital or transmedial poetic projects, including the vast majority of those collected in the *ELC*, volume one, "The Dreamlife of Letters" is non-interactive, non-generative, non-hyperlinked, and distributed in the now unfavoured format of Macromedia Flash, the same format as *Code X*. Even so, this does not mean that "Dreamlife" fails to engage or empower the reader. I disagree, then, with Alexandra Saemmer, who files this kinetic poem under the label "aesthetics of surface," one of four labels she offers for the purpose of categorizing digital texts. In an "aesthetics of surface," the author of a born-digital work "simply ignores" the "instability" of digital dissemination "and creates at once, as if the digital framework was immutable" (478). Nevertheless, because of the Flash format, Saemmer notes differences in the ways that readers can receive or attempt to read "Dreamlife." It is probably a safe assumption that most readers will access "Dreamlife" either through Arras or the ELC, but noting that does not account for the virtually limitless hardware options that readers have available to them. As with every digital project, variations in screen size and resolution, device (computer, tablet, cell phone, television), and environment alter the manner in which a reader accesses, reads, and ultimately makes sense of the text. For example, just as Saemmer notes, the reader encounters blurring and pixelation (what she terms "sporulation") in one part of "Dreamlife" in which many copies of the word "all" appear on the screen at once, where they blur into each other, producing new and indeterminate figures and meanings (482). However, while Saemmer acknowledges that this effect renders a single, authoritative reading impossible to achieve, she neglects the implications of this, arguing only that "The figures I try to identify and describe may be considered as a telltale sign of the *poetic fact* in electronic texts" (481, emphasis Saemmer's). I would point out that this "sporulation" only appears when the poem is viewed on older devices where the animation does not run quite as quickly or smoothly as it may on a newer device. For Saemmer, these inconsistencies do not account for reader freedom but contribute rather to the videation of the born-digital text (482). Yet postanarchist literary theory provides a framework by which we may understand and appreciate the radical reader-centric multiplicities that such a "poetic fact" and such device-driven variances offer.

Dworkin is similarly critical of "Dreamlife," pointing to its debt to a long tradition of highly formalized print-based visual poetry, as well as to the "videated" nature of the text, to argue that "Dreamlife"'s interest lies less in pushing new technological boundaries than it does in looking back:

> Although "Dreamlife" is presented in Macromedia Flash, its linear and noninteractive sequences bear a closer resemblance to cinema and filmstrip animation than to most Web art, and the work displays an overall typographic design palette referencing the mid-century aesthetic of concrete poetry. Its once cutting-edge technology, in short, gestures away from both the very future it defines and the moment its imminent obsolescence will soon mark. ("Imaginary Solution" 53)

The question, in light of Saemmer's and Dworkin's arguments, then becomes: if we are to understand "Dreamlife" and all of its inconsistencies as amounting to no more than a glorified video, then what are we to make of the way it changes from reader to reader?

For Saemmer, the inconsistency (even indecipherability) of "Dreamlife" is merely a result of the reader's inability to access the intentions of the author; this is a claim that would seem strange in any scholarship of print-based texts, and yet Saemmer pines for access to Stefans's original "source file," some manuscript that might affirm how Stefans *wanted* us to read this poem, its original or proper appearance: "the reader is given no opportunity to grasp the meaning the author wants to convey. He is not even able to guess it, for there is no theoretical paratext to warn him about the fact that certain surface events may become invisible" (482). In Saemmer's view, the potential inconsistencies of a digital text from device to device, reader to reader, are not a potential for radically different readings or a revelation of a reader-centric approach to digital literatures, but rather an error or inadequacy on Stefans's part, a failure to instruct his readers on how to read his text. Saemmer ends by arguing that "Stefans should have chosen a video device for this poem in order to preserve the surface events from the fatal 'over-flows' of the device; or he should have indicated the exact electronic framework...to keep his work in conditions approaching those experienced during the creative process, and come within the scope of mimetic aesthetic" (482). In the "mimetic aesthetic," another category she offers for born-digital texts, authors "insist on the 'right' context for the reception of their work" (479). What Saemmer points to here is an important facet of the archival and preservation work required to maintain the software (and in many excellent labs, the hardware, too) required for our study of electronic literature going forward, but her fixation on the obsolescing technology in "Dreamlife" demonstrates, above all, a refusal to value diffuse authorial power.

In my view, "Dreamlife" is a conceptual project that requires a critical interrogation of the role of authorship and authorial intention in the work. If we situate this poem in the context of conceptual poetry as described in chapter three, then we must also work to develop postanarchism as a theory that can be applied to digital reading and digital scholarship, a theory that recognizes digital *and* conceptual authors as first readers, just as we might say of the authors of print-based texts. This means, also, that such authors are no more obligated to instruct readers in the *proper* ways to read their texts than print-based authors would be. As Jacquelyn Ardam writes, the major scholars of conceptual poetry—that is, "Perloff, Goldsmith, and Dworkin"—all "define conceptual writing from the perspective of its creators, via authorial intentions, techniques, and methods, which are more often than not procedural, which is to say, rule- or constraint-based" (134). As I argue in the previous chapter, we need a theory of conceptualism that recognizes that the "concept" of the text does not reside in the head of the author but must be decoded properly by the reader; Ardam makes a similar argument for such born-digital works as "Dreamlife." Questions of readership and reading occupy Ardam throughout "ABCs," where she protests how "These unnerving but important questions," which "seem to be central to this new movement,...have more often than not been overshadowed by questions of intentionality, technique, and procedural rationale" (135). This overshadowing continues to be a concern, despite Kenneth Goldsmith's work to develop a "thinkership" (as opposed to a "readership") of conceptual poetry ("Conceptual Poetics" np). Following Ardam and Place, then, I argue that we must ask not "How are we supposed to read 'Dreamlife'?" but rather, "What does it mean to be a reader of 'Dreamlife'?" The kinetic and digital elements of "Dreamlife" do influence and alter the reading process, even if the poem is not interactive or integrative in the way that Andrews's and Sutherland's works are. In attending to this fact, we may see room for postanarchist, free readership of the digital text even when it does not employ the radical interactive potentials of new media.

One way to respond to the questions I ask above is to read "Dreamlife" in terms of its engagement with a tradition of print-based experimentalism, an approach similar to my earlier study of Andrews's work in relation to concrete poetry and Sutherland's in relation to sound poetry. The ways in which Stefans works through and beyond the issues of the print-based experimental text in "Dreamlife" have been a major feature of the (admittedly limited) scholarship on the poem, and Stefans himself, as we have seen, clearly intended "Dreamlife" to update and extend the concerns of concrete poetics. More specifically, he notes that aesthetic concerns separated the first draft analog form of the poem from the final animation. The former "was in a sort of antique 'concrete' mode" that "resembled a much older aesthetic" (np); the aesthetic of the final Flash poem is, of course, markedly different from that of concretism. First, and most obviously, its movements are literal rather than figurative, and its kinesis is viewable rather than imagined or implied. Second, as Kim Knight points out, "The animation, which is consciously non-interactive, is in some ways a more writer-directed experience than reading concrete poetry in print" (np). Unlike the brief constellation pieces of Gomringer and the de Campos brothers (whom Stefans explicitly identifies as influences), "Stefans's piece cannot be taken in at-a-glance [*sic*]. The user must wait patiently while the poem runs its course" (np).

Significantly, it is right after his discussion of concretism that Stefans turns to consider the role of the reader in this work, albeit reluctantly:

> I don't wish to explain much more about the piece here, except to say that it is not interactive. I decided that it was much more like a short film than an interactive piece, and there didn't seem any natural place to let the viewer in that way...It takes about 11 minutes to run once loaded. You should try to shut your screensaver off, or it may take over the screen sometime into the piece. (np)

Because the poem is available now most commonly through online viewing in a browser—and also because of the widespread availability of much quicker internet than when Stefans first distributed the piece—his note here on "loading" (and his notes elsewhere about "downloading") seem archaic. So too does the idea that readers must "try" to turn their screensavers off. I would be hard-pressed today (and I write this in 2017) to find readers who would be interested in engaging with any digital poem that required them to "try" to turn off a screensaver; "screensaver" use in general is rapidly declining. In light of this, these comments alone draw our attention to the rapid pace of technological change, change that has in recent years produced greater freedom for the reader (freedom from screensavers' intrusions, for instance) and greater variance in the ways readers will encounter the text. This variance is not comparable to the variance that results from the fact that different people read print-based books at different paces and in different spaces or environments. Rather, it reflects the fact that reader interactivity (of the type we see in Andrews and Sutherland) is so pervasive in the realm of digital literature that Stefans feels the need to address the lack of interactivity in his piece. This perception is reinforced by the paratext provided by the *ELC*, which lists "Dreamlife" in its collection with the label keyword "non-interactive."

Perhaps "Dreamlife" is not purposefully interactive, and certainly it is not interactive in the way the two previously discussed born-digital pieces are. Nevertheless, a postanarchist reading challenges us not to accept that "non-interactive" label unquestioningly and may well lead us to conclude that "Dreamlife" is indeed interactive. This is the conclusion arrived at by Mirona Magearu, who labels the piece "transmedial" (348). The concept of transmediality serves the study of electronic literature well, by allowing scholars to distinguish between born-digital works, analog or print-based works, and works like "Dreamlife" (or Moure's *Pillage Laud*, discussed in chapter two) that occupy a liminal space between the two. In applying this concept to "Dreamlife," Magearu notes as others do the limited reader interactivity, but even so she considers the work a transmedial "'Flash translation' or an avatar of DuPlessis's text to which it responds and with which is in dialogue" (348). In support of her classification she also points to the fact that Stefans himself undermines his earlier claim that "Dreamlife" is "not-interactive" when, in a later text, *Fashionable Noise*, he argues that in electronic literature, "unlike with a movie (or at least one in the theatres), you are invited to go back and look at each section as a discrete unit, and in fact when you view the piece a second time—after it has been fully downloaded—the index is one of your options along with 'run the poem'" (33). Since everything he says here applies to "Dreamlife," we may conclude that even Stefans has come to understand the work as one in which reader interaction is a reality that deserves discussion.

Other features of the poem are also important to this issue, although they have not received critical attention up till now. I note, for instance, that, when selected, the poem emerges from the browser as a pop-up; readers are able (browser permitting) to alter the pop-up's shape (changing the rectangle's ratio though never changing the fact that it is a rectangle), change its size, zoom in and out, cover it up with another browser, add music, or enact many other possibilities that would literally alter how they see/read the text. Again, these variations are markedly different from the range of possibilities open to a reader who might, perhaps, listen to music while reading a print book. Those variations are limited by generic norms as well as by the possibilities of the medium. Print books are literally silent; videos and other animations from the last century are almost always accompanied by sound. This can also be said for most online graphics, games, and other videated media.

In making this argument I do not mean to ignore the ways in which the animation of "Dreamlife" from print to Flash does limit the way the reader interacts with it. Here too I agree with Magearu, who considers that, though transmedial, "Dreamlife" "displays minimal interactive qualities" (352). On my reading, however, the significance of this minimal interaction can only be appreciated when we consider the particular kinds of limits placed on the reader. More specifically, I consider "Dreamlife" to produce a liminal space in which the agency of the reader is affirmed through active interaction with the text at the same time that the subjectivity of the reader dissolves within and throughout the text. This is most evident in the time that the poem affords its viewers to read and interpret the words. As Magearu points out, "Unlike the onscreen performance in which letters and words are in constant movement and formation, the print version of the poem displays them in a space in which they can be both read and watched. In this way, the space invites readers to pause at their own speed and reflect on the meaning of the words and on their spatial arrangement" (350). The onscreen performance does not allow this space to reflect. The Flash poem does offer some words a good deal of time on screen: "Gender," for example, repeats and moves along the screen for so long (with bouncing "g"s to add to the effect) that the reader might even start to question whether or not it was a word at all. But many of the words that zoom past us on screen or are manipulated move and change so quickly that they are difficult to focus on. These words are, typically, words from the DuPlessis original that denote identity or identity politics. These include "gender" several times and in several permutations, various pronouns ("you," "I," "me"), the repetition of "I'd" with and without the apostrophe, alongside a reference to Freud, and other theoretical terms including "hyperidentification" and "oedipalized." Each of these words is moved, (re)mixed, and destabilized by the works' animation. The resulting lack of focus or stability suggests a subjectivity in fracture. Ultimately, the generally rapid movement of the letters on the screen and the swift succession of words, an order that remains just outside of the reader's control, attest to the ways in which this digital piece draws readers in only to encourage the dissolution of their subjectivity through viewing.

Insofar as "Dreamlife" encourages dissolution or dis-integration of subjectivity, it is, as Mageary describes, the perfect place for such a dissolution: "The trans-medial space is an ephemeral in-between space, which results out of transactions from source-code space to production space.... This means that the trans-medial space exists and emerges spontaneously" (353). Put this way, the transmedial is revealed as a kind of TAZ. It is thus especially significant, if perhaps contradictory, that Stefans chose the abecedarian form, a form that is precisely *not* spontaneous, transient, or ephemeral. As Ardam observes, the alphabet is a favourite organizing feature of experimental and conceptual poets (everyone from Silliman to Pound has had their way with it), particularly because "The alphabet is not developmental; it is teleological, but it doesn't evolve" (140). Conceptualism's treatment of the alphabet and the abecedarian form has been traditionally irreverent (an oxymoron, maybe, but still appropriate), and Stefans's is no different. This is clearly demonstrated by the poem's "index," which boasts alphabetized but not letter-specific stanzas (though perhaps "stanza" is no longer the appropriate word) and the cheeky option to "run the whole damn thing." Its attack on normalization and organization in this case may be easy and obvious, but it speaks to a larger dissolution of categories and selves that is integral to the way the poem gets read and distributed.

### Andy Campbell, Mez Breeze, and the Constrict(l)ure of Code

To end these case studies, I look at Andy Campbell and Mez Breeze's *The Dead Tower* (2012). Mez, an Australian digital writer, and Campbell, a British digital media artist and the head of Dreaming Methods, stand at the forefront of digital narrative and new media literary games; *The Dead Tower*, one of their first collaborative projects, presents the merging of two important subgenres of electronic literature: codework and games. For this reason, *The Dead Tower* offers exceptional insight into digital literatures' potential to encourage reader interaction in ways radically different from what is available to print-based texts. In *The Dead Tower*, the user is dropped into a dark narrative and gaming world where the wreckage of a bus crash is littered throughout an uneven, rocky landscape. Using the cursor to look around, the direction keys to move, and the spacebar to jump, the user must figure out how to navigate this space with the presumable end-goal of making it to and then up the text-covered tower that gives the work its name. Also scattered throughout the landscape is bright white text written in Mez's trademark codework poetic language, mezangelle, which provides hints about navigation and recounts, only partially and cryptically, the narrative of the bus crash whose wreckage is all around the user navigating the space.

Because this writing is bright white against the dark background of the landscape, we might expect the reader's eyes to be drawn directly to it. Instead, the language of human speech and programmable code tends to merge, sometimes illegibly, with the rocks and cliffs of the landscape. Mez writes in mezangelle often, and outside of this gaming environment she uses this remixed language of speech and code that she has developed to offer readers unexecutable code that is illegible in the two reading forms of digital writing: it is illegible as human language, but also unreadable as computer code. This illegibility, however, when encountered in the context of mezangelle's propensity for linking and connection, increasingly reveals potential meanings, encourages mis- and cross-reading, and invites its readers into radically free interpretive relationships with all of Mez's texts. Thus, throughout the digital space of *The Dead Tower* we encounter an e-literary form that encourages system-jamming and noise poetics that interfere with communicative discourses to reveal the fissures therein. Following such electronic literature theorists as Mark Marino and Rita Raley, I turn to postanarchist literary theory to illuminate mezangelle's call to understand literary language beyond its signifying function. Rather than uniting the disparate functions of poetic language and computer code, I argue, mezangelle reveals the fissures and inadequacies of both languages and renders both unusable in their usual functions. Accordingly, Mez's poetic project is not unlike the noise interference of Howe and Moure that I discuss in chapter two.

Furthermore, *The Dead Tower* does not simply present mezangelle to its readers; instead Mez and Campbell place readers in a video-game-like environment permeated by mezangelle, immersing them in the disorientation of this manipulation of language. *The Dead Tower* is purposely misleading or confusing to its users, offering a reading space that deliberately collapses traditional reading and gaming practices. These learned traditions are symbolically present in the environment through a variety of images, such as an emptied, crashed school bus heavily overlaid with mezangelle or the ominous titular tower that presides over this space. The environment's mezangelle appears as bright white text in the dark world of blacks, greys, and reds; the language's brightness (l)ures the reader into traditional reading practices, but then no useful narrative meaning can be taken from it. Instead, *The Dead Tower* offers no end-goal for its users, who thus must make their own paths and their own meanings as they navigate it.

Mezangelle is a language developed by Mez in order to unite the unique experimental aspects of poetic language and of programming language into one language. To some critics, it is a "mixed" or "hybrid" language, but in the discussion to follow I argue for preferring Illya Szilak's description of it as "digital creole." Probably the most famous example of Mez's codework is *_cross.ova.ing ][4rm.blog.2.log][_*, a work the author describes as "a 'netwurk [*sic*] repository' that's been in operation since 2003" (Author description np). In *cross.ova.ing* Breeze presents her reader with a language that is part code, part poetry, and ultimately neither. As an example, poem seven of the series presents a poetic style indebted to imagism, concretism, and minimalism while at the same time relying on the basic structures of web-based coding languages. Because it is short, I can reproduce it here in full:

> 7. .ge[a{s}.phasi(a)]sha.
>
> 07:11pm 15/01/2008
>
> ..geisha.aphasia.
> ...paper.scissors.glock.
> ....geas, pls.
> .....
> ...
> ..
> . (np)

While the main effect of the piece is translated in its transposition into this book, part of the work is lost not just by taking it out of the larger series, but also by reproducing it in stylized print. That is, part of the effect of the poems in *cross.ova.ing* lies in the series' presentation as a plain text document with none of the font options or style additions to text that may be afforded by rich text format. Leaving the poems in plain text foregrounds the fact that the code therein is not executable: the text is prepped for execution, but a quick look at this code by anyone with a basic understanding of programming language confirms that it will not run.

Despite the gaming environment that mezangelle would become a part of in *The Dead Tower*, less than a decade after Mez began compiling *cross.ova.ing*, her description of *cross.ova.ing* stresses its no-frills presentation:

> this language evolved/s from multifarious computer code>social_networked> imageboard>gamer>augmented reality flavoured language/x/changes. 2 _mezangelle_ means 2 take words>wordstrings>sentences + alter them in such a way as 2 /x/tend + /n/hance meaning beyond the predicted +/or /x/pected. _mezangelling_ @tempts 2 /x/pand traditional text parameters thru layered/alternative/code based meanings /m/bedded in2 meta-phonetic renderings of language. _cross.ova.ing ][4rm.blog.2.log][ /m/ploys a base standard of code>txt in order 2 evoke imaginative renderings rather than motion-based>flashy graphics. (np)

The poem "/m/ploys a base standard of code>txt," Mez asserts, and does so to bring these two languages into conversation, into "/x/changes," altering both to create radical new forms of meaning-making.

Attempts to make meaning from mezangelle, a poetic language of unexecutable code, presents the reader with linguistic constructs that are illegible on two levels: first, as human language with semantic meaning, and second, as programming code readable by machines. This is not to say, however, that mezangelle does not encode messages or communicate meanings. Indeed, the very fact that Mez wants "2 evoke imaginative renderings" indicates a desire to communicate to her readers through an extensive and expansive reading process.

On a fundamental level, mezangelle challenges the way we use language to make semantic and logical sense. As Raley argues, the very fact that mezangelle is, at its most basic level, "communicative" reveals its desire to unearth the illegibilities of the language we already have and use every day: "Mez's use of her invented language directly suggests and reflects the material and quotidian linguistic changes produced by the mingling of the elements of natural and programming codes" (np). I also note the different modes of engagement implied by the different codes Mez mixes, which Stephanie Strickland, a pioneer of electronic literature in theory and practice, usefully identifies when she observes that Mez's writing "leads us to confront the legible with strategies ordinarily reserved for the viewable" (np). As most of our interaction with text today is mediated by technology and thus undergirded by programming language, the explicit, illegible, and unexecutable merger of what Raley terms "natural and programming codes" reveals their inextricability in our lives and not simply in the context of the experimental poetic work.

Of course, some readers who do not have much experience reading code might find mezangelle difficult and alienating at first. But the difficulty has its purpose and its rewards. As critics and users tend to agree, Mez's blended poetic language reveals potential meanings through its networking and connection, encourages mis- and cross-reading, and, ultimately, invites readers into radically free interpretative relationships with the text. Raley insists that mezangelle does "invite reading," even as she acknowledges its challenges: "Mez's techniques invite reading as complex combinatorial anagrams, other instances of excess linguistic disassembly and reassembly...the language flies off in many directions, and the invitation is to read beyond and even against the lateral, particularly given the frequent use of puns and homophones" (np). The political import of this opened reading practice lies in what Raley refers to as Mez's "aesthetic of interference rather than transmission" (np); it is because of this "interference" that mezangelle—and especially the glowing examples of it that punctuate the bleak environment of *The Dead Tower*—brings to the fore the ways that text-based communication through networked computing so often relies on a transparency of its form. Mez's "aesthetic of interference" also recalls the poetic tactics of Howe and Moure, as discussed in chapter two: Mez uses mezangelle to jam the system, to interfere as noise with communicative discourse and in so doing to reveal the fissures therein.

There are two systems that Mez jams with mezangelle, not just one, a point that Raley makes when she observes that, in her demonstration of "the political potentiality of codework, Mez stresses that her practice... disrupts the apparently seamless surface of mediatized mass communication" (np). Here Raley situates Mez's practice in the subgenre of "codework," a concept that is central to establishing the "political potentiality" of the unexecutability of the code elements of mezangelle. Codework is most clearly defined by John Cayley in "The Code is not the Text (unless it is the Text)"—the essay to which Raley is largely responding in her essay quoted above. Cayley labels as codework any "literature which uses, addresses, and incorporates code: as underlying language-animating or language-generating programming, as a special type of language in itself, or as an intrinsic part of the new surface language or 'interface text'...of writing in networked and programmable media" (np). But, as Marino points out, Cayley's critique of mezangelle is hampered by his emphasis on the functional aspect of code: "Cayley's chief complaint is that the analyzed 'code' in many of the celebrated codeworks exists merely on the surface of the work, [the] output....Because the computer code produced by Mez is not executable, she is," in Cayley's view, "dealing with only one aspect of code" (np). Marino grants that, if we follow Cayley in understanding unexecutable code like mezangelle as purely aesthetic, then we must also admit that these "surface depictions of coding elements are but partial representations, presenting a fraction of code's signifying force" (np). But instead of this narrow and limiting approach, Marino argues persuasively that we should, instead, "no longer speak of the code as a text in metaphorical terms, but...begin to analyze and explicate code as a text, as a sign system with its own rhetoric, as verbal communication that possesses significance in excess of its functional utility" (np). What I would further point out is that this approach to reading code that Marino advocates is consistent with postanarchist literary theory's call to understand literary language beyond its signifying function. In essence, therefore, mezangelle does for both poetic language *and* programming language what the other texts in this study do for poetic language only.

So far I have treated separately the natural and the programming languages that Mez mixes, but the disruptive power of mezangelle, its postanarchist import, also lies in the fact that it mixes the two languages as it does. Szilak's approach to digital literature is important here, as Szilak draws on Deleuze and Guattari's theorizing of minor languages and minor literary forms to read *The Dead Tower* as a work that "concretely illustrates" the "'deterritorializing' aspect of minor languages" (np). That is, mezangelle for Szilak is a minor language of its own that "combines the dominant languages of humans and machine—a kind of creole that disrupts the prescribed utility of both word and code" (np). This very combining of languages is in itself a way of destabilizing or "deterritorializing" the purely use-based values of both these systems and of "opening them up to new meaning and play" (np). On Szilak's reading of *The Dead Tower*, the instability, line of flight, and flux suggested by Deleuze and Guattari's "deterritorialization" is experienced in the distress and confusion felt by the user: "the user wanders in the dark trying to make sense of the 3-D game space" where there "are few clues and little narrative save for the trope of being lost and needing to find a way out" (np). While traversing the dark and dangerous-looking world of the game, "the user encounters fragments of text which, because they have computer code embedded in them, serve as labyrinths, both providing a structure and direction to the experience while, at the same time, complicating it" (Szilak np). This type of confusion is, in itself, not much different from the effects of playing any new video game. What differentiates *The Dead Tower* from those other experiences is the presence of mezangelle.

I would further argue that conceptualizing mezangelle as a "creole" language is preferable to characterizing it as a "hybrid language," as Caitlin Fisher does, among others (100). This approach falls victim to the same problems with hybridity that I identify in my discussion of Mullen in chapter two. Conceptualizing mezangelle as a hybrid language relies on maintaining the distinction between poetic and programming languages as two separate languages. This understanding of mezangelle as hybrid ignores the ways in which mezangelle, by mixing the two languages, reveals the intrinsic ties between them. I would argue, then, that rather than uniting their disparate functions, mezangelle reveals the fissures and inadequacies of both languages and renders both "unusable" in their usual functions.

In fact, one of the first pieces of text that the reader/user encounters in *The Dead Tower* flaunts this very function: "this. broken. space. / [chamber (gamer)place + constrict(l)ure].” This early piece of mezangelle reveals how “broken” is the kind of reading “space” recalled by the traditions (of programming, gaming, reading narrative, reading poetry, and so on) that *The Dead Tower* references as it opposes. By her use of punctuation in the form of parentheses and square brackets, Mez not only references computer code but also overlays the sentence with new meanings. Thus, traditional gaming narratives “constrict” readers even as they “lure” them into active engagement and narrative suture. Moreover, as Fisher argues, the opacity with which Mez’s work at such moments disrupts traditional reading practice is a demonstration—another flaunting—of the kind of new, reader-engaged literacies provoked by digital media writing. Obviously, such impediments to traditional or “normal” reading tend to be off-putting to readers, and Fisher points out the fact that Mez frequently gets contacted by readers who question or criticize her refusal to abide by traditional linguistic and narrative function. Providing one response to this criticism, Fisher quotes Mez’s “Puzzle Pieces of a Datableede Jigsaw”: “[meaning code: if narrative is essential to comprehension, then TTT is not for you. turn reading ‘oV’ and filter ‘on’. if, on the other key, you enjoy dream sequences/ sequentials, reverse the last]” (qtd. in Fisher 100). The choices that Mez points to here are implied in Fisher’s comment that Mez “interrupts and impedes smooth transmission of information, rendering meaning opaque and troubling interpretation, which results in another text of jouissance” (100). Readers who find *The Dead Tower* “troubling” need only “reverse the last]” in order to find “jouissance” instead.

The *Dead Tower* is, of course, a collaboration between two artists, and I credit both Campbell and Mez with the way in which the overall design of the experience serves both to trouble and to liberate the user. Just as there are critics who are more troubled than liberated by the unexecutability of Mez’s code, so too are there critics who are troubled by Mez’s mixture of the computer code with narrative conventions. For Robert Sweeny, for instance, the unexecutability of the code in the mezangelle that permeates the virtual environment of *The Dead Tower* and the inadequate narrative or semantic sense of the writing itself are innately linked.

Both inadequate languages refuse the supposed telos of the language systems from which they are taken. As Sweeny observes, the result is a text that is doubly unexecutable: "Breeze's poems bridge the gap between human and computer communication; her dysfunctional text fragments could be read by both human and machine, with both systems reaching a similar confused conclusion as to their meaning" (np). This reading of *The Dead Tower*, however, shares some of the weaknesses we have already observed in Cayley's reading of mezangelle. Thus, instead of concluding, as Sweeny does, with confusion, I argue for reading *The Dead Tower* alongside other texts committed to interventionary reading practices, such as Wershler's "(mal)content." The *Dead Tower* presents a reading space that deliberately collapses traditional reading and gaming practices; these learned traditions are metaphorically present as the emptied, crashed school bus so heavily overlaid with mezangelle. The invitation to read the white text scattered throughout this virtual world is, ultimately, a red (unread) herring; the bright white text in the dark world (l)ures the reader in, but no useful narrative meaning can be taken from it. Similarly, the invitation to navigate this space using the direction keys and the cursor, and especially the directive to use the spacebar to jump that is hidden in some of the *Dead Tower*'s mezangelle, leads the user to treat this like a gaming environment, another red herring that leaves the user without quest or finality.

As I have already suggested, in *The Dead Tower* Campbell and Mez are working from the context of gaming narratives, particularly in the form of first-person shooters and other similar gaming interfaces through which the reader as player navigates these systems. Flores makes a number of important points on this aspect of *The Dead Tower* in his scholarly blog and now encyclopedic resource, *I ♥ E-Poetry*, to which my own analysis is indebted. Specifically, Flores argues that the degree of familiarity that a user of *The Dead Tower* has with first-person shooters and gaming more generally is likely to colour that user's understanding of the work. Gamers might have more difficulty than other users with adjusting to the point of view and navigation functions, he explains, because gamers are used to a more integrated relationship between the two in typical gaming controls; in *The Dead Tower*, atypically, navigation uses the direction keys but adjustment of the point of view uses the mouse or touchpad. Another way in which gamers might respond differently to *The Dead Tower* that Flores points to lies in the fact that the work features the style of imagery and music characteristic of a typical first-person shooter or adventure game. For this reason, Flores provocatively suggests, "gamers are likely to experience phantom sensations" (np), expecting to encounter threat, battle, or at least a more full interaction with the work than just observation and navigation. The users we might expect to be most expert are therefore those who are most likely to be confused.

The partial reliance on gaming culture, controls, and environments is another level on which *The Dead Tower* is purposely misleading or confusing to its users. On this point again I turn to Flores, who acknowledges the "confusion of being dropped into the space" and the "dread produced by the setting and music" (np), but reframes this confusion as a locus of reader freedom, not an impediment to reader engagement. Flores encourages his blog's readers to embrace the confusion that arises as they "play" or "read" *The Dead Tower*: "Explore with confidence that you won't get lost in this space, its psychogeography will guide you....It won't take long to discover that everything is readable in this textual environment, best experienced in a dark space with good speakers or headphones on" (np). I note that the reading environment encouraged both by Flores and by the text itself is one of isolation and individual engagement; nevertheless, the reading process he advocates lends itself to a postanarchist approach, where users make their own paths and their own meanings as they navigate the textual and virtual world.

Finally, *The Dead Tower* works against traditional formations of authorship. Obviously, the fact that *The Dead Tower* is collaborative counteracts conceptions of single and closed authorship, especially because it is unclear which parts of the work are authored by Campbell and which by Mez. And yet Mez Breeze's name is hidden in "mezangelle," which suggests that the bulk of the visible writing here is by her. The fact that mezangelle reveals the presence of a writing subject in the language's name itself also suggests a refusal to withdraw the subject even as digital writing encourages, more and more, the erasure of the producer. As Raley observes, "situating the author 'Mez' within 'mezangelle' as a construction, and... enhancing and embellishing previously composed messages" is "a tactic that positions her simply as a mediating nodal point, a sysadmin with only partial write permissions" (np). Because it "positions her" in this way, the mezangelle in *The Dead Tower*—despite being a radically different form of writing and of text—also situates Mez's writing alongside the feminist writing practices discussed in chapter two. We may recognize in Breeze a similar refusal to withdraw the subject entirely.

Ultimately, as readers navigate this textual space in the virtual world, they are encouraged to make substantial use of their own whims, their own desires, and their own subjectivity. Making their way to the vantage point at the top of the eponymous tower is perhaps only the suggested way of reading the work: suggested because of the title and the bright red appearance of the tower, which is much taller than any of the cliffs or rock formations scattered throughout the space. Once users finally make their way to the top of the tower, though, they are rewarded only with a different vantage point; nothing about the world or the text that fills it changes in any way, and nothing new is presented. In this way, the freedom with which the reader navigates this textual space is symbolic of readerly freedom. This symbolism is heavy-handed, perhaps, but nothing about the ominous music, broken languages, or dark and foreboding atmosphere of *The Dead Tower* is subtle. Instead, the work flaunts its disruptive practices just as it flaunts the freedom of the reader to navigate this space. It requires that the confusion and the scariness of readerly freedom be made explicit. It reveals, in this way, how deliberately frightening it is to free oneself from the "constrict(l)ure" of traditional reading and gaming practices.

As I suggested at the start of this chapter, making reader engagement explicit is the most obvious trait that unites the four disparate projects that have been my focus here. None of these works is particularly subtle in its approach to an engaged readership. From the direct and explicit desire of "Seattle Drift" to have the reader "Do" it, to the clear difference between what is produced when *Code X* is used and when it is left to run in random automated mode, these texts all make obvious that they require agential, interventionary, and engaged readers. Thus the aimless and largely unguided wanderings of the reader's point of view in *The Dead Tower* symbolizes digital media's radical potential to place readers in free virtual spaces. There is no correct path through *The Dead Tower*, no proper arrangement of letters in *Code X* or of words in "Seattle Drift." Even "The Dreamlife of Letters," in its minimal interactivity, represents that liminal space between the static nature of printed text and the apparent ephemerality of the digital. Of course, just as the radically free readership sought by postanarchism is not exclusive to the digital (and can thus, as this study has demonstrated, be found throughout print-based poetry and its variant uses of machine-writing), not all digital media engages with these radical possibilities for interactive readership. What these four works demonstrate is the *potentials* of the digital medium, potentials that should continue to be engaged with, explored, and encouraged in a field of experimental literary production that continues to desire a space for radical, anarchic reading practices.

# Conclusion

TO CLOSE THIS PROJECT, I want to look beyond the sixteen poets who have served as case studies in this project to consider the broader implications for studying, critiquing, and engaging with literature that postanarchism's insights into the radical potentials of the digital for collaboration, reader engagement, and free reading practices might offer the academy. While I concede that the work of humanities departmental reform and of humanities academic publishing has its roots and its efficacy elsewhere, I remain convinced that the politics of postanarchist literary criticism require just such a discussion. Nor am I the first to make such a claim; for a more thorough study of the need to transform literary research, I recommend Kathleen Fitzpatrick's *Planned Obsolescence* (2011), which argues optimistically for a common of academic humanities publishing that embraces the rhizomatic networking and the potential for more direct communal engagement made available through digital potentialities. My own work contributes to the larger project that Fitzpatrick advocates by drawing on postanarchist literary theory as a basis for advocating the kind of literary scholarship that makes clear its investment in collaboration and communal voices—a scholarship that Fitzpatrick also advocates.

Despite the ways that the common suggested by digital technologies and networked computing permeates our day-to-day experience of the world in North America, we still typically understand scholarship in the humanities to be what Dave Parry terms "an individual, indeed often solitary, performance" (np). While collaborative authorship in publications is relatively common in the digital humanities, it is quite rare in more traditional literary studies. This, as Lisa M. Spiro notes (writing in 2009), continues to be true despite the fact that the benefits of collaboration and collaborative authorship in humanities departments and humanities publishing have been discussed for at least fifteen years. As early as 1999, for instance, Cathy N. Davidson's published "What if Scholars in the Humanities Worked Together, in a Lab?" a critique of the academy's commitment to the ideal of the solitary humanist. Davidson convincingly historicizes this figure as a myth grounded in a Romantic conception of authorship, despite the fact that this conception is more or less universally disregarded as archaic among literary critics themselves. As my research here demonstrates, in the last fifty years many poets have worked toward the dissolution of such a Romantic ideal of authorship, both aesthetically and politically. Nonetheless, print-based scholarship in the humanities has tended to prioritize single-author publications, such as this one and the vast majority of the scholarly texts I cite, thereby continuing to fashion scholarship in the humanities as something that happens in private: a special, secret relationship between one scholar and a rather large pile of books.

This is, of course, not the case. First and foremost, for most scholars in the humanities, the primary works that we discuss are increasingly available online or are born-digital projects, facts that make the supposedly private and personal work of the reading and exegetical analysis of print books an ever-obsolescing myth of criticism. Second, the core concept of research is that we use the ideas put forth by other scholars in order to improve our own work, and we as scholars in the humanities participate constantly in workshops, conferences, panels, peer-reviews, seminars, and the friendly exchange of ideas in order to advance our scholarship. Regardless, print-based humanities scholarship remains generally resistant to collaborative authorship in a way that the digital humanities is not. Part of this difference is due to the fact that a single digital project will often require multiple individuals with different kinds of expertise (a programmer, a graphic designer, a linguistic analyst, a literary scholar). But part of it is also due to the fact that digital projects—often using the internet as a networking tool—embrace the potentials of the digital to produce a common readership.

As Parry notes, it is not that digital humanities invented or even reinvented collaborative scholarship, but rather that it makes accessible and visible the collaborative nature of the work that we already do. In the end, while "Digital humanities did not invent collaborative scholarship," it ultimately does or can "make such work more acceptable and transparent" (np). While this project is a study by a single author, I hope that the case studies I offer herein succeed in highlighting the collaborative process involved in the production and reception of these experimental texts. Moreover, I hope that the moments of exegetical analysis throughout this book will be received only as suggestions for extrapolation rather than exhaustive or conclusive interpretations.

Conversely, it is my hope that the gestures toward the radical potentials of machine-writing and, later, networked computing that I examine here will collectively reveal an interest in potentials rather than a utopian understanding of the digital common as an egalitarian space. It would be both idealistic and naive to look only to the radical new potentials of digital scholarship and digital humanities without looking also at what the form obsolesces, namely the need to treat voices—even dissenting voices—as valuable in and of themselves, something face-to-face contact and, to an extent, print-based media tend to encourage. It is much easier to disregard or discredit the relatively temporal or ephemeral digital text than the print-based one. Similarly, the tendency in digital literatures, and especially in author-effacing conceptualist projects, to remix, redistribute, or rework the work of other authors has the dual effect of, first, revealing the artificiality of single-authorship and, second, of not adequately crediting the authors of the conceptual artist's source texts. While this practice is in line with a postanarchist practice of dispelling the authority of the author, it also threatens to silence nondominant voices; the often free or open-sourced distribution of remixed work creates distinctly material problems for authors who are not affiliated with post-secondary institutions or who financially depend on their writing. It may not therefore be a coincidence that, as the third chapter of this book reflects, this practice is dominated by white men affiliated with universities who have significantly less to lose than other writers.

Postanarchism recognizes the potentials of the digital to engage with readers as a more important political and aesthetic poetic goal than the effacement of authorship. This reader engagement hinges on an author's recognition of the digital not as a revolutionary medium in and of itself but as one node in a rhizomatic connection of various media that, in its inherent inter- or trans-mediality, critiques the concept of a singular "medium." Postanarchism positions the digital as anti-medium, conceding that, as the title of Dworkin's book announces, there is *No Medium* (2013), in particular to speak of. Instead, as Dworkin argues persuasively, experimental authorial and artistic practices demonstrate that works cannot be extracted from their material, which is never unitary. Instead, experimental authorship has "fatally complicated any account of single, pure, essential media" (*No Medium* 138). Even works such as the conceptual poetry studied in this project reveal, in their engagement with machine-writing and digital technologies, their reliance on media. In Dworkin's words, "even the most abstract and cerebral works of conceptual art cannot be separated from those material and technical supports. There is no single medium, to be sure, but media are inescapable" (*No Medium* 138). The collaborative, machine, and digital writing practices studied in this book reveal the inescapability of media as central to reader engagement and reveal, too, that the political import of media requires new practices of reading and criticism.

Essentially, machine-writing, electronic literature, and digital poetics all have the potential to contribute toward postanarchist literary criticism's implicit goal of disrupting the very nature of hermeneutical reading practices. The need for a new hermeneutics of media has been stressed by scholars in the digital humanities and scholars of digital poetics alike for some time: Simanowski, for instance, calls for scholars of electronic literature to "shift from linguistic hermeneutics to a hermeneutics of intermedial, interactive, and performative signs" by focusing on "the digital in digital literature" ("Holopoetry," 47–48). Such a shift in hermeneutics, as Simanowski cautions, requires that we also shift the focus of electronic literature scholarship away from the demands made by literature departments that we work to convince the reader of the literariness of the digital text; instead, we need to recognize the literariness of digital literature as tied to the media of its composition and dissemination. Amanda Starling Gould also sees such a shift in hermeneutics as radically altering the study of electronic literature. On her reading, Simanowski's call for a new kind of scholarship of electronic literature "gestures toward the misappropriation of 'electronic' as an organizational modifier in so far as it limits our theoretical boundaries if used as a strict qualifier. By dismissing the premise that electronic literature is literature electrified," Gould notes, Simanowski "points toward a method of analysis that rejects the separation of the electronic medium from the work's literariness and instead appreciates that the literary is indeed inseparable from the mediated, performative (inter) face of the unified work" (np). What Simanowski's call, and Gould's analysis, inevitably lead to is precisely the same privileging of a free, engaged readership we see called for in postanarchist literary theory. Any media-specific analysis is first and foremost a consideration of the reader before the author, and the political import of this shift in focus is the central thesis of postanarchist literary theory.

In the end, despite my efforts to be attentive, detailed, and thoughtful in the analyses contained in the sixteen case studies offered here, I have also tried to embrace aspects of Baldwin's concept of the "Idiocy of the Digital Literary." Writing for the *Digital Humanities Quarterly*, Baldwin encourages the practice of "idiocy" in digital literary scholarship, recommending that we understand the term "idiocy" in three interrelated ways: first, "in the ancient Greek sense of an individual, an ordinary person, a non-professional person, a private person"; second, "in the Dostoyevskian or Sartrean sense of saintliness through naïve questioning. Or even the Iggy Poppian sense of the idiot, bringing a bit of snarling punkiness to digital humanities"; third, and most importantly for my purposes here, "as inescapable and yet obdurate; as singular, immediate, and useless. Idiocy as a passion for reality" (np). Baldwin's call for an idiotic approach to the digital literary is, in essence, a call to return to textual analysis, a return to reading rather than theorization and interpretation, and to reading as an "individual...private person" at that; I do note with some caution, accordingly, that this unabashed interest in the text itself, "the text that digital humanities never tires of" (np), verges on the Romantic. Nevertheless, I agree with Baldwin that digital humanities scholarship and digital literary production has the radical potential to re-energize "the study of literature in a way that goes beyond the various 'isms' of theory," provided it remain "rigorously grounded in method" (np). This is to say that digital humanities scholarship must be significantly more invested in methodologics of reading, rather than theories of readership, grounding its analyses in code, connection, and interactivity rather than pontifications about the radical nature of digital praxis.

What Baldwin hopes to achieve with this emphasis on the text is to avoid the "debates about 'isms'" that have all too often turned into bloody "battles," all too often "fought in literature departments" (np). Certainly, postanarchist literary criticism runs the risk of being added to Baldwin's list of "isms"; but it can escape these battles provided it remains interested in process, in method, and in readership. What postanarchism wants of us most as readers is to be idiots about the poetry we read. The poetry studied in this book does not challenge readers to discern meaning; it challenges readers to respond with their own meanings, to write them into the work, onto the work, to become a part of the work as they read. These poems make idiots of us, the same kind of idiots who would believe they owned vast swathes of Antarctic land because Hakim Bey told them so. And, in the end, it is that idiocy that postanarchism invokes; it is an idiocy that can make great activist readers of us all.

# Notes

## Introduction

1. As evidence of this anarchist vanguardism, consider the classical anarchists' interest in *propagande par le fait*, popularized by French anarchist Paul Brousse and later taken up by many activist circles, anarchist and otherwise: a concept that privileged unique and spectacular resistance tactics, both violent and non-violent, as a means of disseminating political statements.
2. Farr writes: "Bakunin...for many years published a journal called *l'Avant-Garde*, a title he chose, I believe, to refer to his contention that 'the workers themselves' should move to 'the forefront' of the struggle, and not out of some inclination towards elitist 'vanguardism,' of which he was a virulent critic? Yes again. Indeed, the term 'avant-garde' does not mean 'vanguard' or 'elite.'... It is better understood, as Peter Burger argues in *Theory of the Avant-Garde*, as a turn against the institutionalization and commodification of artistic praxis. In this reading, avant-garde formations emerge as a tactical response to the neutralization of dissent that occurs under capitalism, where art (and its intrinsic movement against 'bourgeois' society) is annexed to a sphere separate from life, before being redeployed against its producers as a kind of trophy, an ossified representation" (np).
3. NAMBLA is the North American Man/Boy Love Association.
4. Vanguardism has long been a concern of poststructuralism. For one example of a poststructuralist critique of the vanguardist nature of resistance or oppositional movements, see Paul Bové's foreword to Gilles Deleuze's *Foucault*: "Deleuze emphasizes that Foucault's sense of the diffusion of power is a

challenge not only to Statist theories but also to theories of the oppositional or vanguard party" (xxix).

5. Despite indeterminacy's indebtedness to the scientific meanings of "experiment," its end-goal is markedly different. The scientific experiment seeks category, system, hierarchy, and Truth (bolstered by juridical, medical, logical, and scientific discourses); the experimental poem disrupts these goals.
6. See Voyce's introduction to *Underground Passages* for a thorough discussion of the relationship between literature and anarchism.
7. Dene Grigar is, at time of writing, Director of the Creative Media & Digital Culture Program at Washington State University Vancouver (WSUV), Director of the Electronic Literature Lab, and President of the Electronic Literature Organization. Grigar does the important work of curation of hardware and software for the archivization and preservation of early works of electronic literature.
8. At the heart of these conceptualist approaches to authorship and critiques of representation is the distinction between quotation, plagiarism, and appropriation. This distinction has also become central in the wealth of critiques of conceptualism in popular and academic criticism. Ken Chen's scathing article against the racism of conceptual poets argues that such theories of authorship as Marjorie Perloff's work on conceptualism (in *Unoriginal Genius* and elsewhere) demonstrate an "inability to theorize the ethics of appropriation" (np). Chen adds Dworkin to those contributing to the problem of the conceptual, citing his argument that conceptual poetry is a movement of intellect rather than emotion. But I would like to argue that Dworkin's earlier scholarly work in *Reading the Illegible* demonstrates that if the work of the experimental poet is of the intellect, the work of its readers is highly subjective and highly engaged, precisely in its movement away from the intellectualization of interpretation and toward a theory of *reading* as subjective and affective.

### 1 Precursors to Digital Writing

1. While I position these works as precursors to the digital, I do so based only on chronology. I worry about the language of the "proto-digital" because it has the potential to devalue print work, situating it as only partway to digital. The term "proto-digital" implies that this earlier formal work was inevitably leading to the digital, and viewing it in this way ignores the important fact that print medium is central to these digital experiments. Nichol is a useful

example: his interest in the kinetic, formalist potentials of language and printmaking is what led him to be curious about the digital format. *First Screening* is an extension of those concerns, not the inevitable result of it. Connecting these two related kinds of poetry reveals two things: first, the digital is not a reworking, a reinvention of experimental poetry's experimentation with language, just another remediated tool for that experimentation; and second, the medium is still (most of) the message, with thanks as always to Marshall McLuhan. Words were always moving on the page; the digital just lets us make them move in a different way.

2. The best source for discussions of the anarchist activism of Mac Low, Cage, and Duncan is Antliff. His book-length study, *Anarchy and Art: From the Paris Commune to the Fall of the Berlin Wall* (2007), is nearly encyclopedic. See also Antliff's "Situating Freedom" and Louis Cabri's "Rubus Effect" for more specifics of these authors' engagement with anarchist journals and activist circles. On Nichol's commune and work with Therafields, see Frank Davey.
3. "Diastic" is a paragrammatic procedure Mac Low developed to make deterministic poems. In a diastic poem, a source text is selected, and a seed text is used to select words from the source text. Words are selected based on the placement of the letters, so the first letter of the first word of the seed text is used to find a word in the source text with the same letter at the start of the word. Next, the second word is chosen, provided it has the second letter of the seed text in its own second-letter-position. Mac Low's "Stein 72," for example, uses as its source text part 1, stanza 6 of Gertrude Stein's "Stanzas in Meditation." Its seed text is Mac Low's son's name, Mordecai-Mark. The poem reads: "more not more to-day forget." The poem ends here because the program was unable to find a word after "forget" in which the "c" was in the sixth position (*Thing of Beauty* 401).
4. Mac Low explains the difference thus: "Procedures operating from *any* level of the ego, in the Zen sense, I call 'intentional'; 'nonintentional' refers only to those procedures that do not do so" ("Cage's Writing" 226).
5. As Higgins describes in "A Child's History of Fluxus," "Everything was itself, it wasn't part of something bigger or fancier" (87).
6. I offer here a much-abbreviated paraphrase of the original. See Brooks 38.
7. I use this term in the same way Brian Massumi uses it: "Intensity is qualifiable as an emotional state, and one that is static—temporal and narrative noise. It is a state of suspense, potentially of disruption" (26).

8. The poems also literally serve as notation, and can be read as a musical piece for solo voice, famously performed by Demetrio Stratos and later by Eberhard Blum. Singing *62 Mesostics* requires taking the size and font of the letters to denote volume, tone, and length of each letter's pronunciation.
9. That is, Pound and Lewis, in their brief years leading the Vorticist vanguard, align the vortex with the field of artistic and poetic production, suggesting new and various perspectives, syntactical models, and other radical experimentations. It is also worth noting that, in terms of physics, the creation of vortices is highly dependent on the absence or presence of external forces. Both the artistic movement and the physical phenomenon here are interested in concert and multiplicity, the creation of assemblages in which the parts can never truly be disassembled but never reach amalgamation or homogeneity.
10. At this point, a note on Duncan's mysticism seems necessary. His understanding of the relationship between a singular part and an inarticulable whole are directly related to his understanding of an incomprehensible divine order of which we are only a part. For Duncan, the production of a poem was one articulation of this relationship between the individual and the divine order. "Our consciousness," he writes, "and the poem as a supreme effort of consciousness, comes in a dancing organization between personal and cosmic identity" ("Towards" 78). Ross Hair's "Fallen Love" does excellent work in connecting this mysticism to Duncan's concept of eros.
11. The use of the term "field" here is loaded, as the term carries with it important associations with Duncan's method of "composition by field." I use it to denote a space, but also hope that it carries Duncanian echoes.
12. Painting, for Duncan, is a process of integration in a way that weaving is not. Consider "The Fire (Passages 13)," also in *Bending the Bow*:

    He [Piero di Cosimo] inherits the *sfumato* of Leonardo da Vinci —
    there is a softening of outline,   his color fuses. (*Bending* 41)

    It is worth noting that Duncan's partner Jess's collage artworks similarly resist integration in the way that painting seems to court it.
13. All references in this chapter are to the emulated version of *First Screening* unless otherwise stated.
14. Though what follows is a clearly anachronistic reading, it is fascinating to observe that Nichol's use of the "tune in" language here is an uncanny prediction of digital media, which is now clearly (albeit slowly) obsolescing

syndicated television as it empowers the user; as with *First Screening*, television viewers can now use download and streaming services to "tune in" whenever they like.

## 2 Feminism, Print, Machines

1. For studies on Cage, see my article "John Cage and the Comunis" or Andy Weaver's "Writing through Merce." For studies on Robert Duncan, see Weaver's "Promoting 'a community'" or Eric Keenaghan's "Life, War, and Love."
2. Bob Perelman summarizes the communication between Silliman and Scalapino in *The Marginalization of Poetry*.
3. The debate between Scalapino and Silliman is probably the most succinct discussion of the racialized tension within experimental poetry communities. Scalapino essentially argues that Silliman's position is "authoritarian" and that "those who are without social power are less inclined to see reality as orderly; for example, less inclined to see the social construction as unified.... The conception of a 'unified subject' is merely taught" (52). Silliman published that essay in 1987, and in the thirty years since then a good deal has changed in experimental poetry communities where gender, race, and identity politics in general are concerned; consequently Silliman has had to do a lot of work to distance himself from his earlier position. The Electronic Poetry Center hosts an interview in which Silliman works tirelessly to correct the (probably well-intentioned) normativity of his 1987 essay (Silliman, "Interview [with Gary Sullivan])."
4. All references hereafter to *Eikon Basilike* refer to Howe's text. Any reference to the 1649 text will include the date of publication: the 1649 *Eikon Basilike*. Any reference to Almack's bibliography will be referred to as such. Because the pages of Howe's original edition of *Eikon Basilike* are not numbered, all numerical references to the long poem are to the version of the poem in *The Nonconformist's Memorial*. Any pertinent differences between editions will be noted.
5. The paradox here is that Howe uses an extreme image of state power (Charles I) to represent its dismantling (his execution). This paradox, rather than impeding her argument, strengthens it by demonstrating how quickly and easily the figures of government are altered, deposed, or repurposed, thus revealing their arbitrariness.

6. In *Eikon Basilike*'s original edition, these two crossed-over lines are given their own page to emphasize their importance. In *The Nonconformist's Memorial* they are relegated to the bottom of the page that comes before.
7. All references to *Pillage Laud* refer to the 2011 Book*hug reprint. I will note where this edition differs from the 1999 Moveable Type printing.
8. This interest in paratext is frequently seen in scholars of experimentally-produced or computer-generated texts. See for instance Jerome J. McGann's *The Textual Condition* (1991), or the scholarly writings of Johanna Drucker, Perloff, and others.
9. See also Rachel Zolf's 2011 essay, "'Like plugging into an electric circuit': Fingering out Erín Moure's Lesbo-Digit-O! Smut Poems."
10. Weaver, for example, argues that Moure retains the aesthetics of LANGUAGE poetry without the politics. Because Moure eschews the New Sentence in favour of more traditional syntax, Weaver sees her work as politically ineffectual, presenting the images of radical politics uncritically and thus unpolitically ("Indeterminacy" 293).
11. Lauren Elkin and Scott Esposito's *The End of Oulipo? An Attempt to Exhaust a Movement* (2013) is an informative and thoughtful look at the issue of the sexism of, and feminist responses to, Oulipo. Elkin and Esposito provide some important discussion of the women writers of Oulipo who are rarely discussed in English criticism because they are rarely translated into English from the French.
12. The N + 7 technique was invented by Jean Lescure, the French Oulipian poet; the technique involves replacing each noun in a text (original or source) with the seventh one following it in a dictionary.
13. This antagonism has been usefully summarized by Evie Shockley in her introduction to *Renegade Poetics: Black Aesthetics and Formal Innovation in African American Poetry* (2011).
14. For further discussions of writing blackness as a feature of Mullen's radical poetics, see Shockley's *Renegade Poetics* (2011); essays by Jessica Lewis Luck, Elisabeth A. Frost, and Amy Moorman Robbins; and Mullen's own pivotal essays, "Poetry and Identity" and "African Signs and Spirit Writing."
15. Consider, for example, the role of coal mining as symbolic of poverty in works as early as Emile Zola's *Germinal* (1885), D.H. Lawrence's *Sons and Lovers* (1913), Upton Sinclair's *King Coal* (1917), and Sinclair's posthumous sequel *The Coal War*. We can even see the influence of coal mining and its relationship to

poverty and labour politics in later poetry, exemplified by British poet Tony Harrison's *v.* (1985).

16. The concept of the hybrid is theorized extensively in recent scholarship. The term is often applied to Mullen's work, as where Frost argues that "like the poets of the Black Arts Movement, Mullen experiments with a speech-based idiom, but, like Language-influenced writers, she launches her cultural critique by rejecting the rules of syntax and fashioning a distinctively visual, punning, and allusive play with language" ("'Ruses'" 465). While Frost does argue that this "hybrid" is "shot through with ambivalence" ("'Ruses'" 469) and that it exists "in a realm not of fixed identity...but of language in flux" ("'Ruses'" 471), I worry that by her use of this term Frost implies that Mullen has merged two previously separate perspectives.
17. Mullen tells Henning that the "she" in this poem is also her "artist friend Yong Soon Min," who organized a group meal, called "Kimchi Xtravanganza," for the Korean American Museum (73).

**3 Easy Concepts**

1. Most studies of *Soliloquy* in academic journals, including those by Paul Stephens and Dworkin, cite only the print version of this book. The vast majority of these studies make note of the massive size of *Soliloquy* as a print book, including those by Frank J. Kearful and Andrew Epstein. The only exception to this, as far as I have seen, is Christopher Schmidt's article, which considers, briefly, the relationship between Goldsmith's print and digital versions by way of a fascinating study of the relationship between digital text circulation and the digital-anal sexual interaction described in the text itself and quoted later in this case study.
2. I note here a parallel between Goldsmith's repeated assertions that he needs to purchase more tapes and Patrick Bateman's repeated excuse that he needs to return some videotapes in Bret Easton Ellis's *American Psycho*. This parallel invites comparison between both male protagonists' explicit performance of selfhood, but more work would have to be done to flesh out this comparison.
3. Steven Zultanski provides a useful overview of the controversy surrounding Place's publication of *Statement of Facts* in "Short Statement in Five Parts on *Statement of Facts*" for *Jacket2* and in the *Could Be Otherwise* blog's summary and discussion of Perloff's response (see Spahr, Comment).
4. For further reading on the legibility of serif and sans serif typefaces, see Poole's survey of the literature, *Which Are More Legible: Serif or Sans Serif Typefaces?*

For more information on the politics of the sans serif typeface as indicative of a cultural milieu, see Dworkin, *Reading the Illegible* (xx). For more reading on the best practices for serif and sans-serif typefaces in print and digital publishing, see Robert Bringhurst's quintessential *The Elements of Typographic Style*. The important thing to take from the plethora of resources on serifs in typefaces is that there can be no clear designation of serifs as appropriate for a certain genre or style save cultural traditions and graphical, aesthetic preferences. Place's decision to use serifs in *Statement of Facts*'s paratext and a sans serif typeface for the book's content is thus highly dependent on her own designation of serifs as "epaulets of authority."

5. Although *Statement of Facts* was published by Blanc Press and not by the publishing house Place works for, Les Figues, it is likely that she was aware of the specificities of these paratextual elements.
6. While tangential, it is worth noting Moschovakis's anarchist allegiances as the translator of some of the works of Egyptian-born French anarchist novelist Albert Cossery.
7. "Writing *Eunoia* proved to be an arduous task. I read through all three volumes of the *Webster's Third International Unabridged Dictionary*, doing so five times in order to extract an extensive lexicon of univocal words, each containing only one of the five vowels. I could have automated this process, but I figured that learning the software to write a program would probably take just as long as the manual labor itself—so I simply got started on the project. I arranged the words into parts of speech (noun, verb, etc.); then I arranged these lists into topical categories (creatures, foodstuff, etc.), so that I could determine what stories the vowels could tell. I then spent six years, working four or five hours every night after work, from about midnight on, piecing together a five-chapter novel, doing so until I exhausted this restricted vocabulary" (Bök, qtd. in Voyce, "Xenotext" np).
8. See Braune's "The Meaning Revealed at the *N*th Degree in Christian Bök's *Eunoia*" for this mathematical reading.
9. For more on *Eunoia*'s place in cultural and historical context and tradition, see Perloff's "The Oulipo Factor: The Procedural Poetics of Christian Bök and Caroline Bergvall."
10. Much of the existing Bök scholarship, particularly on *Eunoia*, focuses on the poet's writing practices and the labour of this work. See for instance Brian Kim Stefans and Wershler's "Exchange," Perloff's "The Oulipo Factor," McGann's "*Eunoia*," and Braune's "The Meaning Revealed."

11. This is a charge frequently levelled unfairly and unhelpfully at conceptualist poetry, as in Calvin Bedient's now infamous "Against Conceptualism" for the *Boston Review*.
12. Wershler's contributions to digital humanities include the "Exchange on Circulars" with Brian Kim Stefans, discussed in this case study, the essay "The Locative, the Ambient, and the Hallucinatory in the Internet of Things" (2010), and several book-length studies, including *Free as in Speech and Beer: Open Source, Peer-to-Peer and the Economics of the Online Revolution* (2002), *Internet Directory 2001* (2000), and *Commonspace: Beyond Virtual Community* (2000).
13. This race-based criticism reached its apex following Goldsmith's presentation at Brown University's *Interrupt 3* conference of a reframed and remixed version of the autopsy report of Michael Brown, the unarmed black teenager gunned down by white police officer Darren Wilson in Ferguson, Missouri. The backlash following Goldsmith's presentation is exemplified by Jillian Steinhauer's article in *Hyperallergic* that condemns the white appropriation of black suffering and reproduces many Facebook posts and Tweets that condemn Goldsmith for the same reason. Goldsmith took to Facebook to address the controversy surrounding this performance, arguing that while he did rearrange the autopsy report and dumbed down the medical language, he "did not editorialize," and because "the document" he "read from is powerful," his "reading of it was powerful." He concluded with the assertion that uncreative writing "is the writing that is able to tell the truth in the strongest and clearest way possible." Rather than appeasing his audience, this created a venue for further critiques, with the first response reading: "You're a white person appropriating black suffering for your own personal gain. Spin it however you want, but that's also the truth." Later, King's "Why Are People So Invested in Kenneth Goldsmith? Or, Is Colonialist Poetry Easy?," easily the best online response to the reading, argued that Goldsmith "overstepped in revealing ways, calling attention to the historical power plays he has publicly boasted and by enacting how privilege is expected to invoke and establish power" (np). The situation is thoughtfully summarized and analyzed by Daniel Morris in *Not Born Digital*.
14. The stereotypical representation of the Middle East in *Eunoia* is helpfully summarized in Braune's "The Meaning Revealed."

# Works Cited

Allen, Donald, editor. *The Poetics of the New American Poetry*. Grove Press, 1974.

Almack, Edward. *A Bibliography of the King's Book: or, Eikon Basilike*. 1896. Kessinger Publishing, 2008.

Andrews, Jim. "Digital Langu(image): Language and Image as Objects in a Field." *Vispo.com*, 1998, http://www.vispo.com/writings/essays/jimarticle.htm. Accessed 11 November 2016. Originally published in *Perihelion*, edited by Jennifer Ley, vol. 1, no. 2, 1998.

———. *On Lionel Kearns. Vispo.com*, 2004, http://vispo.com/kearns/index.htm. Accessed 11 November 2016.

———. "Seattle Drift." *Vispo.com*, 1997, http://www.vispo.com/animisms/SeattleDrift.html. Accessed 17 October 2016.

Andrews, Jim, et al. "Introduction: *First Screening*." *Vispo.com*, March 2007, http://vispo.com/bp/introduction.htm. Accessed 25 August 2015.

Antliff, Allan. *Anarchy and Art: From the Paris Commune to the Fall of the Berlin Wall*. Arsenal Pulp Press, 2007.

———. "Situating Freedom: Jackson Mac Low, John Cage, and Donald Judd." *Anarchist Developments in Cultural Studies*, vol. 2, 2011, pp. 39–57.

Ardam, Jacquelyn. "The ABCs of Conceptual Writing." *Comparative Literary Studies*, vol. 51, no. 1, 2014, pp. 132–58.

Ashbery, John. "The Invisible Avant-Garde." *Twentieth-Century American Poetics: Poets on the Art of Poetry*, edited by Dana Gioia, David Mason, and Meg Schoerke, McGraw Hill, 2004, pp. 284–91.

Baldwin, Sandy. "The Idiocy of the Digital Literary (and What Does It Have to Do with Digital Humanities?)" *Digital Humanities Quarterly*, vol. 7, no. 1, 2013, http://www.digitalhumanities.org/dhq/vol/7/1/000155/000155.html. Accessed 25 November 2016.

Bedient, Calvin. "Against Conceptualism: Defending the Poetry of Affect." *Boston Review*, 24 July 2013, http://bostonreview.net/poetry/against-conceptalism. Accessed 17 December 2017.

"beer, *n*." OED. Accessed 16 January 2015.

Bergvall, Caroline, and Erín Moure. "O Yes." *Antiphonies: Essays on Women's Experimental Poetries in Canada*, edited by Nate Dorward, The Gig, 2008, pp. 167–76.

Bernstein, Charles. "Artifice of Absorption." *A Poetics*, Harvard UP, 1993, pp. 9–89.

———. *Close Listening: Poetry and the Performed Word*. Oxford UP, 1998.

Bernstein, David W., and Christopher Hatch, editors. *Writing Through John Cage's Music, Poetry, and Art*. U of Chicago P, 2001.

Betts, Gregory. "I Object: Writing Against the Contemporary." *ESC: English Studies in Canada*, vol. 40, no. 2–3, June/September 2014, pp. 41–63.

Bey, Hakim. *Opium Dens I Have Known*. Shivastan Press, 2014.

———. *Temporary Autonomous Zone; Ontological Anarchy; Poetic Terrorism*. BiblioLife, 2007.

"birr, *v*." OED. Accessed 16 January 2015.

Blum, Eberhard, performer. *Sixty-Two Mesostics Re Merce Cunningham*, composed by John Cage, Hat Art.

Bookchin, Murray. *Post-Scarcity Anarchism*. Black Rose Books, 1971.

———. *Social Anarchism or Lifestyle Anarchism: An Unbridgeable Chasm*. AK Press, 1995.

Bök, Christian. *Eunoia*. Coach House Press, 2001.

———. *Eunoia: The CD*. Coach House Books, 2003. Compact disc.

Bolter, Jay David, and Richard Grusin. *Remediation: Understanding New Media*. MIT Press, 1999.

Bové, Paul. Foreword. *Foucault*, by Gilles Deleuze. MIT Press, 1988, pp. vi–x.

Braune, Sean. "The Meaning Revealed at the *N*th Degree in Christian Bök's *Eunoia*." *Studies in Canadian Literature*, vol. 34, no. 2, 2009, https://journals.lib.unb.ca/index.php/scl/article/view/12705/13632. Accessed 5 October 2016.

Breeze, Mez. Author description. Breeze, *_cross.ova.ing ][4rm.blog.2.log]*. Accessed 26 December 2017.

———. *_cross.ova.ing ][4rm.blog.2.log]. [_XXtracts. Electronic Literature Collection*, edited by Laura Borràs, Talan Memmott, Rita Raley, and Brian Kim Stefans, vol. 2, 2003, http://collection.eliterature.org/2/works/mez_crossovaing.html. Accessed 11 November 2016.

Bringhurst, Robert. *The Elements of Typographic Style*. Hartley & Marks Publishers, 1992.

Brooks, William. "In Re: 'Experimental Music.'" *Contemporary Music Review*, vol. 31, no. 1, February 2012, pp. 37–62.

Brown, Alistair. "Reading the Source of 'Seattle Drift.'" *The Pequod Blog*, 15 September 2012, http://thepequodblog.blogspot.ca/2012/09/reading-source-of-seattle-drift.html. Accessed 17 October 2016.

Bultmann, Rudolf. *Theology of the New Testament*. 1951. Baylor UP, 2007.

Butler, Judith. *Precarious Life: The Powers of Mourning and Violence*. Verso, 2006.

Cabri, Louis. "Rubus Effect Remove Government: Jackson Mac Low, Why?/Resistance, Anarcho-Pacifism." *Crayon: Festschrift for Jackson Mac Low's 75th Birthday*, edited by Andrew Levy and Bob Harrrison, vol. 1, no. 1, 1997, pp. 45–48.

Cage, John. "62 Mesostics Re Merce Cunningham." *M: Writings '67–'72*. Wesleyan UP, 1973, pp. 4–211, *passim*.

———. "Diary: How to Improve the World (You Will Only Make Matters Worse) Continued 1970–71." *M: Writings '67–'72*. Wesleyan UP, 1973, pp. 96–116.

———. Foreword. *M: Writings '67–'72*. Wesleyan UP, 1973, pp. i–viii.

———. "Form is a Language." *John Cage: An Anthology*, edited by Richard Kostelanetz, Da Capo Press, 1991, p. 135.

———. "The Future of Music: Credo." *Silence*, pp. 3–6.

———. "History of Experimental Music in the United States." Cage, *Silence*, pp. 67–75.

———. *Silence: Lectures and Writings*. MIT Press, 1967.

———. *Writing Through Finnegans Wake*. U of Tulsa P, 1978.

Campbell, Andy, and Mez Breeze. *The Dead Tower. Electronic Literature Collection*, edited by Stephanie Boluk, Leonardo Flores, Jacob Garbe, and Anastasia Salter, vol. 3, 2012, http://collection.eliterature.org/3/work.html?work=dead-tower. Accessed 11 November 2016.

Cayley, John. "The Code Is Not the Text (Unless It Is the Text)." *Electronic Book Review*, 10 September 2002, http://electronicbookreview.com/thread/electropoetics/failure. Accessed 11 November 2016.

Chen, Ken. "Authenticity, Obsession, or Conceptualism as Minstrel Show." *The Margins*, 11 June 2015, http://aaww.org/authenticity-obsession. Accessed 25 November 2016.

Clark, Miriam Marty. "The Library and the Wilderness: Susan Howe's Pragmatism." *Contemporary Literature*, vol. 54, no. 2, Summer 2013, pp. 369–96.

Clover, Joshua. "Technical Composition of Conceptualism." *Metamute*, 2 April 2014, http://www.metamute.org/editorial/articles/technical-composition-conceptualism. Accessed 17 December 2017.

"codex, *n.*" OED. Accessed 11 November 2016.

Cohn, Jesse. *Anarchism and the Crisis of Representation: Hermeneutics, Aesthetics, Politics*. Susquehanna UP, 2006.

———. "What Is Anarchist Literary Theory?" *Anarchist Studies*, vol. 15, no. 2, 2007, pp. 115–31.

———. "What is 'Postanarchism' Post?" Review of *From Bakunin to Lacan: Anti-Authoritarianism and the Dislocation of Power*, by Saul Newman. *Postmodern Culture*, vol. 13, no. 1, September 2002, doi:10.1353/pmc.2002.0028. Accessed 25 November 2016.

Collis, Stephen. "A Duncan Etude: Dante and Responsibility." *Jacket*, vol. 26, October 2004, http://jacketmagazine.com/26/dunc-coll.html. Accessed 25 November 2016.

———. *Through Words of Others: Susan Howe and Anarcho-Scholasticism*. English Literary Studies (ELS) Editions, 2006.

Cramer, Florian. "Post-Digital Writing." *Electronic Book Review*, 12 December 2012, http://www.electronicbookreview.com/thread/electropoetics/postal. Accessed 5 October 2016.

Crown, Kathleen. "'This Unstable I-Witnessing': Susan Howe's Lyric Iconoclasm and the Articulating Ghost." *Women's Studies*, vol. 27, no. 5, 1998, pp. 483–506.

Davey, Frank. *Aka bpNichol: A Preliminary Biography*. ECW Press, 2012.

Davidson, Cathy N. "What If Scholars in the Humanities Worked Together, in a Lab?" *The Chronicle Review*, 28 May 1999, http://www.chronicle.com/article/What-If-Scholars-in-the/24009. Accessed 25 November 2016.

Davidson, Ian. *Ideas of Space in Contemporary Poetry*. Palgrave MacMillan, 2007.

de Sade, Marquis. *The 120 Days of Sodom and Other Writings*. Grove / Atlantic, 2007.

Deleuze, Gilles, and Félix Guattari. *A Thousand Plateaus: Capitalism and Schizophrenia*. 1987. Translated by Brian Massumi, U of Minnesota P, 2011.

Derrida, Jacques. *Archive Fever: Freudian Impressions*. Translated by Eric Prenowitz. U of Chicago P, 1998.

———. *Disseminations*. 1972. Translated by Barbara Johnson. U of Chicago P, 1981.

"digital, *n.* and *adj.*" OED. Accessed 11 November 2016.

Doran, Kerry. "Speaking in Code." *Rhizome Blog*, 5 March 2015, http://rhizome.org/editorial/2015/mar/05/speaking-code. Accessed 25 August 2015.

Drucker, Johanna. "Beyond Conceptualisms: Poetics after Critique and the End of the Individual Voice." *The Poetry Project Newsletter*, vol. 231, April/May 2012, pp. 6–9.

"ductor, *n.*" OED. Accessed 16 January 2015.

Duncan, Robert. *Bending the Bow*. New Directions, 1968.

———. *Ground Work: Before the War/In the Dark*. New Directions, 2006.

———. *A Poet's Mind: Collected Interviews with Robert Duncan 1960–1985*, edited by Christopher Wagstaff, North Atlantic Books, 2012.

———. "Some Notes on Notation." *Ground Work*, pp. 3–6.

———. "Towards an Open Universe." *A Selected Prose*, edited by Robert J. Bertholf, New Directions, 1995, pp. 1–12.

DuPlessis, Rachel Blau. "Agency, Social Authorship, and the Political Aura of Contemporary Poetry." *Textual Practice*, vol. 23, no. 6, 2009, pp. 987–99.

Dutton, Paul. "Scratch." 2002. *Scratch*, by Dutton and W. Mark Sutherland, http://www.wmarksutherland.com. Accessed 11 November 2016. Originally printed for Koffler Gallery, curated by Carolyn Bell Farrell.

Dworkin, Craig. "The Imaginary Solution." *Contemporary Literature*, vol. 48, no. 1, Spring 2007, pp. 29–60.

———. *No Medium*. MIT Press, 2013.

———. *Reading the Illegible*. Northwestern UP, 2003.

Eichhorn, Kate. "The Digital Turn in Canadian and Québécois Literature." *The Oxford Handbook of Canadian Literature*, edited by Cynthia Sugars, Oxford UP, 2015, pp. 512–25.

Ellis, Bret Easton. *American Psycho*. Random House, 1991.

Emerson, Lori. "*First Screening*." *Electronic Literature Directory*, 24 July 2009, http://directory.eliterature.org/individual-work/42. Accessed 25 August 2015.

———. "From Apple BASIC to Hypercard, or, Translating Translating bpNichol." *Media Archaeology Lab Blog*, 9 July 2013, http://mediaarchaeologylab.com/blog/translating-translating-bpnichol. Accessed 25 August 2015.

———. "Materiality, Intentionality, and the Computer-Generated Poem: Reading Walter Benn Michaels with Erin Mouré's *Pillage Laud*." *ESC: English Studies in Canada*, vol. 34, no. 4, December 2008, pp. 45–69.

Elkin, Lauren, and Scott Esposito. *The End of Oulipo? An Attempt to Exhaust a Movement*. Zero Books, 2013.

Epstein, Andrew. "Critiquing 'La Vie Quotidienne': Contemporary Approaches to the Everyday." *Contemporary Literature*, vol. 49, no. 3, January 2008, pp. 476-87.

Evren, Süreyyya, and Duane Rouselle. "Introduction: How New Anarchism Changed the World (of Opposition) after Seattle and Gave Birth to Post-Anarchism." *Post-Anarchism: A Reader*, edited by Evren and Rouselle, Pluto Press, 2011, pp. 1–22.

Farr, Roger. "The Intimacies of Noise: A Reply to Jesse Cohn." *Fifth Estate*, vol. 376, 2007, https://www.fifthestate.org/archive/376-halloween-2007/intimacies-noise. Accessed 15 February 2017.

Finkelstein, Norman. "'MAKING THE GHOST WALK ABOUT AGAIN AND AGAIN': History as Séance in the Work of Susan Howe." *Literature Interpretation Theory*, vol. 20, 2009, pp. 215–40.

Fisher, Caitlin. "Electronic Literacies." *Light Onwords/Light Onwards, Living Literacies*, conference proceedings, 14–16 November 2002, http://en.copian.ca/library/research/ltonword/part3/fisher/fisher.pdf. Accessed 11 November 2016.

Fitzpatrick, Kathleen. *Planned Obsolescence: Publishing, Technology, and the Future of the Academy*. New York UP, 2011.

Flores, Leonardo. "'The Dead Tower' by Andy Campbell and Mez Breeze." *I ♥ E-Poetry*, 17 July 2012, http://iloveepoetry.com/?p=302. Accessed 11 November 2016.

———. *Typing the Dancing Signifier: Jim Andrews' (Vis)Poetics*, University of Maryland, College Park, 2010.

Frost, Elisabeth A. "'Ruses of the lunatic muse': Harryette Mullen and Lyric Hybridity." *Women's Studies*, vol. 27, 1998, pp. 465–81.

———. "Signifyin(g) on Stein: The Revisionist Poetics of Harryette Mullen and Leslie Scalapino." *Postmodern Culture*, vol. 5, no. 3, May 1995, doi:10.1353/pmc.1995.0023.

Funkhouser, C.T. *Prehistoric Digital Poetry: An Archaeology of Forms, 1959–1995*. U of Alabama P, 2007.

Gascoigne, George. "The Fruit of Fetters, with the Complaint of the Green Knight and his Farewell to Fancy." *Sixteenth-Century Poetry*, edited by Gordon Braden, Blackwell Publishing, 2005, pp. 106–118. Originally published in *The Posies of George Gascoigne, Esquire*, London, 1575, pp. 175-84.

[Gauden, John?]. *Eikon Basilike: The Pourtraicture of His Sacred Majestie in His Solitude and Sufferings*. 1649. Edited by Edward Almack and A. Moring, 1904.

Graeber, David. "Anarchism, Academia, and the Avant-Garde." *Contemporary Anarchist Studies: An Introductory Anthology of Anarchy in the Academy*, edited by Randall Amster et al., Routledge, 2009, pp. 103–12.

Goldsmith, Kenneth. "Being Boring." *Electronic Poetry Center*, 2004, http://epc.buffalo.edu/authors/goldsmith/goldsmith_boring.html. Accessed 5 October 2016.

———. "Conceptual Poetics." *Poetry Foundation*, 2008, https://www.poetryfoundation.org/harriet/2008/06/conceptual-poetics-kenneth-goldsmith. Accessed 13 December 2017.

———. *Day*. The Figures, 2003.

———. "I am requesting...." Facebook post, 16 March 2015, https://www.facebook.com/kenneth.goldsmith.739/posts/354952974690518. Accessed 2 March 2017.

———. "Sentences on Conceptual Writing." *UbuWeb*, http://www.ubu.com/papers/kg_ol_goldsmith.html. Accessed 5 October 2016.

———. *Soliloquy*. Granary Books, 2001.

———. *Soliloquy*. *Electronic Literature Collection*, edited by N. Katherine Hayles, Nick Montfort, Scott Rettberg, and Stephanie Strickland, vol. 1, 2002, http://collection.eliterature.org/1/works/goldsmith__soliloquy.html. Accessed 5 October 2016.

———. *Uncreative Writing: Managing Language in the Digital Age*. Columbia UP, 2011.

Gossman, Uta. "Susan Howe's Nonconformist Memorials." *Poetic Memory: The Forgotten Self in Plath, Howe, Hinsey, and Glück*. Farleigh Dickinson UP, 2012, pp. 71–130.

Gould, Amanda Starling. "A Bibliographic Overview of Electronic Literature." *Electronic Literature Directory*, 2012, http://directory.eliterature.org/article/4573. Accessed 25 November 2016.

Guthrie, Annie. "Conceptual Poetry Conceptual Interview." *University of Arizona Poetry Center*, reprinted in *The Body in Parts: Poetry + Other*, edited by Maryan Nagy Captain, http://thebodyinparts.tumblr.com/post/7420265211. Accessed 25 November 2016.

Hair, Ross. "Fallen Love: Eros and Ta'wl in the Poetry of Robert Duncan." *Journal of Modern Literature*, vol. 36, no. 3, 2013, pp. 174–93.

Hardt, Michael, and Antonio Negri. *Commonwealth*. Harvard UP, 2009.

Harrison, Tony. *v*. Bloodaxe Books, 1985.

Hart, Matthew. *Nations of Nothing but Poetry: Modernism, Transnationalism, and Synthetic Vernacular Writing*. Oxford UP, 2010.

Hayles, N. Katherine. *Electronic Literature: New Horizons for the Literary.* U of Notre Dame P, 2008.

Hejinian, Lyn. "The Rejection of Closure." *The Language of Inquiry*, U of California P, 2000, pp. 40–58.

Helms, Robert P. "Leaving Out the Ugly Part—Hakim Bey/Peter Lamborn Wilson." *Libcom.org*, 18 October 2005, https://libcom.org/library/leaving-out-ugly-part-hakim-bey. Accessed 21 February 2017.

Henning, Barbara. *Looking Up Harryette Mullen: Interviews on* Sleeping with the Dictionary *and Other Works*. Introduction by Juliana Spahr, Belladonna, 2011.

Heraclitus. *Fragments*, translated and edited by T.M. Robinson, U of Toronto P, 1987.

Higgins, Dick. "A Child's History of Fluxus." *Horizons: The Poetics and Theory of Intermedia*, Southern Illinois University, 1984, p. 87.

Howe, Susan. *A Bibliography of the King's Book; or, Eikon Basilike*. Paradigm Press, 1989.

———. *The Birth-mark: Unsettling the Wilderness in American Literary History.* Wesleyan UP, 1993.

———. *Frame Structures: Early Poems 1974-1979*. New Directions, 1996.

———. *The Nonconformist's Memorial*. New Directions, 1993.

Huth, Geof. "First Meaning: The Digital Poetry Incunabula of bpNichol." *Vispo.com*, http://vispo.com/bp/geof.htm. Accessed 25 August 2015.

Kaufmann, David. "Bullshit and Interest: Casing Vanessa Place." *Postmodern Culture*, vol. 24, no. 2, 2014, np, doi:10.1353/pmc.2014.0006.

Kearful, Frank J. "Poetry: The 1940s to the Present." *American Literary Scholarship*, vol. 2006, no. 1, November 2008, pp. 391-419.

Keenaghan, Eric. "Life, War, and Love: The Queer Anarchism of Robert Duncan's Poetic Action during the Vietnam War." *Contemporary Literature*, vol. 49, no. 4, Winter 2008, pp. 633–58.

King, Amy. "Why Are People So Invested in Kenneth Goldsmith? Or, Is Colonialist Poetry Easy?" *VIDA*, 18 March 2015, http://www.vidaweb.org/why-are-people-so-invested-in-kenneth-goldsmith-or-is-colonialist-poetry-easy. Accessed 2 March 2017.

Kittler, Friedrich. "There Is No Software." *C-Theory: Theory, Technology, Culture*, edited by Arthur and Marilouise Kroker, no. 32, 18 October 1995, http://www.ctheory.net/articles.aspx?id=74. Accessed 11 November 2016.

Knight, Kim. "Research Report: Brian Kim Stefans, 'The Dreamlife of Letters' (2000)." *Transliteracies Project*, 18 February 2007, http://transliteracies.english.ucsb.edu/post/research-project/research-clearinghouse-individual/

research-reports/brian-kim-stefans-the-dreamlife-of-letters-2004-2. Accessed 11 November 2016.

Kostelanetz, Richard. *Conversing with Cage*. 2nd ed., Routledge, 2003.

Lawrence, D.H. *Sons and Lovers*. Gerald Duckworth, 1913.

Lederer, Katy. Review of *Response*, by Juliana Spahr. *Chicago Review*, vol. 44, no.1, 1998, pp. 140–44.

Lennon, Brian. "Screening a Digital Visual Poetics." *Configrations*, vol. 8, no. 1, Winter 2000, pp. 63–85.

Lewallen, Constance. "Cage and the Structure of Chance." Bernstein and Hatch, pp. 234–44.

Luck, Jessica Lewis. "Entries on a Post-Language Poetics in Harryette Mullen's Dictionary." *Contemporary Literature*, vol. 49, no. 3, Fall 2008, pp. 357–82.

Mac Low, Jackson. "Cage's Writings up to the Late 1980s." Bernstein and Hatch, pp. 211–32.

———. "Dialog (with Gil Ott)." *Paper Air*, vol. 2, no. 3, 1980, pp. 18–28.

———. "An Essay Begun in 1965." *Paper Air*, vol. 2, no. 3, 1980, pp. 29–33.

———. "Interview with Nicholas Zurbrugg." *Art, Performance, Media: 31 Interviews*, edited by Nicholas Zurbrugg, U of Minnesota P, 2004, pp. 253–72.

———. "Making Poetry 'Otherwise' (28 January 2001)." *Jacket*, vol. 34, October 2007, http://jacketmagazine.com/34/mac-low-iv.shtml. Accessed 7 February 2016.

———. "The Poetics of Chance & the Politics of Simultaneous Spontaneity, or the Sacred Heart of Jesus (Revised & Abridged)." *Talking Poetics from the Naropa Institute: Annals of the Jack Kerouac School of Disembodied Poetics*, edited by Anne Waldman and Marilyn Webb, Shambala, 1978, pp. 171-92.

———. "Poetry and Pleasure." *Thing of Beauty*, pp. xxvii–xxxvi.

———. Selections from *154 Forties*. *Thing of Beauty*, pp. 337-75.

———. Selections from *The Pronouns: A Collection of 40 Dances for the Dancers*. *Thing of Beauty*, pp. 133–38.

———. Selections from *The Stein Poems*. *Thing of Beauty*, pp. 376–420.

———. "Some Remarks to the Dancers." Allen, pp. 386–91.

———. "Something about the Writings of John Cage." *Writings about John Cage*, edited by Richard Kostelanetz, U of Michigan P, 1993, pp. 283–96.

———. "Statement." Allen, pp. 384–86.

———. *Thing of Beauty: New and Selected Works*, edited by Anne Tardos, U of California P, 2008.

Magearu, Mirona. "Making Digital Poetry: Writing *with* and *through* Spaces." *Journal of Literary Theory*, vol. 6, no. 2, 2012, pp. 337–57.

Marino, Mark. "Critical Code Studies." *Electronic Book Review*, 4 December 2006, http://electronicbookreview.com/thread/electropoetics/codology. Accessed 11 November 2016.

Massumi, Brian. *Parables for the Virtual: Movement, Affect, Sensation*. Duke UP, 2002.

Mayer, Sophie. "Aggregators: RSS (Radically Subversive Syndication) Poetics." *SubStance*, vol. 38, no. 2, 2009, pp. 43–62.

McCaffrey, Steve. "Writing as General Economy." *North of Intention: Critical Writings 1973–1986*. Nightwood, 1986, pp. 201–21.

McGann, Jerome J. "*Eunoia*: Beauty or Truth (or What?)" *The Antioch Review. All Poetry Issue*, vol. 67, no. 1, Winter 2009, pp. 138–52.

———. *The Textual Condition*. Princeton UP, 1991.

mclennan, rob. "'Erín Moure's *Pillage Laud*." *rob mclennan's blog*, 24 June 2011, http://robmclennan.blogspot.ca/2011/06/erin-moure-pillage-laud.html. Accessed 17 January 2015.

"medley, *n.* and *adj.*" OED. Accessed 16 January 2015.

"mêlée, *n.*" OED. Accessed 16 January 2015.

Miller, Tyrus. *Singular Examples: Artistic Politics and the Neo-Avant-Garde*. Northwestern UP, 2009.

Mix, Deborah M. *A Vocabulary of Thinking: Gertrude Stein and Contemporary North American Women's Innovative Writing*. U of Iowa P, 2007.

Moschovakis, Anna. "Poetics of Guilt: Review of *Tragodía 1: Statement of Facts*." *American Book Review*, May-June 2011, pp. 9–10.

Moore, Isabel A. "Lyric Fever: Erin Mouré and the Queer Anatomy of Lyric Life." *Mosaic*, vol. 45, no. 1, March 2012, pp. 35–53.

Morris, Daniel. *Not Born Digital: Poetics, Print Literacy, New Media*. Bloomsbury, 2016.

Moure, Erín [Eirin Moure, Erin Mouré]. *My Beloved Wager: Essays from a Writing Practice*. NeWest, 2009.

———. *Pillage Laud: Cauterizations, Vocabularies, Cantigas, Topiary, Prose*. Moveable Type, 1999.

———. *Pillage Laud: Cauterizations, Vocabularies, Cantigas, Topiary, Prose*. Book*hug, 2011.

———. "Poetry, Memory and the Polis." *Language in Her Eye: Writing and Gender, Views by Canadian Women Writing in English*, edited by Libby Scheier, Sarah Sheard, and Eleanor Wachtel, Coach House Press, 1990, pp. 201–08.

———, translator. *Sheep's Vigil by a Fervent Person*. By Fernando Pessoa. Anansi, 2001. Transelation [*sic*] of *O Gardador de Rebanhos*.

Mouré, Erin, and Bronwen Wallace. *Two Women Talking: Correspondence 1985–87*, edited by Susan McMaster, Living Archives of the Feminist Caucus of the League of Canadian Poets, 1993.

Mullen, Harryette. "African Signs and Spirit Writing." *Callaloo,* vol. 19, no. 3, Summer 1996, pp. 670–89.

———. "Imagining the Unimagined Reader: Writing to the Unborn and Including the Excluded." *boundary 2,* vol. 26, no. 1, 1999, pp. 198–203.

———. "An Interview with Harryette Mullen by Elisabeth A. Frost." *Contemporary Literature,* vol. 41, no. 3, Autumn 2000, pp. 397–421.

———. "Poetry and Identity." *West Coast Line,* vol. 19, 1996, pp. 85–89.

———. *Sleeping with the Dictionary*. U of California P, 2002.

Naylor, Paul. "Susan Howe: Where Are We Now in Poetry?" *Poetic Investigations: Singing the Holes in History*. Northwestern UP, 1999, pp. 43–70.

Newman, Saul. *The Politics of Postanarchism*. Edinburgh UP, 2011.

Ngai, Sianne. *Ugly Feelings*. Harvard UP, 2007.

Nichol, bp (Barrie Phillip). *First Screening: Computer Poems. Vispo.com*. Emulated version, edited by Jim Andrews, http://vispo.com/bp/emulatedversion.htm. Accessed 10 October 2016.

———. *First Screening: Computer Poems. Vispo.com*. Video version, edited by Jim Andrews, http://vispo.com/bp/videoversion.htm. Accessed 10 October 2016.

———. *Konfessions of an Elizabethan Fan Dancer*. 1973. Edited by Nelson Ball, Coach House Press, 2000.

Nicholls, Peter. "Unsettling the Wilderness: Susan Howe and American History." *Contemporary Literature*, vol. 37, no. 4, Winter 1996, pp. 586-601, https://www.jstor.org/stable/1208773. Accessed 17 December 2017.

Olson, Charles. "Projective Verse." *Collected Prose*, edited by Donald Allen and Benjamin Friedlander, U of California P, 1997, pp. 239–49.

Oudart, Clément. "Genreading and Underwriting: A Few Soundings and Probes into Duncan's *Ground Work*." *Jacket*, vol. 32, April 2007, http://jacketmagazine.com/32/oudart-genreading.shtml. Accessed 5 September 2016.

*The Oxford English Dictionary*. 2nd ed., Oxford UP, www.oed.com.

Palmer, Michael. Introduction. Duncan, *Ground Work*, pp. ix–xiv.

Parikka, Jussi. *What Is Media Archaeology?* Polity Press, 2012.

Parry, Dave. "The Digital Humanities or a Digital Humanism." *Debates in the Digital Humanities*, U of Minnesota P, 2012, http://dhdebates.gc.cuny.edu/debates/text/2. Accessed 24 November 2016.

Perelman, Bob. *The Marginalization of Poetry: Language Writing and Literary History*. Princeton UP, 1996.

Perloff, Marjorie. "A Conversation with Kenneth Goldsmith." *Jacket*, no. 21, February 2003, http://jacketmagazine.com/21/perl-gold-iv.html. Accessed 5 October 2016.

———. "Language Poetry and the Lyric Subject: Ron Silliman's Albany, Susan Howe's Buffalo." *Critical Inquiry*, vol. 25, no. 3, Spring 1999, pp. 405–34.

———. "The Oulipo Factor: The Procedural Poetics of Christian Bök and Caroline Bergvall." *Textual Practice*, vol. 18, no. 1, 2004, pp. 23–45.

———. *Radical Artifice: Writing Poetry in the Age of Media*. U of Chicago P, 1994.

———. *Unoriginal Genius: Poetry by Other Means in the New Century*. U of Chicago P, 2010.

Place, Vanessa. "The Death of the Text: Kenneth Goldsmith at the White House." *Harriet: A Poetry Blog*, Poetry Foundation, 19 May 2011, https://www.poetryfoundation.org/harriet/2011/05/the-death-of-the-text-kenneth-goldsmith-at-the-white-house. Accessed 5 October 2016.

———. *Tragodía 1: Statement of Facts*. Blanc Press, 2010.

Poole, Alex. "Which Are More Legible: Serif or Sans Serif Typefaces?" *AlexPoole.info*, 17 February 2008, updated March 2012, http://alexpoole.info/blog/which-are-more-legible-serif-or-sans-serif-typefaces. Accessed 5 October 2016.

Pound, Ezra. *The Cantos of Ezra Pound*. New Directions, 1993.

Raley, Rita. "Interferences: [Net.Writing] and the Practice of Codework." *Electronic Book Review*, 8 September 2004, http://electronicbookreview.com/thread/electropoetics/net.writing. Accessed 11 November 2016.

Read, Herbert. *Anarchy and Order; Poetry and Anarchism*. 1938. Freedom Press, 1947.

Robbins, Amy Moorman. "Harryette Mullen's *Sleeping with the Dictionary* and Race in Language/Writing." *Contemporary Literature*, vol. 51, no. 2, Summer 2010, pp. 341–70.

Robinson, T.M., translator and editor. *Fragments*. By Heraclitus, U of Toronto P, 1987.

Rudy, Susan. "'what can atmosphere with / vocabularies delight?': Excessively Reading Erin Mouré." *Writing in Our Time: Canada's Radical Poetries in English (1957–2003)*, Wilfrid Laurier UP, 2005, pp. 205–15.

Saemmer, Alexandra. "Aesthetics of Surface, Ephemeral, Re-enchantment, and Mimetic Approaches in Digital Literature: How Authors and Readers Deal with the Potential Instability of the Electronic Device." *Neohelicon*, vol. 36, 2009, pp. 477-88, doi:10.1007/s11059-009-0016-2.

Sándor, Katalin. "Moving (the) Text: From Print to Digital." *Between Page and Screen: Remaking Literature through Cinema and Cyberspace*, edited by Kiene Brillenburg Wurth, Fordham UP, 2012, pp. 144–56.

Saussure, Ferdinand de. *Course in General Linguistics*. Translated by Wade Baskin, edited by Perry Meisel and Haun Saussy, Columbia UP, 2011.

"scene, *n*." OED, accessed 11 November 2016.

Schmidt, Christopher. "The Waste-Management Poetics of Kenneth Goldsmith." *Substance #116*, vol. 37, no. 2, 2008, pp. 25–40.

Schmidt, Saint. "Postanarchism Is Not What You Think: The Role of Postanarchist Theory After the Backlash." *The Anarchist Library*, 2008, https://theanarchistlibrary.org/library/saint-schmidt-postanarchism-is-not-what-you-think-the-role-of-postanarchist-theory-after-the-backlash.html. Accessed 25 November 2016.

Shockley, Evie. *Renegade Poetics: Black Aesthetics and Formal Innovation in African American Poetry*. U of Iowa P, 2011.

"sic, *adv.* (and *n.*)." OED. Accessed 16 January 2015.

Silliman, Ron. "Interview (with Gary Sullivan)." *Electronic Poetry Center*, 2000, http://home.jps.net/~nada/silliman.htm. Accessed 25 February 2017.

———. "Poetry and the Politics of the Subject." *Socialist Review*, vol. 88, no. 3, July–September 1988, pp. 61–68.

Silliman, Ron, and Leslie Scalapino. "What/Person? From an Exchange." *Poetics Journal*, vol. 9, 1991, pp. 51–68.

Simanowski, Roberto. *Digital Art and Meaning: Reading Kinetic Poetry, Text Machines, Mapping Art, and Interactive Installations*. U of Minnesota P, 2010.

———. "Fighting/Dancing Words: Jim Andrews' Kinetic, Concrete Audiovisual Poetry." *Dichtung Digital*. Translated by Florian Cramer, 26 November 2001, http://dichtung-digital.de/2002/01/10-Simanowski/cramer.htm. Accessed 17 October 2016.

———. "Holopoetry, Biopoetry and Digital Literatures: Close Reading and Terminological Debates." *The Aesthetics of Net Literature: Writing, Reading and Playing in Programmable Media*, edited by Peter Gendolla and Jörgen Schäfer, Transcript Verlag, 2007, pp. 3–66.

Sinclair, Upton. *The Coal War*. Colorado Associated UP, 1976.

———. *King Coal*. Macmillan, 1917.

"soliloquy, *n*." OED. Accessed 20 November 2017.

Solomon, Andrew. "Their Irony, Humor (and Art) Can Save China." *The New York Times Magazine*, 19 December 1993, http://www.nytimes.com/1993/12/19/

magazine/their-irony-humor-and-art-can-save-china.html. Accessed 17 October 2016.

Spahr, Juliana. "The 90s." *boundary 2*, Fall 2009, pp. 159–82.

———. "A, B, C: Reading Against Emily Dickinson and Gertrude Stein." *A Poetics of Criticism*, edited by Kristin Prevallet, Pam Rehm, Spahr, and Mark Wallace, Leave Books, 1994, pp. 281–92.

———. "A Brief Q&A with Juliana Spahr [by Michael Boyko]." *Tarpaulin Sky*, vol. 3, no. 2, Summer 2005, http://www.tarpaulinsky.com/Summer05/Spahr/Juliana_Spahr_Q-n-A.html. Accessed 21 September 2016.

———. Comment on Response from Marjorie Perloff. *Could Be Otherwise*, 17 June 2010, http://could-be-otherwise.blogspot.ca/2010/06/response-from-marjorie-perloJff.html. Accessed 17 December 2017.

———. *Everybody's Autonomy: Connective Reading and Collective Identity*. U of Alabama P, 2001.

———. *Fuck You—Aloha—I Love You*. Wesleyan UP, 2001.

———. Introduction. Henning, pp. i–iv.

———. *Response*. Sun & Moon Press, 1996.

———. *This Connection of Everyone with Lungs*. U of California P, 2005.

Spinosa, Dani. "John Cage and the Comunis of Communication." *Canadian Review of American Studies*, vol. 46, no. 1, Spring 2016, pp. 22–41.

Spiro, Lisa M. "Collaborative Authorship in the Humanities." *Digital Scholarship in the Humanities: Exploring the digital humanities*, 21 April 2009, https://digitalscholarship.wordpress.com/2009/04/21/collaborative-authorship-in-the-humanities. Accessed 25 November 2016.

Stacey, Robert David. "Toil and Trouble: On Work in Christian Bök's *Eunoia*." *Canadian Poetry*, vol. 62, Spring/Summer 2008, pp. 64–79.

Stefans, Brian Kim. "The Dreamlife of Letters." *Arras.net*, 2000, http://www.arras.net/RNG/flash/dreamlife/dreamlife_index.html. Accessed 17 October 2016.

———. "The Dreamlife of Letters." *Electronic Literature Collection*, vol. 1, Electronic Literature Organization, 2000, http://collection.eliterature.org/1/works/stefans__the_dreamlife_of_letters/dreamlife_index.html. Accessed 17 October 2016.

———. *Fashionable Noise: On Digital Poetics*. Atelos, 2003.

———. "Toward a Poetics for Circulars." *New Media Poetics: Contexts, Technotexts, and Theories*, edited by Adalaide Morris and Thomas Swiss, MIT Press, 2006, pp. 65–94.

Stefan, Brian Kim, and Darren Wershler[-Henry]. "Exchange on Circulars." *New Media Poetics: Contexts, Technotexts, and Theories*, edited by Adalaide Morris and Thomas Swiss, MIT Press, 2006, pp. 73–82.

Steinhauer, Jillian. "Kenneth Goldsmith Remixes Michael Brown Autopsy Report as Poetry." *Hyperallergic*, 16 March 2015, http://hyperallergic.com/190954/kenneth-goldsmith-remixes-michael-brown-autopsy-report-as-poetry. Accessed 2 March 2017.

Stephens, Paul. "Vanguard Total Index: Conceptual Writing, Information Asymmetry, and the Risk Society." *Contemporary Literature*, vol. 54, no. 4, Winter 2013, pp. 752-84.

Strickland, Stephanie. "Moving through Me as I Move." *Electronic Book Review*, 5 November 2004, http://electronicbookreview.com/thread/firstperson/stenorthographic. Accessed 11 November 2016.

Sutherland, Keston. "Theses on Antisubjectivist Dogma." *A Fiery Flying Roule*, 1 May 2013, http://afieryflyingroule.tumblr.com/post/49378474736/keston-sutherland-theses-on-antisubjectivist. Accessed 17 December 2017.

Sutherland, W. Mark. *Code X*. Coach House Press, 2002, http://www.wmarksutherland.com/downloads/Codex/Main.html. Accessed 11 November 2016.

Sweeny, Robert. "Dysfunction in the Networks of Machinic Assemblage." *Visual Arts Research*, vol. 39, no. 1, iss. 76, Summer 2013, pp. 108–21.

Szilak, Illya. "Towards Minor Literary Forms: Digital Literature and the Art of Failure." *Electronic Book Review*, 2 August 2015, http://electronicbookreview.com/thread/electropoetics/failure. Accessed 11 November 2015.

*Tapeworm*. 2008, http://writing.upenn.edu/wh/involved/series/art/tapeworm/tapewormcatalogue.pdf. Accessed 26 December 2017. Originally published by University of Pennsylvania English and Creative Writing Departments for exhibit curated by Kaegan Sparks.

Tardos, Anne. Foreword. Mac Low, *Thing of Beauty*, pp. xv–xvii.

Trimarco, Paola. *Digital Textuality*. Palgrave MacMillan, 2015.

Vanderborg, Susan. "Transformations of the Poetry Book as General Economy: Darren Wershler-Henry's *The Tapeworm Foundry*." *Contemporary Literature*, vol. 52, no. 1, Spring 2011, pp. 146–74.

Van Looy, Jan, and Jan Baetens. "Introduction: Close Reading Electronic Literature." *Close Reading New Media: Analyzing Electronic Literature*, edited by Van Looy and Baetens, Leven UP, 2003.

"vo., *adv.*" OED. Accessed 11 November 2016.

"vo., *n.*" OED. Accessed 11 November 2016.

"voce, *n.*[2]" OED. Accessed 11 November 2016.

Voyce, Stephen. *Poetic Community: Avant-Garde Activism and Cold War Culture*. U of Toronto P, 2013.

———. "The Xenotext Experiment: An Interview with Christian Bök." *Postmodern Culture*, vol. 17, no. 2, 2007, doi:10.1353/pmc.2007.0025.

Weaver, Andy. "Darren Wershler-Henry's *The Tapeworm Foundry*, the Lyotardian Sublime, and the Ethical Importance of the Inhuman." *Canadian Poetry*, vol. 66, Spring/Summer 2010, pp. 98–116.

———. "The Indeterminacy of Poetics: Six Experimental Poets." Dissertation. U of Alberta, 2005.

———. "Promoting 'a community of thoughtful men and women': Anarchism in Robert Duncan's *Ground Work* Volumes." *ESC: English Studies in Canada*, vol. 34, no. 4, December 2008, pp. 71–95.

———. "Re: Re[2]: justafewquestions." Received by Dani Spinosa, 1 January 2015.

———. "Writing through Merce: John Cage's Silence, Differends, and Avant-Garde Idioms." *Mosaic*, vol. 45, no. 2, June 2012, pp. 19–37.

Weir, David. *Anarchy and Culture: The Aesthetic Politics of Modernism*. U of Massachusetts P, 1997.

Wershler[-Henry], Darren. *Commonspace: Beyond Virtual Community*. Financial Times Management, 2002.

———. *Free as in Speech and Beer: Open Source, Peer-to-Peer and the Economics of the Online Revolution*. Pearson, 2002.

———. *Internet Directory, 2001*. Prentice Hall, 2000.

———. "The Locative, the Ambient, and the Hallucinatory in the Internet of Things." *Design and Culture*, vol. 2, iss. 2, 2010, pp. 199-216.

———. *The Tapeworm Foundry, andor, The Dangerous Prevalence of Imagination*. House of Anansi, 2000.

———. *The Tapeworm Foundry, andor, The Dangerous Prevalence of Imagination*. ubu editions, 2002, http://www.ubu.com/ubu/pdf/wershler_tapeworm.pdf. Accessed 9 October 2016.

Wittgenstein, Ludwig. *Zettel*. Translated by G. E. M. Anscombe, edited by Anscombe and G. H. von Wright, U of California P, 1967.

Wooler, Katherine. "Communication Codes and Critical Editing: Recognizing Materiality in the Work of bpNichol." MA thesis. Dalhousie U, 2013.

Zola, Emile. *Germinal*. Paris, 1885.

Zolf, Rachel. "'Like plugging into an electric circuit': Fingering out Erín Moure's Lesbo-Digit-*O*! Smut Poems." *21st-Century Poetics*. Spec. issue of *Canadian Literature*, no. 210-11, Autumn/Winter 2011, pp. 230-41.

Zultanski, Steven. "Short Statement in Five Parts on *Statement of Facts*: A Review of Vanessa Place's *Statement of Facts*." *Jacket 2*, 16 October 2012, http://jacket2.org/reviews/short-statement-five-parts-statement-facts. Accessed 10 October 2016.

# Permissions

"62 Mesostics re Merce Cunningham" from *M: Writings '62–'72* © 1973 by John Cage. Published by Wesleyan University Press. Used by permission.

By Mark Sutherland, from *Code X*, © 2002 by Mark Sutherland. Reprinted with permission of the author.

By Barrie Philip (bp) Nichol from *First Screenings: Computer Poems*, © 1984 by bpNichol. Reprinted by permission of Eleanor Nichol, the Nichol estate, and Jim Andrews et al. at Vispo.

By Robert Duncan from *Ground Work: Before the War / In the Dark*, copyright © 1968, 1969, 1970, 1971, 1972, 1974, 1975, 1976, 1977, 1978, 1979, 1980, 1981, 1982, 1983, 1984, 1985, 1987, 1988 by Robert Duncan. Reprinted by permission of New Directions Publishing Corp.

"Introduction" by Michael Palmer, from *Ground Work: Before the War / In the Dark* by Robert Duncan, copyright © 2006 by New Directions Publishing Corp. Reprinted by permission of New Directions Publishing Corp.

By Susan Howe, from *The Nonconformist's Memorial*, copyright © 1993 by Susan Howe. Reprinted by permission of New Directions Publishing Corp.

By Erin Mouré, from *Pillage Laud*, copyright © 1999, 2011 by Erin Moure. Reprinted by permission of Book Thug.

Juliana Spahr, excerpts from *Response*. Copyright © 1996 by Juliana Spahr. Reprinted with the permission of The Permissions Company, Inc. on behalf of Green Interger, www.greeninterger.com.

By Jim Andrews, from *Seattle Drift*, copyright © 1997 by Jim Andrews. Reprinted by permission of the author.

*Ugly Feelings* by Sianne Ngai, Cambridge, Mass.: Harvard University Press, Copyright © 2005 by the President and Fellows of Harvard College.

# Index

Page numbers with *f* refer to figures.

Other Titles from The University of Alberta Press

**Personal Modernisms**

*Anarchist Networks and the Later Avant-Gardes*

JAMES GIFFORD

Oft-neglected Personalist writers of 1930s–40s comprise a missing link between modernist and postmodernist literatures

**Counterblasting Canada**

*Marshall McLuhan, Wyndham Lewis, Wilfred Watson, and Sheila Watson*

GREGORY BETTS, PAUL HJARTARSON & KRISTINE SMITKA, Editors

Situating the intellectual inheritance of Canadian vorticists in a multidisciplinary assemblage of authors and artists.

**Poets Talk**

*Conversations with Robert Kroetsch, Daphne Marlatt, Erin Mouré, Dionne Brand, Marie Annharte Baker, Jeff Derksen, and Fred Wah*

PAULINE BUTLING & SUSAN RUDY

Seven poets of diverse region, gender, sexual orientation, race, and generation. *Poets Talk* brings new insights to the value of inspiration, imagination, and poetic re-invention.

*A volume in cuRRents, a Canadian literature series*

*More information at www.uap.ualberta.ca*